SOURCES IN WESTERN CIVILIZATION

The Twentieth Century,
1914–1964

THE

Sources in Western Civilization

GENERAL EDITOR, *Herbert H. Rowen*

RUTGERS UNIVERSITY

TWENTIETH CENTURY

1914·1964

EDITED BY

Arthur P. Mendel

THE UNIVERSITY OF MICHIGAN

THE FREE PRESS, NEW YORK

Collier-Macmillan Limited, London

printing number

5 6 7 8 9 10

CONTENTS

SOURCES IN WESTERN CIVILIZATION

The Twentieth Century,
1914–1964

INTRODUCTION

"History repeats itself." "There is nothing new under the sun." "Everything changes, yet everything remains the same." Whether we agree or disagree with these familiar sayings, they raise some of the essential questions about our contemporary world. How does our era compare with those that went before? How much continuity and how much change do we find when we contrast our own century with the earlier centuries of Western civilization? Is ours a revolutionary age, or is it a legitimate and respectful offspring of past generations?

When we look back on two terrible World Wars, on concentration and extermination camps unprecedented in their horror, on the most oppressive and totalitarian political systems that man has ever known, and on such cultural phenomena as surrealist and abstract art, free-association literature, and atonal music, the argument for change and revolution may seem quite convincing. Yet the continual advance of science and technology, the prevalence of secularism, rationalism, and materialism, the obvious vitality of nationalism, and, above all, the spread of all these key themes of Western civilization into the economically underdeveloped, formerly colonial areas of Asia and Africa clearly link our era with the main themes of Western civilization since the Renaissance.

An even more difficult problem than deciding between continuity and change is identifying the sources of main tendencies and the causes of key events in our era. Any chronological division is arbitrary and unsatisfactory. While this volume begins with World War I, it will be necessary when introducing various subjects to glance back for a moment to earlier periods, primarily to the last decades of the nineteenth century, when some of the main cultural and political features of our time began to emerge.

I. WORLD WAR I

The close association between the events of our century and those of the nineteenth century is dramatically exemplified in World War I, the fateful conflict that begins this most recent phase of our history. Such events as the assassination of the heir to the throne of the Austro-Hungarian Empire certainly played their role, but for deeper causes one must look back at least to the preceding century. After the formation of the German Empire in 1871, Germany experienced astounding economic progress. By 1914 its production of iron and steel surpassed that of Britain and France combined, German exports competed with English goods in traditional English markets, and an ambitious program of naval construction challenged England's control of the seas. Finally, German plans for extending the Berlin-Constantinople railroad by a line from the Bosporus to Baghdad threatened British interests in Persia and, some thought, even in India. The friction between Germany and France also dates back to the closing decades of the last century. A main issue was the French desire to regain Alsace-Lorraine, ceded to Germany in 1871. The loss of the rich iron and coal deposits in those provinces made France dependent on imports of these vital raw materials. In addition, France and Germany gradually moved toward serious friction in North Africa.

When we turn to Russia and the Balkans, we find the same long-range causes: the slow decline of Turkish influence in the Near East, leaving a "power vacuum"; Russia's "panslavist" ambitions in the Balkans; nationalist stirrings among the Slavs in the Turkish and the Austro-Hungarian Empires; and Austria's clear realization that all of these tendencies threatened the very life of her Empire.

In response to these and other economic, political, and psychological forces, the nations formed alliances so tightly knit that any local crisis involving only a few could easily lead to a world-wide catastrophe involving them all. The key features of these alliances also originated in the previous decades. The conflict between Austria and Russia in the Balkans forced Germany to choose between the two. Understandably it chose Austria, thereby alienating Russia and undermining Bismarck's League of the Three Emperors (Germany, Russia, Austria). France, meanwhile, settled its quarrels with Britain in North Africa and entered into close financial and later (1894) military agreements with Russia, thereby gaining a strong ally in the

East in the event of conflict with Germany. Finally, faced with the growing challenge from Germany, Britain allied with France (1904) and, three years later, with Russia, after they had resolved their differences in Persia. The result was the Triple Entente, comprising Britain, France, and Russia. At first this emerging alliance faced the so-called Triple Alliance of Germany, Austria, and Italy. But Italy, moved by ambitions in North Africa and claiming territory under Austrian control, gradually divorced itself from the two Germanic Empires.

As these alliances were taking shape, repeated local crises occurred in the Balkans, North Africa, and elsewhere, intensifying the resentments felt by each group of powers against the other. In 1905–1906 and 1911 France and Germany opposed each other in Morocco. In 1908 Austria annexed the nominally Turkish territory of Bosnia and Herzegovina. The Serbs, who looked to these areas as their next acquisitions on the way to forming a South Slavic nation, were enraged; while Russia, which had a tacit agreement with Austria that it would gain something for itself in return for permitting the annexation, was left empty-handed and humiliated. These events were virtually repeated in 1912–1913, when, after the second Balkan War, Austria forced Serbia to give up the Adriatic sea coast it had taken as part of the spoils of the disintegrating Turkish Empire. Both times Serbia sought Russian support. Both times Russia refused to risk war, realizing that it was not yet economically or militarily ready to fight the German-Austrian alliance. The third crisis came on June 28, 1914, when Archduke Francis Ferdinand, the heir to the throne of the Austro-Hungarian Empire, was killed at Sarajevo by a terrorist group that included Serbian army officers. This time there was a different result. Russia supported Serbia. Germany supported Austria. The "chain reaction" of the alliance system led to explosion, and World War I began [1].*

If the causes of World War I can be found emerging clearly toward the close of the nineteenth century, the consequences of the war were to be felt by the entire world until the present. Above all, it marked for many the end of an era of hope and optimism. The human cost included military casualties of nine million dead and twenty million wounded, and an incalculable number who died and suffered as a result of wartime conditions. To these human losses one

* Bracketed numbers refer to the numbers of the selections in the text.

must add the enormous destruction of resources and material wealth together with the collapse of the world economy following the war. But this by no means closes the list of the costs of the war. As we shall see, the Communist victory in Russia and the rise of Fascism in Italy and Germany probably would not have occurred except in the conditions produced by the war. Nor are the nihilism, cynicism, escapism, and almost pathological pessimism that swept the world of literature, art, and thought and that characterized so many lives in the ensuing decades understandable apart from the experience of the war and its aftermath.

2. RUSSIA

Chronologically the first principal consequences of the war were the Russian Revolution and the Bolshevik conquest of power. Since the consequences of these events are of the utmost importance today, more space must be given to them than might otherwise be justified in a brief survey.

It is seldom realized nowadays how rapidly Russia was progressing in the decades before the war. An ambitious program of industrialization started in the 1890's, and an even more dramatic program of rural reorganization begun a decade later were gradually transforming Russia into a Western, industrial, urban society. Moreover, a liberal revolution in 1905 had resulted in the establishment of the Duma, the first Russian parliament, which, for all its shortcomings, was a major advance towards representative government. Finally, in the fields of music, art, and letters, Russians not only matched their Western European counterparts but often surpassed them.

Now it is certainly true that these economic, social, and political processes were causing important dislocations in rural and urban Russia. It is also true that the government of Tsar Nicholas II was unusually incompetent. Nevertheless, it is very doubtful whether Tsarism would have been overthrown had it not been for the extra burdens of the war. In spite of the significant economic progress, Russia was ill prepared for war. Each month brought more shortages and greater resentment both at the front and in the towns and villages. One should keep in mind the fact that Russian armies comprised, in the main, the same peasant class which had been exploited to pay for the industrialization program and had suffered many hardships caused by the rural transformation.

It would be inaccurate, however, to say simply that these wartime burdens led to the revolution which overthrew Tsarism. In fact, after the German advance of 1915, radical changes were made in the government; competent ministers were brought in who worked closely with the Duma and with various citizens' groups to improve the war effort. Had this situation continued, there is good reason to believe that Russia could have remained in the war through 1917 and, in view of the United States entry into the war the following year, ended the war among the victors.

But the hopeful situation did not last. Extraordinary circumstances intervened to alter the course of Russia and world history. The heir to the throne suffered from hemophilia, and a Russian "holy man" named Rasputin, as clever as he was unscrupulous, convinced the Tsar's wife that he had power to stop the fateful bleeding. She not only believed in him as a healer but also trusted his judgment in political affairs and urged Nicholas to do so too. Competent ministers were replaced by Rasputin's followers, and hostility against the Tsar and his government rose rapidly. By the end of 1916 this opposition included representatives of the highest social, political, economic, and military circles, who realized that the influence of the Tsarina and Rasputin was disastrous. The "holy man" was assassinated, but his appointees remained and with them the detrimental influence of the Tsarina.

In February, 1917, the population of Petrograd (formerly St. Petersburg), began to demonstrate against the wartime shortages. Tsar Nicholas completely misread the nature of the crisis. He tried to crush the demonstrations and ordered dissolution of the Duma, the only body that still inspired in the people some loyalty to the existing political system. The troops sent to crush the demonstrators mutinied, and the Duma refused to disband. Faced with this defiance and finally realizing the extent of the opposition as well as the weakness of his own position, Nicholas II abdicated. Tsarism was no more, though at least part of the prerevolutionary political structure was retained in the Provisional Government, which included members of the elected Duma.

The revolution of February, 1917, was led by the established middle and upper classes of society, who opposed the Tsarist government primarily because of its intolerable wartime policies. But it was too late to undo the harm done. In any case, the members of the Provisional Government lacked the ability and the mass support to meet the staggering problems — unreliable troops, shortages in the cities and workers' demonstrations, and widespread discontent in the countryside, including a wave of land seizures by the peasantry. Gradually the united front which had brought an end to Tsarism disintegrated. Moderate center and right-wing groups, increasingly dissatisfied with the policies of the Provisional Government, particularly after it came under the control of the socialist Kerensky, turned for leadership to General Kornilov, the head of the army. In September Kornilov made an unsuccessful attempt to seize power. In the meantime groups that opposed the Provisional Government because of its unwillingness to withdraw from the war and to enact radical economic measures looked increasingly to the Bolsheviks, the extreme left party. However, notwithstanding this growing support, the Bolsheviks, with the exception of Lenin, were reluctant to take advantage of the crisis and seize power. As Marxists, they were convinced that a socialist revolution had no place in a backward, underdeveloped, rural economy; for, according to Marx, socialism could come only in an advanced industrial economy where capitalism had provided the industrial foundation upon which a planned socialist economy could be successfully established and social justice achieved. It was only by intense arguments, threats of resignation, and similar means of persuasion that Lenin won the Bolshevik leaders to his side.

This Bolshevik victory became the model for Marxist revolutions from that time until the present. Economic, social, and political developments in Western Europe had disproved Marx. Working-class conditions improved rather than worsened, and violent revolution leading to the rapid transformation of society seemed increasingly out of place in these economically advanced and politically democratic "open" societies. The Bolshevik uprising, on the contrary, was essentially a "populist" revolution of the type envisioned by Russian rural socialists of the nineteenth century; it was a revolution fed by the resentment of the mass peasant population and led by a small, tightly knit organization of full-time revolutionaries. The urban working class formed only a small percentage of the Russian population in 1917. Furthermore, they were a class socially and psychologically still at the very earliest stages of capitalist development rather than at the late stage Marx considered an essential condition for a truly socialist revolution [2].

The program that the Bolshevik party promised to realize once it was in power painted a "brave new world." The people were to rule themselves through Soviets (councils) completely responsive to popular will. They were to take a direct part in the day-to-day administration of society, much as citizens in the West participate in juries. All officials were to be subject to immediate recall if they did not satisfy the people. In addition, they were to be paid no more than good workers. The workers in turn were to control industrial production, thereby eliminating the high-salaried managerial class. In place of the stratified and oppressive army, there was to be a volunteer citizen militia with elected officers, distinguished by neither high salaries nor insignia of rank. Minority peoples who wished to secede from the Russian state would be free to do so.

Perhaps all these promises were cynical deceptions; perhaps they were seriously meant for an ultimate future. The Bolshevik leaders knew that such measures could not be put into effect in an underdeveloped rural country like Russia, so recently emerged from "feudal" serfdom. In fact, Bolshevik leaders frequently admitted that if socialism was to be established in Russia, a socialist revolution must first occur in an economically advanced country like Germany. As a result of war losses and deprivations, Germany seemed to be on the eve of such a revolution. However, Lenin himself lessened the likelihood of such a revolution by concluding the Brest-Litovsk peace with Germany in 1918, which took Russia out of the war and significantly alleviated the burdens on the German state and population. Lenin's reason for making this highly unfavorable peace was clear: if he did not end the war burdens on Russia, his party would face the same internal opposition which he had exploited in his seizure of power. In short, he preferred to keep power in Russia even if the means of doing so undermined the chance of a rebellion in industrial Germany, the very event which he and most Marxists considered a prerequisite for establishing socialism in Russia.

The fears of many Western and earlier Russian socialists thus became a reality. As a result of a premature revolution, "socialists" found themselves in control of a backward economy and faced with the task of creating an industrial system that, so it had been assumed in Marxist theory, should have been established by the capitalists. In order to build industry, the socialists would have to exploit the masses in the same way that, they claimed, the capitalist industrializers had done. All the hopeful promises were abandoned. Workers' control in industries gave way to bureaucratic administration of the entire economy. Elected Soviets and direct popular government was replaced by the unlimited dictatorial rule of the Communist Party. The citizen militia was reorganized by Trotsky into a rigorously disciplined army led by former Tsarist officers. Minority nationalities were forcefully kept in the empire — Soviet now rather than Tsarist — regardless of their desire to secede.

It is true that this betrayal of revolutionary goals was also fostered by the civil war and the foreign intervention that began almost immediately after the Bolsheviks won power. However, it has been argued that politically the civil war and the intervention did more good than harm to the position of the Bolshevik party. The anti-Bolshevik Russian armies were too disunited and the foreign detachments too small to defeat the Bolshevik forces militarily, but they did allow the Communists to present themselves as defenders of the motherland against foreign invaders and as defenders of the peasantry against alleged plans of the anti-Bolsheviks to restore seized lands to their former owners. The civil war and the intervention also provided excellent justification for destroying the political foes of the Bolsheviks and for retreating from revolutionary promises which in any case could not be met in the underdeveloped state of the Russian economy and society.

By 1921 the civil war was over. The economy was in ruins after seven years of constant fighting. Production was only a small part of what it had been before 1914. Shortages were universal, and millions faced actual starvation. Moreover, the small remaining hope for socialist revolutions in the economically advanced West had proven to be an illusion. Finally, there was no longer justification for repression, shortages, and exploitation. Mass discontent was rife in the countryside, in Petrograd, and even in the armed forces, resulting in the rising of the Kronstadt naval garrison against the Bolshevik government. Lenin's response to this crisis set a pattern often followed by his successors. On the one hand, he strengthened organization and control of the Communist Party by outlawing all opposition factions within it. On the other hand, he made another broad retreat, the New Economic Policy (NEP). The essential goal of the NEP was to increase the flow of goods between town and village and thereby to eliminate the politically dangerous shortages of goods. Light industry and marketing, both rural and urban, were freed from bureaucratic direction and returned to "free enterprise," while the banks, heavy industry, and foreign trade were retained by the state. The program achieved its purpose. Production and distribution rose

rapidly, and by the time of Lenin's death in 1924 the threat of revolution against the Bolsheviks was gone. For the next seven years
Soviet society enjoyed relative political relaxation and economic revival and indulged in a variety of imaginative experiments in social
organization and cultural expression.

Political life in Russia knew no such relaxation, for it was dominated by the struggle over Lenin's succession. Although Lenin did
not die until January, 1924, the battle began in earnest after he
suffered two strokes in 1922. It was generally believed that his successor would be Trotsky, the organizer of the Soviet army, one of the
party's most brilliant theoreticians and forceful public speakers, and
the leader of the military-revolutionary committee that had directed
the October Revolution. However, his extreme views on such issues
as world revolution, labor mobilization, and rapid industrialization as
well as the envy of other Bolshevik leaders led to the formation of
a powerful group, headed by Zinoviev and Kamenev, which opposed
Trotsky as supreme leader.

A relatively minor ally of Zinoviev and Kamenev was Stalin,
commissar of nationalities, who became general secretary of the
party in 1922. By pursuing a policy of moderation after his return
from Siberian exile in 1917 and by staying behind the scenes in
apparently unimportant administrative jobs in the party government,
Stalin seemed to threaten no one. Behind this façade, however, he
gradually used his position as general secretary to fill key party posts
with personal supporters. Since it was Lenin's Communist Party that
controlled Russia, whoever controlled the party dominated the
country. People might thrill to the speeches of Trotsky or others,
but Russia was not a country of democratic elections, where such
admiration might lead to political power; it was a country ruled by
a party whose members obeyed the orders of the man who controlled their fate. Stalin advanced to total power in three phases.
From 1922 until 1925 he joined Zinoviev and Kamenev against
Trotsky. Then, in alliance with the party's moderate right-wing, he
turned against Zinoviev and Kamenev, his recent allies. The right-
wing moderates, his final rivals, were defeated by 1928, when Stalin
became the unlimited dictator.

It was now time to pursue a new program of action. The New
Economic Policy, having revived the economy, had served its purpose.
For a variety of economic, ideological, political, and international
reasons, Stalin now began his gargantuan task of industrializing the

country through a series of Five Year Plans and rural collectivization. The two are inextricably related, since the purpose of replacing small peasant farms with large collective farms was to permit the state to use rural production as it desired, whether for food and resources needed by new industrial centers or for export needed to pay for import of industrial equipment. It was hoped that the entire agrarian economy would be turned into a network of state farms, in which peasants would work much as did factory workers. However, the fierce peasant resistance, which became a virtual war between the party and the peasantry, millions of whom were sent to Siberian labor camps and eventual death, forced Stalin to retreat. Instead of the state farm, the so-called *artel* became the main form of collective farming. It allowed the peasants to keep small private garden plots and a specified number of farm animals, permitted them to sell the produce of this private activity on open markets, and retained the basic village character of rural life. To this day, however, the party continues its ultimate plans to eliminate these vestiges of private property "capitalism" and to establish a universal state farm system throughout Russia.

Collectivization and rapid industrialization were of course only a part of the Stalinist system. Equally important was the "great retreat" in various social and economic areas. This was yet another shift away from the original goals of the revolution. Wide wage inequalities and sharp class distinctions were re-established. The importance of the traditional system of marriage and family relations was stressed. Individual responsibility in all areas replaced the earlier Marxist focus on class, mass, and social conditions. Finally, the novel experiments in education and in the arts gave way to uniformity, regimentation, and dismal mediocrity. Probably the most characteristic features of Stalinism were the ubiquitous secret police, which actually replaced the Communist Party as Stalin's main instrument of political rule, and the "treason trials," confessions, and forced labor camps that processed and housed his victims.

Thus, in large part because it collapsed under the added burdens of World War I, a Russian society that had been gradually moving in the direction of a "Western" community politically free and economically developed, gave way to a system of absolute party dictatorship and a degree of ideological and cultural regimentation and police oppression not even dreamed of by Tsarist bureaucrats [2].

3. THE RISE OF FASCISM

Hitler's Germany and Mussolini's Italy, the other principal examples of totalitarianism in our century, also find part of their roots in the burdens and the dislocations of World War I.

Although one of the victors, Italy came out of the war humiliated because of her poor showing on the battlefield and her failure to win colonial territories in Africa. Moreover, the drastic shortages of goods together with financial disorganization brought about rampant inflation. Jobs were scarce, and the unemployed reacted with strikes and the seizure of land and even factories. Since the government was too weak and disunited to take determined action, the propertied class and the extreme nationalists sought someone who could re-establish order and rebuild national pride. Mussolini, who presented himself as this man of order and patriotism, had earlier been a socialist, but, after witnessing the failure of the radical left movements in the years 1919 to 1921, he revamped his program to meet the interests of the extreme nationalists and the property owners. With bands of unemployed war veterans dressed in black shirts, Mussolini in 1922 undertook his famous "march on Rome" and forced the incompetent King Victor Emanuel III to name him premier.

Once in office, he immediately began to establish an unlimited Fascist Party dictatorship. In certain respects the Fascist system can be compared to that of the Communists in Russia. Only one party was legal; all means of communication and cultural expression had to conform to the ideals and ideas of the Fascist Party; opposition or threat of opposition was stifled by the secret police. To protect the interests of the property owners, Mussolini abolished the trade unions. The entire economy was placed under a network of Fascist councils that sought to raise the efficiency and productivity of both agriculture and industry. In addition to the difference of their attitudes toward private property, a clear distinction between Communism and Fascism can be seen in the central themes of their respective ideologies. [3]

Politically far more important and far worse an outrage than Mussolini's system was the Nazi variety of Fascism established in Germany in 1933. Here, too, we must turn to World War I to find the main causes. The peace made at Versailles was deeply resented by a people who, after centuries of disunity, had experienced an exhilarating half-century of proud achievement. Germany had to acknowledge full responsibility for the war, give up all her colonies, return Alsace-Lorraine to France, give Poland territories taken in the eighteenth century, and pay an indemnity set in 1921 at $33 billion. In addition, the German navy was radically reduced; German munitions factories were placed under Entente supervision; and Germany was forbidden to own submarines, military aircraft, tanks, and artillery.

This blow at national pride was only part of the conditions that helped foster Fascism. As in Italy — and, indeed, throughout Western Europe — wild inflation and widespread unemployment wiped out lifelong savings and drastically depressed living standards. Particularly agonizing were the conditions of the returning veterans after their long sufferings at the front. The resulting sense of hopelessness and insecurity created an atmosphere hardly congenial to the successful functioning of a free society. In 1919 a noble effort to create such a society was undertaken with the establishment of a republic. The emperor was replaced by an elected president, and the elected legislature became much more important than it had been under the Empire. But, weak and disunited from the start, the Weimar Republic failed during the ten years of its existence to win the broad support that democracy requires. Nationalism and militaristic sentiments proved more powerful.

German national pride received still another blow when the Ruhr Valley was occupied in 1923 by French, Belgian, and Italian troops after Germany refused to continue paying war reparations. However, after an international loan was arranged to aid Germany in meeting these obligations, economic stability was re-established, and Germany became one of the more prosperous nations in Europe. Beneath the surface of this relative prosperity, however, nationalist feelings continued to be extremely strong. Among the nationalist groups was the so-called National Socialist German Workers Party, the Nazis. Its leader was Adolf Hitler, a frustrated artist, a war veteran, and a skillful demagogue. In 1923, following Mussolini's example of the "march on Rome," he attempted to seize control of the country by an uprising in Munich. He failed and was sentenced to a year in prison, which he spent writing *Mein Kampf* (My Struggle) and preparing for the next opportunity. He seemed to meet the psychological needs of important segments of the German people by the endlessly repeated claim that the Jews were to blame for all the evils that had befallen Germany and by his demands for the return of all her colonies to Germany, the removal of all arms restrictions, the acquisition by the German fatherland of all areas inhabited by Germans as well as of non-German areas needed as *Lebensraum* (living space) for the "superior" Nordic race.

As long as economic conditions improved, Hitler was unable to win the vast support needed for gaining power. With the onset of the world economic depression in the early 1930's, however, Hitler's following rose rapidly. The parliamentary elections of 1930 saw Nazi seats in the Reichstag increase from 12 to 107. In the presidential election of 1932, Hitler almost defeated the incumbent President Hindenburg, the venerable hero of the "Great War." In the parliamentary elections of the same year, the Nazi party won 230 of the 648 Reichstag seats, more than any single party had ever received under the Weimar Republic. In response to this indication of popular support, as well as direct pressures from powerful groups and individuals, Hindenburg named Hitler as chancellor (premier). Hitler filled the police and propaganda agencies with his Nazis and began to terrorize his opponents in an effort to gain still greater power in the Reichstag. In the secret and still relatively free elections of March, 1933, the Nazis and the Nationalists together won 52 per cent of the vote. Almost immediately thereafter, Hitler demanded that the Reichstag grant him four-year dictatorial powers. Only the 94 Social Democrats (anti-Communist Marxists) in the Reichstag voted against this demand.

The essential features of the Nazi system were like those of the totalitarian regimes already discussed. All the institutions of a free society were abolished, including free elections, trade unions, free speech and press, civil rights, and independent courts. Only the Nazi Party was permitted, and its members controlled all important positions. As in the other totalitarian states, the secret police played a key role in crushing any hint of opposition, and all means of communication, education, and cultural expression were rigidly controlled and used as instruments for propagating and molding desired public opinion. Hitler's rule differed from Communist totalitarianism, though not from Italian Fascism, in the close association between the Nazis and the great industrialists and financiers; his support was particularly great among the arms manufacturers. The unique feature of Hitler's rule was his effort to put his racial theories into practice by attempting to murder the entire Jewish population wherever he gained control.

4. ENGLAND AND FRANCE BETWEEN THE WARS

Our story thus far has been a depressing one of social breakdown, totalitarianism, and terror. How different were developments in the other main countries of Western Europe?

Economic conditions in England after the war were not much different from those in Germany and Italy: economic crisis, inflation, and unemployment prevailed there too. England also experienced a shock to its pride when the United States replaced it as the world's leading economic and financial power. The first attempts to revive the economy were made by Conservative governments under Bonar Law and Stanley Baldwin. But their program of reducing government expenses in such areas as social services only served to depress further the condition of the working class. As a result of accumulated mass dissatisfaction, the Conservatives lost in 1924 to a coalition of Labour and Liberal parties headed by Ramsay MacDonald. Liberal legislation, however, failed to improve conditions sufficiently. In addition, the Conservatives skillfully used widespread opposition to the government's recognition of Soviet Russia and to new economic ties with the Communist state to drive the coalition from office in 1925. Labor regained control of the government under Ramsay MacDonald in 1929, but he refused to introduce the social and economic measures demanded by most of his supporters. Consequently, he split with his Labour Party in 1931 and formed a coalition dominated by the Conservatives. The political situation remained essentially unchanged until World War II, as the Conservatives Stanley Baldwin and Neville Chamberlain succeeded Ramsay MacDonald.

Developments in France during these interwar years closely paralleled those in Great Britain. Devastated by a war that had been largely fought on French soil, burdened by a staggering war debt and inflation, and unable to modernize the backward small-scale economic enterprises in industry and agriculture, France experienced the same economic problems that oppressed the other countries of the West. As in the case of England, control was held by conservative governments, with the exception of two short periods of "Left" governments under Edouard Herriot in 1925–1926 and Léon Blum in 1936–1937. On the eve of World War II, therefore, the leading European democracies, France and Great Britain, were

plagued by economic depression, unstable political systems, disunited and discontented populations, and a military and diplomatic
system woefully inadequate to meet the challenge that Hitler was
soon to hurl at them.

5. THE LEAGUE OF NATIONS AND FASCIST AGGRESSION

One institution, the League of Nations, had seemed for a time
to hold out some hope of checking aggression. Organized at the
time of the Versailles Conference, the League and its affiliate institutions, such as the World Court, had helped to put treaty stipula-
tions into effect, to settle various border and financial disputes, and
to promote welfare activities, particularly among war refugees. The
League suffered a crippling blow, however, when the United States
refused to join it. In any case, it lacked the power to enforce the
measures it deemed necessary for preserving the peace.

In 1931 the League met its first great challenge. Japan invaded
Manchuria, violating its pledge both as a League member and as a
signatory of the Kellogg-Briand pact of 1928, which rejected war
as an instrument of national policy. Britain and France were unwilling to support forceful action without the participation of the United
States. President Hoover refused, however, to join any military or
economic measures against Japan. Japan's action went completely
unpunished.

Mussolini was the next challenger. In 1935 he invaded Ethiopia.
Britain and France attempted to apply economic sanctions, but they
were unable to get the agreement of the United States to a boycott
on shipments of petroleum, without which Mussolini could not continue to wage war.

The next year, in 1936, Hitler drew the lesson from the inability
of the Western democracies to join together against aggression. Violating the restrictions of the Versailles treaty, he sent armed forces into
the demilitarized Rhineland. France asked Britain for support, but
she held back. Force again proved more effective than principle.
Now events moved more swiftly toward catastrophe. Five months
after the Rhineland venture, General Franco began his conservative
and militarist revolution against the republican government of
Spain. Mussolini and Hitler sent large amounts of military aid,
partly to help destroy democratic government in Spain and partly to

test new military equipment. The republican "Loyalists" sought comparable aid from the democratic countries, but Britain, France, and the United States, although they were fully aware of German and Italian support of Franco, followed a policy of strict neutrality. While accepting neutrality in principle, the Soviet Union helped the Loyalists with airplanes, tanks, instructors, and small arms. However, their shipments proved too small to match the opposing supplies from the Fascist powers. With the fall of Barcelona in early 1939, the Loyalist cause was defeated.

Meanwhile, Hitler had not been idle. In 1937 he annexed Austria. Britain and France denounced the action, which was an explicit violation of the Versailles treaty. Later that year Hitler demanded from Czechoslovakia the cession of the German inhabited Sudetenland. The Czechs refused and prepared to fight. Hitler then unleashed an hysterical German nationalist campaign in apparent preparation for war. On September 28, 1938, several days before the deadline in Hitler's ultimatum to the Czechs, Premier Neville Chamberlain of Great Britain met at Munich with Hitler, Mussolini, and Premier Daladier of France. He pursuaded Daladier to accept Hitler's terms and thus in effect to withdraw French support, promised by treaty, from Czechoslovakia, which thereupon gave up the Sudetenland.

In the spring of the following year Hitler violated his "sacred pledge" to respect the rump Czechoslovak state. In March, 1939, the German army invaded and occupied the abandoned Czech republic. Less than a month later, Hitler demanded control of Danzig, then under the League of Nations, and the return of the "Polish Corridor," a section of the territory granted to the newly reformed Poland after World War I, which separated East Prussia from the rest of Germany. The Soviet Union, well aware that Hitler coveted Poland as part of an eventual Slavic *Lebensraum* which included the U.S.S.R., but also recalling the betrayal of Czechoslovakia at Munich and realizing its own unreadiness economically and militarily for war, signed a ten-year neutrality pact with Hitler on August 23, 1939. A week later, on September 1, the German *blitzkrieg* ("lightning war") struck Poland. Britain and France, though no better prepared than Russia and less directly threatened, honored their treaty obligations to Poland and declared war on Germany two days later.

6. WORLD WAR II

The unprecedented horrors experienced during the years of World War II climaxed the series of disasters that had befallen the West since World War I. Until the middle of 1942 the forces of Fascism continued advancing with the same dynamism that had marked their bold drive in the 1930's. Less than a month after the invasion began, Poland fell. During April, 1940, Hitler took Denmark and Norway. In May he opened his mighty attack against France, Belgium, Luxemburg, and the Netherlands. By brilliant strategy he isolated the main body of the French forces in Belgium and in five days routed the remaining French troops. Some 300,000 British troops escaped by a desperate evacuation at Dunkirk.

On June 17, little more than a month after it was invaded, France surrendered. To prepare for the conquest of England, the Nazis began a series of destructive air raids upon London and other cities but soon were engaged in a difficult contest with the Royal Air Force for control of the air over the Channel. At the same time a submarine campaign against British shipping was begun in an attempt to starve England into submission. Winston Churchill, who had replaced Chamberlain as prime minister in May, sent the bulk of the British tanks and artillery which might be needed to meet a Nazi invasion of England itself, to North Africa. This extraordinarily courageous gamble paid off when the British Eighth Army successfully stopped an Italian advance into Egypt the following winter. Seeing that Britain was holding firm, Hitler turned in his own great gamble eastward. On June 22, 1941, having conquered the Balkan countries, he attacked the Soviet Union with one of the greatest concentrations of military power ever assembled. By the end of the year, Leningrad was surrounded and put under a dreadful starvation siege, and Moscow itself faced attack.

Impressed by the seemingly invincible forces of Fascism, Japan, the third member of the Axis alliance, deemed the moment right for her own leap to glory and power. Japan had been advancing slowly since 1940 against British, French, and Dutch territories in Southeast Asia. Convinced that its strength would now bring it control of at least the entire Pacific area, Japan sent its planes in an attack against the American naval base at Pearl Harbor on December 7, 1941. The next day the United States declared war on Japan. On

December 11, Germany and Italy announced a state of war with the United States, and the following day the United States replied in kind.

Many months passed before the United States began to play a significant part in the war. Fascism, meanwhile, moved forward. After a winter of waiting, the Germans reopened the attack in Russia in June, 1942. By August they had reached Stalingrad. For six months the battle raged, street to street, door to door — but the Russians held. By January, 1943, the entire character of the war had changed. By means of a wide pincer movement the Russians captured some 300,000 Germans whom Hitler had refused to allow to retreat from Stalingrad. The Russian counteroffensive was beginning.

The tide also turned in North Africa in 1942. With considerable United States support, the British defended El Alamein, located just sixty miles from Alexandria, Egypt, and by the end of the year forced the German General Rommel to retreat. The United States also began to advance against the Japanese in the Pacific. For several months after Pearl Harbor, Japan had conquered everywhere — Wake Island, Guam, the Philippines, Hong Kong, Malaya, Singapore, Burma. But in June, 1942, as they were preparing to renew the attack on Hawaii, the Japanese encountered the American fleet off Midway Island and suffered a disastrous defeat. In August the United States began its offensive.

During the next two and a half years the Allies slowly pushed ahead toward victory. While the Russians, who still carried the main burden of fighting in Europe, forced the Nazis back on the Eastern Front, the British and American forces drove the Italians and, after the Italian surrender, the Germans up the Italian peninsula. On June 6, 1944, the long-delayed "second front" was opened in the west with a massive landing on the Normandy coast. Heavy bombing combined with persistent attacks on both fronts defeated the Germans militarily, economically, and psychologically. In April, 1945, the Russians entered Berlin. From the west, combined forces of British, French, and American troops broke the German defenses, crossed the Rhine, and moved on to meet the Russians at the Elbe. On May 8, Germany surrendered.

Only the defeat of Japan remained to be accomplished. In October, 1944, several months after the second front had been opened in Europe, the Japanese fleet was virtually destroyed in the Battle of Leyte Gulf. The invasion of Japan lay ahead. To avoid the high human costs any such invasion would demand, the United States decided to terrorize the Japanese into surrender by dropping the first atomic bomb ever used in war. On August 6, 1945, Hiroshima was decimated. Three days later a second atomic bomb struck Nagasaki. On August 14, 1945, Japan surrendered.

It has been estimated that some 22 million people, about half of them civilians, died during the war. Russia alone lost 15 million. As for the material costs, a modest estimate is that $2 thousand billion were lost in destruction, not to speak of an incalculable amount of labor and capital that might have gone into creative economic and welfare investments.

7. THE ARTS AND SCIENCES

From the suffering of World War I, through the distress of economic depression and the victory of police totalitarianism, to the unimaginable agonies of extermination camps, massive bombing of civilians, and atomic warfare — such has been the story of our century from 1914 to the end of World War II. It is little wonder that art, literature, and music reflect turmoil and disorganization, or that the intellectual history of our century is dominated by an obsession with irrationalism, crisis, chaos, and despair [4, 5, 6].

Yet it would be inaccurate and unfortunate to focus attention exclusively on the darker aspects of civilization in these decades. During these same years science and technology not only continued their progress but made astounding and unprecedented leaps forward. The smallest particles of matter and the vast reaches of outer space were being daily forced to divulge their secrets. Moreover, although such progress provided men with enormously destructive weapons, it also contributed greatly to a rapid improvement in living standards and human health. Machines continued to relieve men of the burden of work, allowing ever longer periods of leisure in which they might realize their finer potentialities [7].

As always, every advance entailed new problems. The application of new medical and sanitation techniques to the underdeveloped areas of the world promoted a dangerous "population explosion" [8]. The progress of science fostered a distressing cleavage of educated society into "two cultures" and has raised a variety of problems resulting from automation [7].

8. THE ADVANCE OF SOCIAL JUSTICE

It is not only in the areas of science and technology that one finds positive and, in spite of the new dangers, encouraging developments to weigh in the balance against the outrageous events and depressing tendencies of our century. Through these decades of strife, pain, and oppression one can see clearly a persistent, if uneven, advance of social justice. The assumptions that supported the laissez-faire society of the preceding century have been constantly undermined by a more venerable judgment which insists that each man is his brother's keeper. As we have seen above, new tendencies in so many areas of life and thought have dramatically challenged the beliefs of the eighteenth-century Enlightenment, the conviction that all men are by nature of equal mind and virtue and may therefore participate in the affairs of society and enjoy its benefits. But it is the realization of these very ideals that one witnesses in the continuing democratization of education, the broadening of civil rights and liberties, and the countless and diverse welfare measures legislated throughout the world. All this must be included in the balance when one judges these decades [10].

When we turn to the years following the World War II, we find the same dilemma of judgment. How should one weigh vast suffering and unprecedented dangers against exhilarating progress in a wide range of areas?

9. COMMUNIST AGGRESSION AND WESTERN ALLIANCES

In the area of international relations, the situation after World War II was in some ways even worse than it had been after World War I. In 1945, the Soviet Union, in spite of its immense war losses, immediately took advantage of the postwar conditions to expand its sphere of control. During the counteroffensives against the retreating German invaders from 1943 until early 1945, Soviet troops occupied most of Eastern Europe and the Balkans. Russia then began to transform, by carefully planned and effected stages, the independent countries in this region into completely subordinate satellites, in violation of promises made to the Allies at a number of wartime conferences, notably at Yalta in February, 1945. By 1947 the U.S.S.R. had established an empire which included Poland, Czechoslovakia, Rumania, Hungary, Bulgaria, Yugoslavia, and Eastern Germany, in addition to the Baltic countries which Russia had annexed on the eve of the war. In 1949 the Communist bloc was vastly enlarged by the victory of the Chinese Communists over the government of Chiang Kai-shek.

From this powerful base, international Communism persistently sought to move ahead to further territorial gains, convinced that every advance was part of the inevitable course of history. In the West, the first intended victim was Berlin. British, French, and American troops occupied the western portions of the former German capital, pending a final peace treaty with Germany and the unification of Eastern and Western Germany by free elections. First by financial restrictions and then by a full land blockade, the Russians tried in 1948 to force the Allies to leave Berlin; but an Allied "air bridge" defeated the Russian plan.

In the East the first major advance of Communism after the victory in China in 1949 was the invasion of South Korea by North Korean troops in June, 1950. Drawing erroneous conclusions from official United States comments, the invaders believed that the United States would not intervene. Fortunately for the defense of South Korea, at the time the United Nations Security Council was called into emergency session to deal with the invasion the Soviet Union was boycotting the United Nations in order to protest the exclusion of Communist China from the United Nations. Thus free of the Russian veto, the Security Council voted to authorize member nations to furnish aid to South Korea.

Through most of 1950 the invaders advanced rapidly, by September confining the South Koreans to a small area in the southeast around Pusan. But after the landing of United Nations forces under United States command, the North Koreans were quickly forced back. In October the United Nations troops reached the border between Manchuria and Korea. At this point the entire character of the war changed when Communist China sent "volunteers" to serve with the North Koreans. General Douglas MacArthur, the commander of the U.N. force, urged the United States to respond to Chinese air action by bombing Chinese bases in Manchuria. Fearing that such raids upon Chinese territory might lead to a full-scale conflict between the United States and China, with further dangers inherent in Chinese-Russian alliance treaties, President Truman dismissed MacArthur from command of United States forces. By mid-1951 a stalemate had been reached. In July truce talks began, and on July 27,

1953, an agreement was reached establishing the border between the Communist North and non-Communist South Korea.

Since the Korean truce Communism has experienced both advances and defeats in the East. The defeat of the French in Indochina allowed the Communists to take control of North Vietnam. Since 1961 the Communists have continued efforts to win both the rest of Vietnam and the bordering state of Laos as the first steps in a drive to take all of Southeast Asia.

If the threat of totalitarian aggression was far greater than it was after World War I, the strength and determination of the Western democracies were also greater. While totalitarianism advanced in Europe as a result of Russia's wartime success against the Germans, the forces of democracy rapidly gained strength in large part as a result of immense economic growth in the United States. The first dramatic indication of the new leading role of the United States in world affairs came in January, 1947. The British government, burdened by war losses and economic problems, declared itself no longer able to defend Greece and Turkey against Communist threats. On March 12, 1947, President Truman proclaimed the "Truman Doctrine" and obtained a $400 million grant from Congress to help check Communism in the Mediterranean [9]. The period of military containment of the U.S.S.R. began. Three months later, the United States took its second major step in this direction when George Marshall, the Secretary of State, offered broad economic aid to all countries of Europe [9]. Thanks to this aid, the Western European states were able to re-establish their economies and to avoid the conditions which had undermined Europe economically, politically, and psychologically after World War I.

These programs were only the beginning of cooperation between the United States and European powers in efforts to achieve recovery and to establish economic and military defense alliances. On April 4, 1949, the United States joined with twelve nations of Europe, Canada, and Iceland to form the North Atlantic Treaty Organization, which became the West's principal military defense against Russian expansion in the West. In May, 1950, the French statesman Robert Schuman proposed and helped bring into existence the European Coal and Steel Community, which pools the resources of France, Italy, the German Federal Republic, Belgium, Luxemburg, and the Netherlands in those fundamental industries. On March 2 the European Economic Community (the "Common Market") was

formed, with the aim of gradually eliminating customs duties between the member nations and establishing a common external
tariff. By the early 1960's important gains were made toward this
end. Even Great Britain was preparing to join the Common Market,
over the intense criticism of those fearful of the effect this would
have on Commonwealth trade relations and the open opposition of
the French president, General De Gaulle. As part of this general
trend, a "parliament of Europe" was established in March, 1948,
with seats distributed on a party rather than national basis.

10. THE UNITED NATIONS

For many people the most hopeful of all international organizations formed in this century has been the United Nations, the
central meeting ground of opposing power blocs. Discussed origi-
nally in 1944 by the "Big Four" (Great Britain, Russia, the United
States, and China) at Dumbarton Oaks in Washington, the United
Nations held its first meeting in 1945 in San Francisco. On October
24, 1945, the required number of member nations ratified the
Charter of the U.N.

Impeded by big-power vetos, plagued by financial shortages, and
hampered by inadequate enforcement powers, the United Nations
has nonetheless proved to be far more effective than the League of
Nations. Through such agencies as the Technical Assistance Administration, the International Bank of Reconstruction and Development, the Food and Agriculture Organization, and the Educational,
Scientific and Cultural Organization, the United Nations has done
much to further world economic development, health and social
welfare, and international cooperation [10]. Moreover, the United
Nations has demonstrated its ability to arbitrate serious disputes and
even, on occasion, to enforce decisions, as in the Korean War, the
Kashmir controversy between India and Pakistan, the Palestine partition war, and conflict in the former Belgian Congo.

11. ECONOMIC PROSPERITY

While the integration of Western Europe was progressing
steadily, the individual countries experienced steadily increasing
economic prosperity. Though greater in some countries than in
others, the situation was everywhere in striking contrast to what it

had been following World War I. Political conditions were also far healthier, although also unevenly so. In England, despite the well-nigh limitless admiration felt by the British for Winston Churchill, their wartime leader, Churchill's Conservative Party lost to Labour in the 1945 elections. A wave of welfare and socialist legislation followed that included socialization of medicine, nationalization of the coal mines and the Bank of England, and a radical shift in the tax rates to the advantage of the lower-income groups. These measures, which produced a social revolution of a kind in England, when combined with Marshall Plan aid and the indirect benefit of a general rise in the prosperity of Europe and America, rapidly eliminated some of England's most pressing postwar domestic problems. In 1951 a more contented population returned the Conservatives to power. The Conservatives retained many of the socialist and welfare measures instituted by the Labour government [11, 12].

As after World War I, conditions in France were more difficult than in England. Besides the economic burdens and the wartime destruction, there was the psychological impact of the rapid defeat of 1940 and the extensive collaboration with the Nazis during the years of German occupation. The left-wing parties, particularly the Communists, gained a large vote. The postwar French governments were less successful than the British Labour Party government in meeting the new problems. One reason was that the question of colonialism plagued the French far more than it did the British. Where England moved slowly but surely to transform its empire into a voluntary Commonwealth, important segments of French society forced the government to resist adamantly the movement for decolonialization. France granted independence to Indochina only after a humiliating defeat on the battlefield in 1951. Even more difficult were bitter conflicts in North Africa. In 1956 Morocco and Tunisia won their independence, but efforts to achieve Algerian independence led to a revolt of the French army against the government in 1958 and the return of General Charles De Gaulle to power. To the surprise of many, however, De Gaulle used the greatly enlarged executive authority he secured as president of the new Fifth Republic in order to grant independence to a number of French African colonies and to move toward accepting Algerian independence as well. Conservative forces hostile to De Gaulle's new policy formed the Secret Army Organization (OAS), an underground organization. Its purpose was to prevent the establishment of an independent Algeria by all methods, including widespread terror and assassination. OAS terror became particularly intense following the truce arranged in early 1962 between the French government and the leaders of the Algerian independence movement, but Algerian sovereignty was nonetheless approved by the French electorate in a referendum.

Perhaps, paradoxically, the most striking postwar economic recovery occurred in the western part of defeated Germany. Nothing contrasts more starkly with the post-World War I situation. Half-hearted execution of decisions to limit and even dismantle large-scale German industry, a vast influx of foreign capital in loans and investments, the introduction of more modern equipment in the place of machinery destroyed in the war — these were major factors in promoting recovery. The political picture, however, was as unfavorable as the economic scene was favorable. By 1948, the eastern and western parts of Germany were virtually severed as a result of the "cold war." The German Federal Republic was established at the end of 1949 under the elected leadership of Dr. Konrad Adenauer. A month later Russia responded with the establishment of the German Democratic Republic. Thereafter the reunification of the two halves remained a dream, while the fate of the Western-controlled sectors of Berlin, deep within East Germany, became the object of sharp conflict. At the close of 1961 the Russians tried once again to force the West out of Berlin. A wall was built separating East and West Berlin, and Soviet Premier Khrushchev announced his intention of signing a separate peace treaty with East Germany that would give the German Democratic Republic control over the access routes to Berlin.

12. NUCLEAR WEAPONS

In contrast to the situation after World War I, when economic and political turmoil was the central problem, we face today a confrontation of great powers possessing weapons of fantastic destructive capacity. By the early 1960's both Russia and the United States possessed large stockpiles of nuclear weapons each a thousand times more powerful than the atomic bombs dropped on Hiroshima and Nagasaki. A 60- or 70-megaton hydrogen bomb exploded by the Soviet Union in 1961 showed that even more dreadful weapons were being made. With means available to deliver these bombs from land, sea, air, and even from outer space, and with miscalculation, technological failure of control, or irrational action ever-present possibilities, arms control, test and bomb bans, and general disarmament became compelling concerns in the 1960's [14].

13. THE PRESENT INTERNATIONAL SITUATION

While some looked hopefully to international disarmament agreements or at least to agreements for the elimination of nuclear arms, others drew some degree of optimism from developments within the Soviet Union and its satellite empire. When Stalin died in 1953 a new era seemed to have begun. The power of the secret police was significantly reduced, a remarkable "thaw" took place in literature and in other areas of art and thought, and terror was to some extent replaced by economic incentives as a means of winning more active support from the people for the Communist Party and its programs. Some believe that we are witnessing a gradual change within Russia in the direction of a rather typical urban "bourgeois" society, concerned more with improving material conditions at home than with achieving further gains abroad.

Those who argue for this analysis find support in the apparent breakdown of Stalin's highly centralized satellite empire. The first great blow to Stalin's empire was struck in 1948, when Yugoslavia, while retaining its Communist dictatorship, broke with Stalin and began a series of domestic reforms. The next blow came in 1956, when, in part inspired by "de-Stalinization" in Russia, anti-Soviet movements that led to risings in Poland and Hungary emerged in Eastern Europe. These revolts, though put down, compelled Russia to grant greater autonomy to its satellites. In the late 1950's a new and far more threatening danger for Soviet Russia arose in the Eastern branch of world Communism. The Chinese Communist leaders not only demanded equality with Soviet leaders but insisted that their strategies and tactics in a host of basic issues were superior to those of the Russians, whom they accused of cowardice and revisionism. The more optimistic observers in the West therefore look forward to a decline in Russian expansion as a result of several related developments: the competition from Chinese Communists, such that further Communist victories in the East would only strengthen China and weaken Russia within the international Communist movement; the apparent weakening of Russia's control over the

East European satellites; the enormous risks of nuclear holocaust if aggressive policies are pursued; the increasingly effective demand of the Russian people for greater attention to their own needs; and, finally, the Soviet belief that they can win increasing support throughout the world by their achievements in science and technology and economic growth.

14. THE NEW NATIONS

The areas of the world where Soviet Russia hopes to gain most by its successes in the peaceful pursuits of science and industry are the economically underdeveloped, formerly colonial, countries. The surge of these areas into prominence may be seen from a long historical point of view as representing a stage in the persistent expansion of Western ideas and ideals. The sense of nationalism, the desire for high material living standards, the opposition to traditional customs, and the attraction to secularism, rationalism, and "scientism" — all revolutionary changes in these countries reflect essentially Western concepts and attitudes. Meeting in Indonesia in April, 1955, African and Asian representatives of the underdeveloped nations met to outline a common program. In the long run this may prove to have been the most important single development in our century [13].

1

The War that No One Wanted

THERE ARE few more compelling concerns today than the causes of war
and the ways of averting them. This is particularly true of wars resulting
from miscalculations and from misunderstanding of the goals and
intentions of other states. Those most actively concerned with this
danger look to a study of the causes of past wars for guidance. Most
frequently they turn to World War I, for the "Great War" is considered an example of world-wide conflicts resulting from precisely such
confusion and misunderstanding. The way that World War I began is
reflected in the following excerpts from correspondence exchanged on the
very eve of the war.

Diplomatic Documents:
July 28–August 4, 1914

*The Chancellor to the Governments of Germany.
Confidential. Berlin, July 28, 1914]*

 YOU WILL make the following report to the Government to
which you are accredited:

In view of the facts which the Austrian Government has published in its note to the Servian [Serbian] Government, the last
doubt must disappear that the outrage to which the Austro-Hungarian
successor to the throne has fallen a victim, was prepared in Servia, to
say the least with the connivance of members of the Servian Government and army. It is a product of the pan-Serb intrigues which for

From COLLECTED DIPLOMATIC DOCUMENTS RELATING TO THE OUTBREAK
OF THE EUROPEAN WAR (London, 1915), German "White Book" section, pp. 425–426, 431–433, 436–439; Russian "Orange Book" section,
entries 53, 60–63, 66, 70, 76. Reprinted by permission of Her Majesty's
Stationery Office.

a series of years have become a source of permanent disturbance for the Austro-Hungarian Monarchy and for the whole of Europe.

The pan-Serb chauvinism appeared especially marked during the Bosnian crisis. Only to the far-reaching self-restraint and moderation of the Austro-Hungarian Government and the energetic intercession of the Powers is it to be ascribed that the provocations to which Austro-Hungary was exposed at that time, did not lead to a conflict. The assurance of future well-behaviour, which the Servian Government gave at that time, it has not kept. Under the very eyes, at least with the tacit sufferance of official Servia, the pan-Serb propaganda has meanwhile continued to increase in scope and intensity. It would be compatible neither with its dignity nor with its right to self-preservation if the Austro-Hungarian Government persisted to view idly any longer the intrigues beyond the frontier, through which the safety and the integrity of the Monarchy are permanently threatened. With this state of affairs, the action as well as the demands of the Austro-Hungarian Government can be viewed only as justifiable.

The reply of the Servian Government to the demands which the Austro-Hungarian Government put on the 23rd inst., through its representative in Belgrade, shows that the dominating factors in Servia are not inclined to cease their former policies and agitation. There will remain nothing else for the Austro-Hungarian Government than to press its demands, if need be, through military action, unless it renounces for good its position as a great Power.

Some Russian personalities deem it their right as a matter of course and a task of Russia's, to actively become a party to Servia in the conflict between Austria-Hungary and Servia. For the European conflagration which would result from a similar step by Russia, the "Nowoje Wremja" believes itself justified in making Germany responsible in so far as it does not induce Austria-Hungary to yield.

The Russian press thus turns conditions upside down. It is not Austria-Hungary which has called forth the conflict with Servia, but it is Servia which, through unscrupulous favour toward pan-Serb aspirations, even in parts of the Austro-Hungarian Monarchy, threatens the same in her existence and creates conditions, which eventually found expression in the wanton outrage at Sarajewo. If Russia believes that it must champion the cause of Servia in this matter, it certainly has the right to do so. However, it must realise that it makes the Serb activities its own, to undermine the conditions of existence of the Austro-Hungarian Monarchy, and that thus it bears the sole responsibility if out of the Austro-Servian affair, which all other Great Powers desire to localise, there arises a European war. This responsibility of Russia's is evident and it weighs the more heavily as Count Berchtold has officially declared to Russia that Austria-Hungary has no intention to acquire Servian territory or to touch the existence of the Servian Kingdom, but only desires peace against the Servian intrigues threatening its existence.

The attitude of the Imperial Government in this question is clearly indicated. The agitation conducted by the pan-Slavs in Austria-Hungary has for its goal, with the destruction of the Austro-Hungarian Monarchy, the scattering or weakening of the Triple Alliance with a complete isolation of the German Empire in consequence. Our own interest therefore calls us to the side of Austria-Hungary. The duty, if at all possible, to guard Europe against a universal war, points to the support by ourselves of those endeavours which aim at the localisation of the conflict, faithful to the course of those policies which we have carried out successfully for forty-four years in the interest of the preservation of the peace of Europe.

Should, however, against our hope, through the interference of Russia the fire be spread, we should have to support, faithful to our duty as allies, the neighbour-monarchy with all the power at our command. We shall take the sword only if forced to it, but then in the clear consciousness that we are not guilty of the calamity which war will bring upon the peoples of Europe.

Telegram of the Russian Ambassador at Paris to Russian Minister for Foreign Affairs.
Paris, July 16 (29), 1914]

For the information of the President of the French Republic on his return, the French Minister for Foreign Affairs had prepared a short summary of the present political situation, approximately in the following terms: Austria, fearing internal disintegration, seized upon the assassination of the Archduke as an excuse for an attempt to obtain guarantees, which may assume the form of an occupation of Servian military lines or even Servian territory. Germany is supporting Austria. The preservation of peace depends upon Russia alone, for the question at issue must be "localised" between Austria and Servia; that question is the punishment of Servia for her previous policy and the obtaining of guarantees for the future. Germany concludes from this that a moderating influence should be exerted at St. Petersburg. This sophism has been refuted both in Paris and in London. In Paris, Baron von Schoen vainly endeavoured to induce France to adopt joint action with Germany towards Russia for the preservation of peace. The same attempts were made in London. In both capitals the answer was given that any action taken should be at Vienna, as it was Austria's inordinate demands, her refusal to discuss Servia's few reservations, and her declaration of war, that threatened to provoke a general war. France and England are unable to bring any moderating pressure to bear upon Russia, as, so far, that Power has shown the greatest moderation, more particularly in her advice to Servia to accept as much as was possible of the Austrian note. Apparently Germany has now given up the idea of pressure upon Russia only and inclines towards mediatory action both at St. Petersburg and at Vienna, but at the same time both Germany and Austria are endeavouring to cause the question to drag on. Germany is opposing the conference without suggesting any other practical course of action. Austria is continuing discussions at St. Petersburg, which are manifestly of a procrastinating nature. At the same time she is taking active steps, and if these steps are tolerated, her claims will increase proportionately. It is highly desirable that Russia should lend all her support to the proposal for mediation which will be made by Sir E. Grey. In the contrary event, Austria, on the plea of "guarantees," will be able, in effect, to alter the territorial status of eastern Europe.

Telegram of the Russian Minister for Foreign Affairs to Russian Ambassadors at Berlin, Vienna, Paris, London, and Rome. St. Petersburg, July 17 (30), 1914]

The German Ambassador, who has just left me, has asked whether Russia would not be satisfied with the promise which Austria might give — that she would not violate the integrity of the Kingdom of Servia — and whether we could not indicate upon what conditions we would agree to suspend our military preparations. I dictated to him the following declaration to be forwarded to Berlin for immediate action:

"Si l'Autriche, reconnaissant que la question austroserbe a assumé le caractère d'une question européenne, se déclare prête à éliminer de son ultimatum les points qui portent atteinte aux droits souverains de la Serbie, la Russie s'engage à cesser ses préparatifs militaires."

"If Austria, recognising that the Austro-Servian question has assumed the character of a question of European interest, declares herself ready to eliminate from her ultimatum points which violate the sovereign rights of Servia, Russia engages to stop her military preparations."

Please inform me at once by telegraph what attitude the German Government will adopt in face of this fresh proof of our desire to do the utmost possible for a peaceful settlement of the question, for we cannot allow such discussions to continue solely in order that Germany and Austria may gain time for their military preparations.

Telegram of the Russian Ambassador at Berlin to Russian Minister for Foreign Affairs.
Berlin, July 17 (30), 1914]

I learn that the order for the mobilisation of the German army and navy has just been issued.

Telegram of the Russian Ambassador at Berlin to Russian Minister for Foreign Affairs.
Berlin, July 17 (30), 1914]

The Minister for Foreign Affairs has just telephoned that the news of the mobilisation of the German army and fleet, which has just been announced, is false; that the news sheets had been printed in advance so as to be ready for all eventualities, and that they were put on sale in the afternoon, but that they have now been confiscated.

Telegram of the Russian Ambassador at Berlin to Russian Minister for Foreign Affairs.
Berlin, July 17 (30), 1914]

I have received your telegram of 16th (29th) July, and have communicated the text of your proposal to the Minister for Foreign Affairs, whom I have just seen. He told me that he had received an identic telegram from the German Ambassador at St. Petersburg, and he then declared that he considered it impossible for Austria to accept our proposal.

Secret telegram to Russian Representatives abroad.
July 19 (August 1), 1914]

At midnight the German Ambassador announced to me, on the instruction of his Government, that if within 12 hours, that is by midnight on Saturday, we had not begun to demobilise, not only against Germany, but also against Austria, the German Government would be compelled to give the order for mobilisation. To my enquiry whether this meant war, the Ambassador replied in the negative, but added that we were very near to it.

His Majesty to the Czar. July 28th, 10:45 P.M.]

I have heard with the greatest anxiety of the impression which is caused by the action of Austria-Hungary against Servia. The inscrupulous agitation which has been going on for years in Servia, has led to the revolting crime of which Archduke Franz Ferdinand has become a victim. The spirit which made the Servians murder their own King and his consort still dominates that country. Doubtless You will agree with me that both of us, You as well as I, and all other sovereigns, have a common interest to insist that all those who are responsible for this horrible murder shall suffer their deserved punishment.

On the other hand I by no means overlook the difficulty encountered by You and Your Government to stem the tide of public opinion. In view of the cordial friendship which has joined us both for a long time with firm ties, I shall use my entire influence to induce Austria-Hungary to obtain a frank and satisfactory understanding with Russia. I hope confidently that You will support me in my effort to overcome all difficulties which may yet arise.

Your most sincere and devoted friend and cousin

(Signed) WILHELM

The Czar to His Majesty. Peterhof Palace,
July 29th, 1 P.M.]

I am glad that You are back in Germany. In this serious moment I ask You earnestly to help me. An ignominious war has been declared against a weak country and in Russia the indignation which I fully share is tremendous. I fear that very soon I shall be unable to resist the pressure exercised upon me and that I shall be forced to take measures which will lead to war. To prevent a calamity as a European war would be, I urge You in the name of our old friendship to do all in Your power to restrain Your ally from going too far.

(Signed) NICOLAS

His Majesty to the Czar. July 29th, 6:30 P.M.]

I have received Your telegram and I share Your desire for the conservation of peace. However: I cannot — as I told You in my first telegram — consider the action of Austria-Hungary as an "ignominious war." Austria-Hungary knows from experience that the promises of Servia as long as they are merely on paper are entirely unreliable.

According to my opinion the action of Austria-Hungary is to be considered as an attempt to receive full guaranty that the promises of Servia are effectively translated into deeds. In this opinion I am strengthened by the explanation of the Austrian Cabinet that Austria-Hungary intended no territorial gain at the expense of Servia. I am therefore of opinion that it is perfectly possible for Russia to remain a spectator in the Austro-Servian war without drawing Europe into the most terrible war it has ever seen. I believe that a direct understanding is possible and desirable between Your Government and Vienna, an understanding which — as I have already telegraphed You — my Government endeavours to aid with all possible effort. Naturally military measures by Russia, which might be construed as a menace by Austria-Hungary, would accelerate a calamity which both of us desire to avoid and would undermine my position as mediator which — upon Your appeal to my friendship and aid — I willingly accepted.

(Signed) WILHELM

His Majesty to the Czar. July 30th, 1 A.M.]

My Ambassador has instructions to direct the attention of Your Government to the dangers and serious consequences of a mobilisation. I have told You the same in my last telegram. Austria-Hungary has mobilised only against Servia, and only a part of her army. If Russia, as seems to be the case, according to Your advice and that of Your Government, mobilises against Austria-Hungary, the part of the mediator with which You have entrusted me in such friendly manner and which I have accepted upon Your express desire, is threatened if not made impossible. The entire weight of decision now rests upon Your shoulders, You have to bear the responsibility for war or peace.

(Signed) WILHELM

The Czar to His Majesty. Peterhof, July 30th, 1914,
1:20 P.M.]

I thank You from my heart for Your quick reply. I am sending to-night Tatisheff (Russian honorary aide to the Kaiser) with instructions. The military measures now taking form were decided upon five days ago, and for the reason of defence against the preparations of Austria. I hope with all my heart that these measures will not influence in any manner Your position as mediator which I appraise very highly. We need Your strong pressure upon Austria so that an understanding can be arrived at with us.

NICOLAS

Telegram of the Chancellor to the Imperial Ambassador
at St. Petersburg on July 31st, 1914. Urgent]

In spite of negotiations still pending and although we have up to this hour made no preparations for mobilisation, Russia has mobilised her *entire* army and navy, hence also against us. On account of these Russian measures, we have been forced, for the safety of the country, to proclaim the threatening state of war, which does not yet imply mobilisation. Mobilisation, however, is bound to follow if Russia does not stop every measure of war against us and against Austria-Hungary within 12 hours, and notifies us definitely to this effect. Please to communicate this at once to M. Sasonof and wire hour of communication.

Telegram of the Chancellor to the Imperial Ambassador
in Paris on July 31st, 1914. Urgent]

Russia has ordered mobilisation of her entire army and fleet, therefore also against us in spite of our still pending mediation. We

have therefore declared the threatening state of war which is bound
to be followed by mobilisation unless Russia stops within 12 hours
all measures of war against us and Austria. Mobilisation inevitably
implies war. Please ask French Government whether it intends to
remain neutral in a Russo-German war. Reply must be made in 18
hours. Wire at once hour of inquiry. Utmost speed necessary.

Note presented by the German Ambassador at St. Petersburg on July 19 (August 1), at 7:10 P.M.]

The Imperial German Government have used every effort
since the beginning of the crisis to bring about a peaceful settlement.
In compliance with a wish expressed to him by His Majesty the
Emperor of Russia, the German Emperor had undertaken, in concert
with Great Britain, the part of mediator between the Cabinets of
Vienna and St. Petersburg; but Russia, without waiting for any
result, proceeded to a general mobilisation of her forces both on
land and sea. In consequence of this threatening step, which was not
justified by any military proceedings on the part of Germany, the
German Empire was faced by a grave and imminent danger. If the
German Government had failed to guard against this peril, they
would have compromised the safety and the very existence of Germany. The German Government were, therefore, obliged to make
representations to the Government of His Majesty the Emperor of
All the Russias and to insist upon a cessation of the aforesaid military acts. Russia having refused to comply with (not having considered it necessary to answer) this demand, and having shown by
this refusal (this attitude) that her action was directed against Germany, I have the honour, on the instructions of my Government to
inform your Excellency as follows:

His Majesty the Emperor, my august Sovereign, in the name of the
German Empire, accepts the challenge, and considers himself at war
with Russia.

Announcement by the Russian Minister for Foreign Affairs respecting recent events. July 20 (August 2), 1914]

A garbled version of the events of the last few days having
appeared in the foreign press, the Russian Minister for Foreign

Affairs considers it his duty to publish the following brief account of the diplomatic discussions during the period under review: —

On the 10th (23rd) July, 1914, the Austro-Hungarian Minister at Belgrade presented a note to the Prime Minister of Servia, in which the Servian Government were accused of having fostered the pan-Serb movement, which had led to the assassination of the heir to the Austro-Hungarian throne. Austria-Hungary, therefore, demanded of the Servian Government, not only the condemnation in the most formal manner of the above-mentioned propaganda, but also the adoption, under Austrian supervision, of a series of measures for the discovery of the plot, for the punishment of any Servian subjects who had taken part in it, and for the prevention of any future attempts at assassination upon Austrian soil. A time limit of forty-eight hours was given to the Servian Government within which to reply to this note.

The Russian Government, to whom the Austro-Hungarian Ambassador at St. Petersburg had communicated the text of the note seventeen hours after its presentation at Belgrade, having taken note of the demands contained therein, could not but perceive that some of these demands were impossible of execution as regards their substance, whilst others were presented in a form which was incompatible with the dignity of an independent State. Russia considered that the humiliation of Servia, involved in these demands, and equally the evident intention of Austria-Hungary to secure her own hegemony in the Balkans, which underlay her conditions, were inadmissable. The Russian Government, therefore, pointed out to Austria-Hungary in the most friendly manner that it would be desirable to re-examine the points contained in the Austro-Hungarian note. The Austro-Hungarian Government did not see their way to agree to a discussion of the note. The moderating influence of the four Powers at Vienna was equally unsuccessful.

Despite the fact that Servia had reprobated the crime, and had shown herself ready to give Austria satisfaction to an extent beyond the expectations, not only of Russia, but also of the other Powers — despite these facts, the Austro-Hungarian Minister at Belgrade considered the Servian reply insufficient and left the town.

Recognising the exaggerated nature of the demands made by Austria, Russia had previously declared that she could not remain indifferent, while not desisting from doing her utmost to find a peaceful issue which might prove acceptable to Austria, and spare the latter's self-respect as a Great Power. At the same time Russia let it be clearly understood that she could accept a peaceful settlement of the question only so far as it involved no humiliation of Servia as an independent State. Unhappily all the efforts of the Russian Government to this end were fruitless. The Austro-Hungarian Government, which had shunned any attempt at conciliatory intervention by the Powers in the Austrian dispute with Servia, proceeded to mobilise and declared war officially against Servia, and the following day Belgrade was bombarded. The manifesto which accompanied the declaration of war openly accuses Servia of having prepared and carried out the crime of Serajevo. Such an accusation of a crime at common law, launched against a whole people and a whole State, aroused, by its evident inanity, widespread sympathy for Servia throughout all classes of European society.

In consequence of this behavior of the Austro-Hungarian Government, in spite of Russia's declaration that she could not remain indifferent to the fate of Servia, the Russian Government considered it necessary to order mobilisation in the military districts of Kieff, Odessa, Moscow, and Kazan. This decision was rendered necessary by the fact that since the date when the Austro-Hungarian note was communicated to the Servian Government, and since the first steps taken by Russia, five days had elapsed, and yet the Vienna Cabinet had not taken one step to meet Russia halfway in her efforts towards peace. Indeed, quite the contrary; for the mobilisation of half of the Austro-Hungarian army had been ordered.

The German Government were kept informed of the steps taken by Russia. At the same time it was explained to them that these steps were only the result of the Austrian preparations, and that they were not in any way aimed at Germany. Simultaneously, the Russian Government declared that Russia was ready to continue discussions with a view to a peaceful settlement of the dispute, either in the form of direct negotiations with Vienna or, as suggested by Great Britain, in the form of a conference of the four Great Powers not directly interested, that is to say, Great Britain, France, Germany, and Italy.

This attempt on the part of Russia was, however, equally unsuccessful. Austria-Hungary declined a further exchange of views with Russia, and the Vienna Cabinet was unwilling to join the proposed conference of the Powers.

Nevertheless Russia did not abandon her efforts for peace. When questioned by the German Ambassador as to the conditions on which we would still agree to suspend our preparations, the Minister for Foreign Affairs declared that these conditions were Austria's recognition that the Austro-Serbian question had assumed a European character, and a declaration by her that she agreed not to insist upon such of her demands as were incompatible with the sovereign rights of Servia.

Germany considered this Russian proposal unacceptable to Austria-Hungary. At that very moment news of the proclamation of general mobilisation by Austria-Hungary reached St. Petersburg.

All this time hostilities were continuing on Servian territory, and Belgrade was bombarded afresh.

The failure of our proposals for peace compelled us to extend the scope of our precautionary military measures.

The Berlin Cabinet questioned us on this, and we replied that Russia was compelled to begin preparations so as to be ready for every emergency.

But while taking this precautionary step, Russia did not on that account abandon her strenuous efforts to find some solution of the situation, and she announced that she was ready to accept any proposed settlement of the problem that might be put forward, provided it complied with the conditions laid down by her.

In spite of this conciliatory communication, the German Government on the 18th (31st) July demanded of the Russian Government that they should suspend their military measures by midday on the 19th July (1st August), and threatened, should they fail to comply, to proceed to general mobilisation.

On the following day, the 19th July (1st August), the German Ambassador, on behalf of his Government, forwarded a declaration of war to the Minister for Foreign Affairs.

Speech of the Imperial Chancellor before the German Reichstag. August 4th, 1914]

A stupendous fate is breaking over Europe. For forty-four years, since the time we fought for and won the German Empire and our position in the world, we have lived in peace and have protected the peace of Europe. In the works of peace we have become strong and powerful, and have thus aroused the envy of others. With patience we have faced the fact that, under the pretence that Germany was desirous of war, enmity has been awakened against us in the East and the West, and chains have been fashioned for us. The wind then sown has brought forth the whirlwind which has now broken loose. We wished to continue our work of peace, and, like a silent vow, the feeling that animated everyone from the Emperor down to the young-est soldier was this: Only in defence of a just cause shall our sword fly from its scabbard.

The day has now come when we must draw it, against our wish, and in spite of our sincere endeavours. Russia has set fire to the building. We are at war with Russia and France — a war that has been forced upon us.

Gentlemen, a number of documents, composed during the pres-sure of these last eventful days, is before you. Allow me to empha-size the facts that determine our attitude.

From the first moment of the Austro-Servian conflict we declared that this question must be limited to Austria-Hungary and Servia, and we worked with this end in view. All Governments, especially that of Great Britain, took the same attitude. Russia alone asserted that she had to be heard in the settlement of this matter.

Thus the danger of a European crisis raised its threatening head.

As soon as the first definite information regarding the military preparations in Russia reached us, we declared at St. Petersburgh in a friendly but emphatic manner that military measures against Austria would find us on the side if our ally, and that military preparations against ourselves would oblige us to take counter-measures; but that mobilization would come very near to actual war.

Russia assured us in the most solemn manner of her desire for peace, and declared that she was making no military preparations against us.

In the meantime, Great Britain, warmly supported by us, tried to mediate between Vienna and St. Petersburgh.

On July 28th the Emperor telegraphed to the Czar asking him to take into consideration the fact that it was both the duty and the right of Austria-Hungary to defend herself against the pan-Serb agitation, which threatened to undermine her existence. The Emperor drew the Czar's attention to the solidarity of the interests of all monarchs in face of the murder of Serajevo. He asked for the latter's personal assistance in smoothing over the difficulties existing between Vienna and St. Petersburgh. About the same time, and before receipt of this telegram, the Czar asked the Emperor to come to his aid and to induce Vienna to moderate her demands. The Emperor accepted the role of mediator.

But scarcely had active steps on these lines begun, when Russia mobilized all her forces directed against Austria, while Austria-Hungary had mobilized only those of her corps which were directed against Servia. To the north she had mobilized only two of her corps, far from the Russian frontier. The Emperor immediately informed the Czar that this mobilization of Russian forces against Austria rendered the role of mediator, which he had accepted at the Czar's request, difficult, if not impossible.

In spite of this we continued our task of mediation at Vienna and carried it to the utmost point which was compatible with our position as an ally.

Meanwhile Russia of her own accord renewed her assurances that she was making no military preparations against us.

We come now to July 31st. The decision was to be taken at Vienna. Through our representations we had already obtained the resumption of direct conversations between Vienna and St. Petersburgh, after they had been for some time interrupted. But before the final decision was taken at Vienna, the news arrived that Russia had mobilized her entire forces and that her mobilization was therefore directed against us also. The Russian Government, who knew from our repeated statements what mobilization on our frontiers meant, did not notify us of this mobilization, nor did they even offer any explanation. It was not until the afternoon of July 31st that the Emperor received a telegram from the Czar in which he guaranteed that his army would not assume a provocative attitude towards us. But mobilization on our frontiers had been in full swing since the night of July 30th–31st.

While we were mediating at Vienna in compliance with Russia's request, Russian forces were appearing all along our extended and almost entirely open frontier, and France, though indeed not actually mobilizing, was admittedly making military preparations. What was our position? For the sake of the peace of Europe we had, up till then, deliberately refrained from calling up a single reservist. Were we now to wait further in patience until the nations on either side of us chose the moment for their attack? It would have been a crime to expose Germany to such peril. Therefore, on July 31st we called upon Russia to demobilize as the only measure which could still preserve the peace of Europe. The Imperial Ambassador at St.

Petersburgh was also instructed to inform the Russian Government that in case our demand met with a refusal, we should have to consider that a state of war (*Kriegszustand*) existed.

The Imperial Ambassador has executed these instructions. We have not yet learnt what Russia answered to our demand for demobilization. Telegraphic reports on this question have not reached us even though the wires still transmitted much less important information.

Therefore, the time limit having long since expired, the Emperor was obliged to mobilize our forces on the 1st August at 5 P.M.

At the same time we had to make certain what attitude France would assume. To our direct question, whether she would remain neutral in the event of a Russo-German War, France replied that she would do what her interests demanded. That was an evasion, if not a refusal.

In spite of this, the Emperor ordered that the French frontier was to be unconditionally respected. This order, with one single exception, was strictly obeyed. France, who mobilized at the same time as we did, assured us that she would respect a zone of 10 kilometres on the frontier. What really happened? Aviators dropped bombs, and cavalry patrols and French infantry detachments appeared on the territory of the Empire! Though war had not been declared, France thus broke the peace and actually attacked us.

Regarding the one exception on our side which I mentioned, the Chief of the General Staff reports as follows: —

"Only one of the French complaints about the crossing of the frontier from our side is justified. Against express orders, a patrol of the 14th Army Corps, apparently led by an officer, crossed the frontier on August 2nd. They seem to have been shot down, only one man having returned. But long before this isolated instance of crossing the frontier had occurred, French aviators had penetrated into Southern Germany and had thrown bombs on our railway lines. French troops had attacked our frontier guards on the Schlucht Pass. Our troops, in accordance with their orders, have remained strictly on the defensive." This is the report of the General Staff.

Gentlemen, we are now in a state of necessity (*Notwehr*), and necessity (*Not*) knows no law. Our troops have occupied Luxemburg and perhaps have already entered Belgian territory.

Gentlemen, that is a breach of international law. It is true that the French Government declared at Brussels that France would respect Belgian neutrality as long as her adversary respected it. We knew, however, that France stood ready for an invasion. France could wait, we could not. A French attack on our flank on the lower Rhine might have been disastrous. Thus we were forced to ignore the rightful protests of the Governments of Luxemburg and Belgium. The wrong — I speak openly — the wrong we thereby commit we will try to make good as soon as our military aims have been attained.

He who is menaced as we are and is fighting for his highest possession can only consider how he is to hack his way through (*durchhauen*).

Gentlemen, we stand shoulder to shoulder with Austria-Hungary.

As for Great Britain's attitude, the statements made by Sir Edward Grey in the House of Commons yesterday show the standpoint assumed by the British Government. We have informed the British Government that, as long as Great Britain remains neutral, our fleet will not attack the northern coast of France, and that we will not violate the territorial integrity and independence of Belgium. These assurances I now repeat before the world, and I may add that, as long as Great Britain remains neutral, we would also be willing, upon reciprocity being assured, to take no warlike measures against French commercial shipping.

Gentlemen, so much for the facts. I repeat the words of the Emperor: "With a clear conscience we enter the lists." We are fighting for the fruits of our works of peace, for the inheritance of a great past and for our future. The fifty years are not yet past during which Count Moltke said we should have to remain armed to defend the inheritance that we won in 1870. Now the great hour of trial has struck for our people. But with clear confidence we go forward to meet it. Our army is in the field, our navy is ready for battle — behind them stands the entire German nation — the entire German nation united to the last man.

Gentlemen, you know your duty and all that it means. The proposed laws need no further explanation. I ask you to pass them quickly.

2

Communism and Democracy

WHILE THE conflict between international Communism and the free
nations of the world became particularly acute after World War II, the
sources of this conflict go back at least as far as the Bolshevik victory 'n
Russia in 1917. From the outset it has been clear that this bitter controversy is in large part promoted by ideological differences — different
ways of looking at the world and different meanings given to words,
ideas, and ideals. An example of this difference is seen in the following
excerpt from Lenin's State and Revolution, where Lenin contrasts the
Bolshevik views on politics and the state with those prevalent in democratic countries. Written in late 1917, in the period immediately preceding the October Bolshevik Revolution, these selections also anticipate
much of the later history of Soviet Russia.

Twentieth-century totalitarian movements, both Communist and Fascist,
have not been secretive about their ideals, goals, and specific techniques.
No one who reads the selection from Joseph Stalin's works should
wonder either about the goals Soviet Communists hope to attain or
the ways they believe they can be attained. The excerpts are from Stalin's
Foundations of Leninism, first delivered as a series of lectures in 1924. In
spite of the early date of this publication, its contents have remained
until the present an essential part of Soviet "orthodoxy."

a V. I. Lenin, State and Revolution

The higher phase of Communist society]

 MARX continues:

... In the higher phase of communist society, after the enslav-
ing subordination of the individual to the division of labor and,
therewith, also the antithesis between mental and physical labor,
has vanished; after labor has become not only a means of life

From Arthur P. Mendel (ed.), ESSENTIAL WORKS OF MARXISM (New
York, 1961), pp. 177–183, 267–281. Copyright © 1961 by Bantam
Books, Inc. Reprinted by permission of Bantam Books, Inc.

but life's prime need; after the productive forces have increased together with the advance of the individual's all-around development, and all the springs of co-operative wealth flow abundantly — only then can the narrow horizon of bourgeois right be crossed completely and society inscribe on its banners: "From each according to his ability, to each according to his needs!"

Only now can we appreciate to the full the correctness of Engels' remarks in which he mercilessly ridiculed the absurdity of combining the words "freedom" and "state." So long as the state exists there is no freedom. When there will be freedom, there will be no state.

The economic basis for the complete withering away of the state is that high stage of development of communism when the antithesis between mental and physical labor disappears, when there disappears consequently one of the principal sources of modern *social* inequality — a source, moreover, which cannot on any account be removed immediately by the mere conversion of the means of production into public property, by the mere expropriation of the capitalists.

This expropriation will create *the possibility* of an enormous development of the productive forces. And when we see how incredibly capitalism is already *retarding* this development, when we see how much progress could be achieved on the basis of the level of technique now already attained, we are entitled to say with the fullest confidence that the expropriation of the capitalists will inevitably result in an enormous development of the productive forces of human society. But how rapidly this development will proceed, how soon it will reach the point of breaking away from the division of labor, of doing away with the antithesis between mental and physical labor, of transforming labor into "the prime necessity of life" — we do not and *cannot* know.

That is why we are entitled to speak only of the inevitable withering away of the state, emphasizing the protracted nature of this process and its dependence upon the rapidity of development of the *higher phase* of communism, and leaving completely open the question of the time required for, or the concrete forms of, the withering away, because there is *no* material for answering these questions.

It will become possible for the state to wither away completely when society adopts the rule: "From each according to his ability, to each according to his needs," *i.e.*, when people have become so accustomed to observing the fundamental rules of social intercourse and when their labor becomes so productive that they will voluntarily work *according to their ability.* "The narrow horizon of bourgeois right," which compels one to calculate with the cold-heartedness of a Shylock whether one has not worked half an hour more than somebody else, whether one is not getting less pay than somebody else — this narrow horizon will then be crossed. There will then be no need for society to regulate the quantity of products to be received by each: each will take freely "according to his needs."

From the bourgeois point of view, it is easy to declare that such a social order is "sheer utopia" and to sneer at the socialists for promising everyone the right to receive from society, without any control over the labor of the individual citizen, any quantity of truffles, automobiles, pianos, etc. Even to this day, most bourgeois "savants" confine themselves to sneering in this way, thereby displaying both their ignorance and their mercenary defense of capitalism.

Ignorance — for it has never entered the head of any socialist to "promise" that the higher phase of the development of communism will arrive; whereas the great socialists, in *foreseeing* that it will arrive presuppose not the present productivity of labor *and not the present* ordinary run of people, who, like the seminary students in Pomyalovsky's stories, are capable of damaging the stocks of public wealth "just for fun" and of demanding the impossible.

Until the "higher" phase of communism arrives, the socialists demand the *strictest* control by society *and by the state* of the measure of labor and the measure of consumption; but this control must *start* with the expropriation of the capitalists and with the establishment of workers' control over the capitalists, and it must be exercised not by a state of bureaucrats, but by a state of *armed workers.*

The mercenary defense of capitalism by the bourgeois ideologists (and their hangers-on, like the Tseretelis, Chernovs and Co.) consists precisely in that they *substitute* controversies and discussions about the distant future for the vital and burning question of *present-day* politics, *viz.,* the expropriation of the capitalists, the conversion of *all* citizens into workers and employees of *one* huge "syndicate" — the whole state — and the complete subordination of the entire work of this syndicate to a genuinely democratic state, to *the state of the Soviets of Workers' and Soldiers' Deputies.*

Actually, when a learned professor, followed by the philistine, who, in turn, is followed by the Tseretelis and Chernovs, talks about unreasonable utopias, the demagogic promises of the Bolsheviks, and the impossibility of "introducing" socialism, it is the higher stage or phase of communism they have in mind, which no one has ever promised or even thought to "introduce," because it generally cannot be "introduced."

And this brings us to the question of the scientific difference between socialism and communism, which Engels touched on in his above-quoted argument about the incorrectness of the name "Social Democrat." Politically the difference between the first, or lower, and the higher phase of communism will in time, probably, be tremendous; but it would be ridiculous to take cognizance of this difference now, under capitalism, and only individual anarchists, perhaps, could invest it with primary importance (if there still remain people among the anarchists who have learned nothing from the "Plekhanovite" conversion of the Kropotkins, the Graveses, the Cornelissens and other "stars" of anarchism into social-chauvinists or "anarcho-trenchists," as Ge, one of the few anarchists who have still preserved a sense of honor and a conscience, has put it).

But the scientific difference between socialism and communism is clear. What is usually called socialism was termed by Marx the "first" or lower phase of communist society. In so far as the means of production become *common* property, the word "communism" is also applicable here, providing we do not forget that this is *not* complete communism. The great significance of Marx's explanations is that here, too, he consistently applies materialist dialectics, the theory of development, regarding communism as something which develops *out of* capitalism. Instead of scholastically invented, "concocted" definitions and fruitless disputes about words (what is socialism? what is communism?), Marx gives an analysis of what might be called the stages of the economic ripeness of communism.

In its first phase, or first stage, communism *cannot* as yet be fully ripe economically and entirely free from traditions or remnants of capitalism. Hence, the interesting phenomenon that communism in its first phase retains "the narrow horizon of *bourgeois* right." Of course, bourgeois right in regard to the distribution of articles of *consumption* inevitably presupposes the existence of the *bourgeois state,* for right is nothing without an apparatus capable of *enforcing* the observance of the standards of right.

It follows that under communism there remains for a time not only bourgeois right, but even the bourgeois state without the bourgeoisie!

This may sound like a paradox or simply a dialectical conundrum, of which Marxism is often accused by people who do not take the slightest trouble to study its extraordinarily profound content. But as a matter of fact, remnants of the old surviving in the new confront us in life at every step, both in nature and in society. And Marx did not arbitrarily insert a scrap of "bourgeois" right into communism, but indicated what is economically and politically inevitable in a society emerging *out of the womb* of capitalism.

Democracy is of enormous importance to the working class in its struggle against the capitalists for its emancipation. But democracy is by no means a boundary not to be crossed: it is only one of the stages on the road from feudalism to capitalism and from capitalism to communism.

Democracy means equality. The great significance of the proletariat's struggle for equality and of equality as a slogan will be clear if we correctly interpret it as meaning the abolition of *classes*. But democracy means only *formal* equality. And as soon as equality is achieved for all members of society *in relation* to ownership of the means of production, that is, equality of labor and equality of wages, humanity will inevitably be confronted with the question of advancing farther, from formal equality to actual equality, *i.e.,* to the realization of the rule, "from each according to his ability, to each according to his needs." By what stages, by means of what practical measures humanity will proceed to this supreme aim — we do not and cannot know. But it is important to realize how infinitely mendacious is the ordinary bourgeois conception of socialism as something lifeless, petrified, fixed once for all, whereas in reality *only* under socialism will there begin in all spheres of public and personal life a rapid, genuine, really mass forward movement, embracing first the *majority* and then the whole of the population.

Democracy is a form of the state, one of its varieties. Consequently, like every state, it represents the organized, systematic use of violence against persons. But it also signifies the formal recognition of the equality of citizens, the equal right of all to determine the structure of the state and to administer it. This, in turn, results in the fact that, at a certain stage in the development of democracy, it first welds together the class that wages a revolutionary struggle against capitalism — the proletariat, and enables it to crush, to smash to bits, to wipe off the face of the earth the bourgeois, even the republican bourgeois, the state machine, the standing army, the police and the bureaucracy, and to substitute for them a *more* democratic state machine, but a state machine nevertheless, in the shape of the armed masses of workers who develop into a militia in which the entire population takes part.

Here "quantity turns into quality": *such* a degree of democracy involves leaving the boundaries of bourgeois society and beginning its socialist reconstruction. If really *all* take part in the administration of the state, capitalism cannot retain its hold. And the development of capitalism itself creates, in turn, the *premises* that *enable* "all" to take part in the administration of the state. Some of these premises are universal literacy, which has already been achieved in a number of the most advanced capitalist countries, and the "training and disciplining" of millions of workers by the huge, complex, socialized apparatus of the postal service, railways, big factories, large-scale commerce, banking, etc., etc.

Given these *economic* premises it is quite possible, after the overthrow of the capitalists and the bureaucrats, to proceed immediately, overnight, to replace them in the *control* of production and distribution, in the work of *keeping account* of labor and products by the armed workers, by the whole of the armed population. (The question of control and accounting should not be confused with the question of the scientifically trained staff of engineers, agronomists and so on. These gentlemen, working today in obedience to the wishes of the capitalists, will work even better tomorrow in obedience to the wishes of the armed workers.)

Accounting and control — that is the *main* thing required for "arranging" the smooth working, the correct functioning of the *first phase* of communist society. *All* citizens are transformed here into hired employees of the state, which consists of the armed workers. *All* citizens become employees and workers of a *single* nationwide state "syndicate." All that is required is that they should work equally, do their proper share of work, and get equally paid. The accounting and control necessary for this have been *simplified* by capitalism to the extreme and reduced to the extraordinarily simple operations — which any literate person who knows arithmetic can perform — of supervising, recording, and issuing appropriate receipts.[17]

When the *majority* of the people begin independently and everywhere to keep such accounts and maintain such control over the capitalists (now converted into employees) and over the gentry intellectuals who preserve their capitalist habits, this control will really become universal, general, popular. And there will be no way of getting away from it; there will be "nowhere to go."

The whole of society will have become a single office and a single factory, with equality of labor and equality of pay.

But this "factory" discipline, which the proletariat, after defeating the capitalists and overthrowing the exploiters, will extend to the whole of society, is by no means our ideal, or our ultimate goal. It is but a necessary *step* for the purpose of thoroughly purging society of all the infamies and abominations of capitalist exploitation *and for further* progress.

From the moment all members of society, or even only the vast majority, have learned to administer the state *themselves,* have taken this work into their own hands, have "arranged" control over the insignificant minority of capitalists, the gentry who wish to preserve their capitalist habits and the workers who have been profoundly corrupted by capitalism — from this moment the need for government of any kind begins to disappear altogether. The more complete the democracy, the nearer the moment approaches when it becomes unnecessary. The more democratic the "state," consisting of the armed workers and "no longer a state in the proper sense of the word," the more rapidly does *every* form of state begin to wither away.

For when *all* have learned to administer and actually do administer independently social production, independently keep accounts and exercise control over the idlers, gentlefolk, swindlers and other such "guardians of capitalist traditions," the escape from this popular accounting and control will inevitably become so incredibly difficult, such a rare exception, and will probably be accompanied by such swift and severe punishment (for the armed workers are practical men and not sentimental intellectuals, and they will scarcely allow anyone to trifle with them), that the *necessity* of observing the simple, fundamental rules of human intercourse will very soon become a *habit.*

And then the door will be wide open for the transition from the

first phase of communist society to its higher phase, and with it, to
the complete withering away of the state.

b   J. Stalin, The Foundations of Leninism

Strategy and tactics]

FROM THIS theme I take six topics:
  a) strategy and tactics as the science of leading the class struggle of the proletariat;
  b) strategy and the stages of the revolution;
  c) tactics and the flow and ebb of the movement;
  d) strategic leadership;
  e) tactical leadership;
  f) reformism and revolutionism.

1) Strategy and tactics as the science of leading the class struggle of
the proletariat] The period dominated by the Second International
was mainly a period of the formation and training of the proletarian
political armies under conditions of more or less peaceful development. It was the period of parliamentarism as the predominant form
of the class struggle. Questions of great class conflicts, of preparing
the proletariat for revolutionary clashes, of the means for achieving
the dictatorship of the proletariat, did not seem to be on the order
of the day at that time. The task was confined to utilizing all means
of legal development for the purpose of forming and training the
proletarian armies, to utilizing parliamentarism in conformity with
the conditions under which the status of the proletariat remained,
and, as it seemed, had to remain, that of an opposition. It scarcely
needs proof that in such a period and with such a conception of the
tasks of the proletariat there could be neither an integral strategy
nor any elaborated tactics. There were fragmentary and detached
ideas about tactics and strategy, but no tactics or strategy as such.

The mortal sin of the Second International was not that it pursued
at that time the tactics of utilizing parliamentary forms of struggle,
but that it overestimated the importance of these forms, that it considered them virtually the only forms; and that when the period of

open revolutionary battles set in and the question of extraparliamentary forms of struggle came to the fore, the parties of the Second International turned their backs on these new tasks, refused to shoulder them.

Only in the subsequent period, the period of direct action by the proletariat, the period of proletarian revolution, when the question of overthrowing the bourgeoisie became a question of immediate practical action, when the question of the reserves of the proletariat (strategy) became one of the most burning questions, when all forms of struggle and organization, parliamentary and extraparliamentary (tactics), had quite clearly manifested themselves — only in this period could any integral strategy and elaborated tactics for the struggle of the proletariat be worked out. It was precisely in this period that Lenin brought out into the light of day the brilliant ideas of Marx and Engels on tactics and strategy that had been suppressed by the opportunists of the Second International. But Lenin did not confine himself to restoring particular tactical propositions of Marx and Engels. He developed them further and supplemented them with new ideas and propositions, combining them all into a system of rules and guiding principles for the leadership of the class struggle of the proletariat. Lenin's pamphlets, such as *What Is To Be Done?*, *Two Tactics, Imperialism, The State and Revolution, The Proletarian Revolution and the Renegade Kautsky, "Left-Wing" Communism,* undoubtedly constitute priceless contributions to the general treasury of Marxism, to its revolutionary arsenal. The strategy and tactics of Leninism constitute the science of leading the revolutionary struggle of the proletariat.

2) Strategy and the stages of the revolution] Strategy is the determination of the direction of the main blow of the proletariat at a given stage of the revolution, the elaboration of a corresponding plan for the disposition of the revolutionary forces (main and secondary reserves), the fight to carry out this plan throughout the given stage of the revolution.

*   *   *

3) Tactics and the flow and ebb of the movement] Tactics are the determination of the line of conduct of the proletariat in the comparatively short period of the flow or ebb of the movement, the rise or decline of the revolution, the fight to carry out this line by re-

placing old forms of struggle and organization by new ones, old slogans by new ones, by combining these forms, etc. While the object of strategy is to win the war against tsarism, let us say, or against the bourgeoisie, to carry through the struggle against tsarism or against the bourgeoisie to its end, tactics pursue less important objects, for their aim is not the winning of the war as a whole, but the winning of some particular engagements or some particular battles, the carrying through successfully of some particular campaigns or actions corresponding to the concrete circumstances in the given period of a rise or decline of the revolution. Tactics are a part of strategy, subordinate to it and serving it.

*   *   *

4) Strategic leadership] The reserves of the revolution are:

direct: a) the peasantry and in general the intermediate strata of the population within the country; b) the proletariat of neighboring countries; c) the revolutionary movement in the colonies and dependent countries; d) the conquests and gains of the dictatorship of the proletariat — part of which the proletariat may give up temporarily, while retaining superiority of forces, in order to buy off a powerful enemy and gain a respite; and

indirect: a) the contradictions and conflicts among the nonproletarian classes within the country, which can be utilized by the proletariat to weaken the enemy and to strengthen its own reserves; b) contradictions, conflicts and wars (the imperialist war, for instance) among the bourgeois states hostile to the proletarian state, which can be utilized by the proletariat in its offensive or in maneuvering in the event of a forced retreat.

*   *   *

The task of strategic leadership is to make proper use of all these reserves for the achievement of the main object of the revolution at the given stage of its development.

What does making proper use of reserves mean?

It means fulfilling certain necessary conditions, of which the following must be regarded as the principal ones:

Firstly] The concentration of the main forces of the revolution at the enemy's most vulnerable spot at the decisive moment, when the revolution has already become ripe, when the offensive is going full-steam ahead, when insurrection is knocking at the door, and when bringing the reserves up to the vanguard is the decisive condition of success. The Party's strategy during the period from April to October 1917 can be taken as an example of this manner of utilizing reserves. Undoubtedly, the enemy's most vulnerable spot at that time was the war. Undoubtedly, it was on this question, as the fundamental one, that the Party rallied the broadest masses of the population around the proletarian vanguard. The Party's strategy during that period was, while training the vanguard for street action by means of mani-festations and demonstrations, to bring the reserves up to the van-guard through the medium of the Soviets in the rear and the soldiers' committees at the front. The outcome of the revolution has shown that the reserves were properly utilized.

Here is what Lenin, paraphrasing the well-known theses of Marx and Engels on insurrection, says about this condition of strategically utilizing the forces of revolution:

1) Never *play* with insurrection, but, when beginning it, firmly realize that you must *go to the end*.

2) Concentrate a great *superiority of forces* at the decisive point, at the decisive moment, otherwise the enemy, who has the advantage of better preparation and organization, will de-stroy the insurgents.

3) Once the insurrection has begun, you must act with the greatest *determination*, and by all means, without fail, take the *offensive*. "The defensive is the death of an armed rising."

4) You must try to take the enemy by surprise and seize the moment when his forces are scattered.

5) You must strive for *daily* successes, even if small (one might say hourly, if it is the case of one town), and at all costs retain the "*moral ascendancy*."

Secondly] The selection of the moment for the decisive blow, the moment for starting the insurrection, so timed as to coincide with the moment when the crisis has reached its climax, when the vanguard is prepared to fight to the end, the reserves are prepared to support the vanguard, and maximum consternation reigns in the ranks of the enemy.

The decisive battle, says Lenin, may be deemed to have fully matured *if* "(1) all the class forces hostile to us have become sufficiently weakened themselves in a struggle which is beyond their strength"; *if* "(2) all the vacillating, wavering, unstable, intermediate elements — the petty bourgeoisie, the petty-bourgeois democrats as distinct from the bourgeoisie — have sufficiently exposed themselves in the eyes of the people, have sufficiently disgraced themselves through their practical bankruptcy"; *if* "(3) among the proletariat a mass sentiment in favor of supporting the most determined, supremely bold, revolutionary action against the bourgeoisie has arisen and has begun to grow vigorously. Then revolution is indeed ripe. Then, indeed, if we have correctly gauged all the conditions indicated above . . . and if we have chosen the moment rightly, is our victory assured."

* * *

Thirdly] Undeviating pursuit of the course adopted, no matter what difficulties and complications are encountered on the road towards the goal. This is necessary in order that the vanguard not lose sight of the main goal of the struggle and the masses not stray from the road while marching towards that goal and striving to rally around the vanguard. Failure to observe this condition leads to a grave error, well known to sailors as "losing one's bearings."

* * *

Fourthly] Maneuvering the reserves with a view to effecting a proper retreat when the enemy is strong, when retreat is inevitable, when to accept battle forced upon us by the enemy is obviously disadvantageous, when, with the given relation of forces, retreat becomes the only way to escape a blow against the vanguard and retain the vanguard's reserves.

"The revolutionary parties," says Lenin, "must complete their education. They have learned to attack. Now they have to realize that this knowledge must be supplemented with the knowledge of how to retreat properly. They have to realize — and the revolutionary class is taught to realize it by its own bitter experience — that victory is impossible unless they have learned both how to attack and how to retreat properly."

The object of this strategy is to gain time, to disrupt the enemy, and to accumulate forces in order later to assume the offensive.

* * *

5) Tactical leadership] Tactical leadership is a part of strategic leadership, subordinated to the tasks and the requirements of the latter. The task of tactical leadership is to master all forms of struggle and organization of the proletariat and to ensure that they are used properly so as to achieve, with the given relation of forces, the maximum results necessary to prepare for strategic success.

What is meant by making proper use of the forms of struggle and organization of the proletariat?

It means fulfilling certain necessary conditions, of which the following must be regarded as the principal ones:

Firstly] To put in the forefront precisely those forms of struggle and organization which are best suited to the conditions prevailing during the flow or ebb of the movement at a given moment, and which therefore can facilitate and ensure the bringing of the masses to revolutionary positions, the bringing of the millions to the revolutionary front, and their disposition at the revolutionary front.

The point here is not that the vanguard should realize the impossibility of preserving the old regime and the inevitability of its overthrow. The point is that the masses, the millions, should understand this inevitability and display their readiness to support the vanguard. But the masses can understand this only from their own experience. The task is to enable the vast masses to realize from their own experience the inevitability of the overthrow of the old regime, to promote such methods of struggle and forms of organization as will make it easier for the masses to realize from experience the correctness of the revolutionary slogans.

* * *

Secondly] To locate at any given moment the particular link in the chain of processes which, if grasped, will enable us to keep hold of the whole chain and to prepare the conditions for achieving strategic success.

The point here is to single out from all the tasks confronting the Party the particular immediate task, the fulfillment of which constitutes the central point, and the accomplishment of which ensures the successful fulfillment of the other immediate tasks.

*　　*　　*

Such are the principal conditions which ensure correct tactical leadership.

6) Reformism and revolutionism] What is the difference between revolutionary tactics and reformist tactics?

Some think that Leninism is opposed to reforms, opposed to compromises and to agreements in general. This is absolutely wrong. Bolsheviks know as well as anybody else that in a certain sense "every little helps," that under certain conditions reforms in general, and compromises and agreements in particular, are necessary and useful.

> "To carry on a war for the overthrow of the international bourgeoisie," says Lenin, "a war which is a hundred times more difficult, protracted and complicated than the most stubborn of ordinary wars between states, and to refuse beforehand to maneuver, to utilize the conflict of interests (even though temporary) among one's enemies, to reject agreements and compromises with possible (even though temporary, unstable, vacillating and conditional) allies — is not this ridiculous in the extreme? Is it not as though, when making a difficult ascent of an unexplored and hitherto inaccessible mountain, we were to refuse beforehand ever to move in zigzags, ever to retrace our steps, ever to abandon the course once selected and to try others?"

Obviously, therefore, it is not a matter of reforms or of compromises and agreements, but of the use people make of reforms and agreements.

To a reformist, reforms are everything, while revolutionary work is something incidental, something just to talk about, mere eyewash. That is why reforms resulting from reformist tactics under the conditions of bourgeois rule are inevitably transformed into an instrument for strengthening that rule, an instrument for distintegrating the revolution.

To a revolutionary, on the contrary, the main thing is revolutionary work and not reforms; to him reforms are a by-product of the revolution. That is why reforms resulting from revolutionary tactics under the conditions of bourgeois rule are naturally transformed into an instrument for disintegrating that rule, into an instrument for strengthening the revolution, into a strongpoint for the further development of the revolutionary movement.

The revolutionary will accept a reform in order to use it as an aid in combining legal work with illegal work, in order to intensify, under its cover, the illegal work for the revolutionary preparation of the masses for the overthrow of the bourgeoisie.

That is the essence of making revolutionary use of reforms and agreements under the conditions of imperialism.

The reformist, on the contrary, will accept reforms in order to renounce all illegal work, to thwart the preparation of the masses for the revolution and to rest in the shade of "bestowed" reforms.

That is the essence of reformist tactics.

Such is the position in regard to reforms and agreements under the conditions of imperialism.

The situation changes somewhat, however, after the overthrow of imperialism, under the dictatorship of the proletariat. Under certain conditions, in a certain situation, the proletarian power may find itself compelled temporarily to leave the path of the revolutionary reconstruction of the existing order of things and to take the path of its gradual transformations, the "reformist path," as Lenin says in his well-known article "The Importance of Gold," the path of flanking movements, of reforms and concessions to the nonproletarian classes — in order to disintegrate these classes, to give the revolution a respite, to recuperate one's forces and prepare the conditions for a new offensive. It cannot be denied that in a sense this is a "reformist" path. But it must be borne in mind that there is a fundamental distinction here, which consists in the fact that, in this case, the reform emanates from the proletarian power, that it strengthens the proletarian power and procures for it a necessary respite, and that its purpose is to disintegrate, not the revolution, but the nonproletarian classes.

Under such conditions a reform is thus transformed into its opposite.

The proletarian power is able to adopt such a policy because, and only because, the scope of the revolution in the preceding period was great enough and therefore provided a sufficiently wide expanse within which to retreat, substituting for offensive tactics the tactics of temporary retreat, the tactics of flanking movements.

Thus, while formerly, under bourgeois rule, reforms were a by-product of revolution, now, under the dictatorship of the proletariat, the source of reforms is the revolutionary gains of the proletariat, the reserves accumulated in the hands of the proletariat and consisting of these gains.

3

The Ideals of Fascism

FASCISM began in Milan in 1919 when Benito Mussolini organized the Fascio di Combattimento. Its name derives from the Latin fasces, the bunch of rods representing authority in ancient Rome. Before becoming the Fascist leader of Italy, Mussolini had achieved high ranks in the Italian Socialist Party, including editorship of the party's newspaper Avanti. As a socialist, he belonged to the radical wing that called for violence and "direct action" as the best means of gaining power. These views won him the praise of Russian Bolsheviks, who regarded him as one of their most likely supporters among Italian socialists. He lost his position as editor of Avanti in 1914 when he changed his views on war from "anti-imperialist" to interventionist. His controversy with the socialists continued after the war, mainly through a newspaper he had founded during the war, Il Popolo d'Italia. He won control of Italy in October, 1922.

Benito Mussolini, The Doctrine of Fascism

(i) Fundamental ideas]

1] LIKE EVERY sound political conception, Fascism is both practice and thought; action in which a doctrine is immanent, and a doctrine which, arising out of a given system of historical forces, remains embedded in them and works there from within. Hence it has a form correlative to the contingencies of place and time, but it has also a content of thought which raises it to a formula of truth in the higher level of the history of thought. In the world one does not act spiritually as a human will dominating other wills without a conception of the transient and particular reality under which it is necessary to act, and of the permanent and universal reality in which the first has its being and its life. In order to know men it is neces-

From Michael Oakeshott (ed.), THE SOCIAL AND POLITICAL DOCTRINES OF CONTEMPORARY EUROPE (New York, 1950), pp. 164–165, 170–179. Reprinted by permission of the Cambridge University Press.

sary to know man; and in order to know man it is necessary to know reality and its laws. There is no concept of the State which is not fundamentally a concept of life: philosophy or intuition, a system of ideas which develops logically or is gathered up into a vision or into a faith, but which is always, at least virtually, an organic conception of the world.

2] Thus Fascism could not be understood in many of its practical manifestations as a party organization, as a system of education, as a discipline, if it were not always looked at in the light of its whole way of conceiving life, a spiritualized way. The world seen through Fascism is not this material world which appears on the surface, in which man is an individual separated from all others and standing by himself, and in which he is governed by a natural law that makes him instinctively live a life of selfish and momentary pleasure. The man of Fascism is an individual who is nation and fatherland, which is a moral law, binding together individuals and the generations into a tradition and a mission, suppressing the instinct for a life enclosed within the brief round of pleasure in order to restore within duty a higher life free from the limits of time and space: a life in which the individual, through the denial of himself, through the sacrifice of his own private interests, through death itself, realizes that completely spiritual existence in which his value as a man lies.

3] Therefore it is a spiritualized conception, itself the result of the general reaction of modern times against the flabby materialistic positivism of the nineteenth century. Anti-positivistic, but positive: not sceptical, nor agnostic, nor pessimistic, nor passively optimistic, as are, in general, the doctrines (all negative) that put the centre of life outside man, who with his free will can and must create his own world. Fascism desires an active man, one engaged in activity with all his energies: it desires a man virilely conscious of the difficulties that exist in action and ready to face them. It conceives of life as a struggle, considering that it behoves man to conquer for himself that life truly worthy of him, creating first of all in himself the instrument (physical, moral, intellectual) in order to construct it. Thus for the single individual, thus for the nation, thus for humanity. Hence the high value of culture in all its forms (art, religion, science), and the enormous importance of education. Hence also the essential value of work, with which man conquers nature and creates the human world (economic, political, moral, intellectual).

4] This positive conception of life is clearly an ethical conception.

It covers the whole of reality, not merely the human activity which controls it. No action can be divorced from moral judgement; there is nothing in the world which can be deprived of the value which belongs to everything in its relation to moral ends. Life, therefore, as conceived by the Fascist, is serious, austere, religious: the whole of it is poised in a world supported by the moral and responsible forces of the spirit. The Fascist disdains the "comfortable" life.

5] Fascism is a religious conception in which man is seen in his immanent relationship with a superior law and with an objective Will that transcends the particular individual and raises him to conscious membership of a spiritual society. Whoever has seen in the religious politics of the Fascist regime nothing but mere opportunism has not understood that Fascism besides being a system of government is also, and above all, a system of thought.

6] Fascism is an historical conception, in which man is what he is only in so far as he works with the spiritual process in which he finds himself, in the family or social group, in the nation and in the history in which all nations collaborate. From this follows the great value of tradition, in memories, in language, in customs, in the standards of social life. Outside history man is nothing. Consequently Fascism is opposed to all the individualistic abstractions of a materialistic nature like those of the eighteenth century; and it is opposed to all Jacobin utopias and innovations. It does not consider that "happiness" is possible upon earth, as it appeared to be in the desire of the economic literature of the eighteenth century, and hence it rejects all teleological theories according to which mankind would reach a definitive stabilized condition at a certain period in history. This implies putting oneself outside history and life, which is a continual change and coming to be. Politically, Fascism wishes to be realistic doctrine; practically, it aspires to solve only the problem which arise historically of themselves and that of themselves find or suggest their own solution. To act among men, as to act in the natural world, it is necessary to enter into the process of reality and to master the already operating forces.

7] Against individualism, the Fascist conception is for the State; and it is for the individual in so far as he coincides with the State, which is the conscience and universal will of man in his historical existence. It is opposed to classical Liberalism, which arose from the necessity of reacting against absolutism, and which brought its historical purpose to an end when the State was transformed into the conscience and will of the people. Liberalism denied the State in the interests of the particular individual; Fascism reaffirms the State as the true reality of the individual. And if liberty is to be the attribute of the real man, and not of that abstract puppet envisaged by individualistic Liberalism, Fascism is for liberty. And for the only liberty which can be a real thing, the liberty of the State and of the individual within the State. Therefore, for the Fascist, everything is in the State, and nothing human or spiritual exists, much less has value, outside the State. In this sense Fascism is totalitarian, and the Fascist State, the synthesis and unity of all values, interprets, develops and gives strength to the whole life of the people.

8] Outside the State there can be neither individuals nor groups (political parties, associations, syndicates, classes). Therefore Fascism is opposed to Socialism, which confines the movement of history within the class struggle and ignores the unity of classes established in one economic and moral reality in the State; and analogously it is opposed to class syndicalism. Fascism recognizes the real exigencies for which the socialist and syndicalist movement arose, but while recognizing them wishes to bring them under the control of the State and give them a purpose within the corporative system of interests reconciled within the unity of the State.

9] Individuals form classes according to the similarity of their interests, they form syndicates according to differentiated economic activities within these interests; but they form first, and above all, the State, which is not to be thought of numerically as the sum-total of individuals forming the majority of a nation. And consequently Fascism is opposed to Democracy, which equates the nation to the majority, lowering it to the level of that majority; nevertheless it is the purest form of democracy if the nation is conceived, as it should be, qualitatively and not quantitatively, as the most powerful idea (most powerful because most moral, most coherent, most true) which acts within the nation as the conscience and the will of a few, even of One, which ideal tends to become active within the conscience and the will of all — that is to say, of all those who rightly constitute a nation by reason of nature, history or race, and have set out upon the same line of development and spiritual formation as one conscience and one sole will. Not a race, nor a geographically determined region, but as a community historically perpetuating itself, a multitude unified by a single idea, which is the will to existence and to power: consciousness of itself, personality.

10] This higher personality is truly the nation in so far as it is the State. It is not the nation that generates the State, as according to the old naturalistc concept which served as the basis of the political theories of the national States of the nineteenth century. Rather the nation is created by the State, which gives to the people, conscious of its own moral unity, a will and therefore an effective existence. The right of a nation to independence derives not from a literary and ideal consciousness of its own being, still less from a more or less unconscious and inert acceptance of a *de facto* situation, but from an active consciousness, from a political will in action and ready to demonstrate its own rights: that is to say, from a state already coming into being. The State, in fact, as the universal ethical will, is the creator of right.

11] The nation as the State is an ethical reality which exists and lives in so far as it develops. To arrest its development is to kill it. Therefore the State is not only the authority which governs and gives the form of laws and the value of spiritual life to the wills of individuals, but it is also a power that makes its will felt abroad, making it known and respected, in other words, demonstrating the fact of its universality in all the necessary directions of its development. It is consequently organization and expansion, at least virtually. Thus it can be likened to the human will which knows no limits to its development and realizes itself in testing its own limitlessness.

12] The Fascist State, the highest and most powerful form of personality, is a force, but a spiritual force, which takes over all the forms of the moral and intellectual life of man. It cannot therefore confine itself simply to the functions of order and supervision as Liberalism desired. It is not simply a mechanism which limits the sphere of the supposed liberties of the individual. It is the form, the inner standard and the discipline of the whole person; it saturates the will as well as the intelligence. Its principle, the central inspiration of the human personality living in the civil community, pierces into the depths and makes its home in the heart of the man of action as well as of the thinker, of the artist as well as of the scientist: it is the soul of the soul.

13] Fascism, in short, is not only the giver of laws and the founder of institutions, but the educator and promoter of spiritual life. It wants to remake, not the forms of human life, but its content, man, character, faith. And to this end it requires discipline and authority that can enter into the spirits of men and there govern unopposed. Its sign, therefore, is the Lictors' rods, the symbol of unity, of strength and justice.

* * *

(ii) Political and social doctrines]

3] Above all, Fascism, in so far as it considers and observes the future and the development of humanity quite apart from the political considerations of the moment, believes neither in the possibility nor in the utility of perpetual peace. It thus repudiates the doctrine of Pacifism — born of a renunciation of the struggle and an act of cowardice in the face of sacrifice. War alone brings up to their highest tension all human energies and puts the stamp of nobility upon the peoples who have the courage to meet it. All other trials are substitutes, which never really put a man in front of himself in the alternative of life and death. A doctrine, therefore, which begins with a prejudice in favour of peace is foreign to Fascism; as are foreign to the spirit of Fascism, even though acceptable by reason of the utility which they might have in given political situations, all internationalistic and socialistc systems which, as history proves, can be blown to the winds when emotional, idealistic and practical movements storm the hearts of peoples. Fascism carries over this anti-pacifist spirit even into the lives of individuals. The proud motto of the *Squadrista,* "Me ne frego" [I ignore it], written on the bandages of a wound is an act of philosophy which is not only stoical, it is the epitome of a doctrine that is not only political: it is education for combat, the acceptance of the risks which it brings; it is a new way of life for Italy. Thus the Fascist accepts and loves life, he knows nothing of suicide and despises it; he looks on life as duty, ascent, conquest: life which must be noble and full: lived for oneself, but above all for those others near and far away, present and future.

4] The "demographic" policy of the regime follows from these premises. Even the Fascist does in fact love his neighbour, but this "neighbour" is not for him a vague and ill-defined concept; love for one's neighbour does not exclude necessary educational severities, and still less differentiations and distances. Fascism rejects universal concord, and, since it lives in the community of civilized peoples, it keeps them vigilantly and suspiciously before its eyes, it follows their states of mind and the changes in their interests and it does not let itself be deceived by temporary and fallacious appearances.

5] Such a conception of life makes Fascism the precise negation of that doctrine which formed the basis of the so-called Scientific or Marxian Socialism: the doctrine of historical Materialism, according to which the history of human civilizations can be explained only as the struggle of interest between the different social groups and as arising out of change in the means and instruments of production. That economic improvements — discoveries of raw materials, new methods of work, scientific inventions — should have an importance of their own, no one denies, but that they should suffice to explain human history to the exclusion of all other factors is absurd: Fascism believes, now and always, in holiness and in heroism, that is in acts in which no economic motive — remote or immediate — plays a part. With this negation of historical materialism, according to which men would be only by-products of history, who appear and disappear on the surface of the waves while in the depths the real directive forces are at work, there is also denied the immutable and irreparable "class struggle" which is the natural product of this economic conception of history, and above all it is denied that the class struggle can be the primary agent of social changes. Socialism, being thus wounded in these two primary tenets of its doctrine, nothing of it is left save the sentimental aspiration — old as humanity — towards a social order in which the sufferings and the pains of the humblest folk could be alleviated. But here Fascism rejects the concept of an economic "happiness" which would be realized socialistically and almost automatically at a given moment of economic evolution by assuring to all a maximum prosperity. Fascism denies the possibility of the materialistic conception of "happiness" and leaves it to the economists of the first half of the eighteenth century; it denies, that is, the equation of prosperity with happiness, which would transform men into animals with one sole preoccupation: that of being well-fed and fat, degraded in consequence to a merely physical existence.

6] After Socialism, Fascism attacks the whole complex of democratic ideologies and rejects them both in their theoretical premises and in their applications or practical manifestations. Fascism denies that the majority, through the mere fact of being a majority, can rule human societies; it denies that this majority can govern by means of a periodical consultation; it affirms the irremediable, fruitful and beneficent inequality of men, who cannot be levelled by such a mechanical and extrinsic fact as universal suffrage. By democratic regimes we mean those in which from time to time the people is given the illusion of being sovereign, while true effective sovereignty lies in other, perhaps irresponsible and secret, forces. Democracy is a regime without a king, but with very many kings, perhaps more exclusive, tyrannical and violent than one king even though a tyrant. This explains why Fascism, although before 1922 for reasons of expediency it made a gesture of republicanism, renounced it before the March on Rome, convinced that the question of the political forms of a State is not pre-eminent to-day, and that studying past and present monarchies, past and present Republics it becomes clear that monarchy and republic are not to be judged *sub specie aeternitatis* [as universals], but represent forms in which the political evolution, the history, the tradition, the psychology of a given country are manifested. Now Fascism overcomes the antithesis between monarchy and republic which retarded the movements of democracy, burdening the former with every defect and defending the latter as the regime of perfection. Now it has been seen that there are inherently reactionary and absolutistic republics, and monarchies that welcome the most daring political and social innovations.

7] "Reason, Science," said Renan (who was inspired before Fascism existed) in one of his philosophical Meditations, "are products of humanity, but to expect reason directly from the people and through the people is a chimera. It is not necessary for the existence of reason that everybody should know it. In any case, if such an initiation should be made, it would not be made by means of base democracy, which apparently must lead to the extinction of every difficult culture, and every higher discipline. The principle that society exists only for the prosperity and the liberty of the individuals who compose it does not seem to conform with the plans of nature, plans in which the species alone is taken into consideration and the individual seems to be sacrificed. It is strongly to be feared lest the last word of democracy thus understood (I hasten to say that it can also be understood in other ways) would be a social state in which a degenerate mass would have no other care than to enjoy the ignoble pleasures of vulgar men."

Thus far Renan. Fascism rejects in democracy the absurd conventional lie of political equalitarianism clothed in the dress of collective irresponsibility and the myth of happiness and indefinite progress. But if democracy can be understood in other ways, that is, if democracy means not to relegate the people to the periphery of the State, then Fascism could be defined as an "organized, centralized, authoritarian democracy."

8] In face of Liberal doctrines, Fascism takes up an attitude of absolute opposition both in the field of politics and in that of economics. It is not necessary to exaggerate — merely for the purpose of present controversies — the importance of Liberalism in the past century, and to make of that which was one of the numerous doctrines sketched in that century a religion of humanity for all times, present and future. Liberalism flourished for no more than some fifteen years. It was born in 1830, as a reaction against the Holy Alliance that wished to drag Europe back to what it had been before 1789, and it had its year of splendour in 1848 when even Pius IX was a Liberal. Immediately afterwards the decay set in. If 1848 was a year of light and of poetry, 1849 was a year of darkness and of tragedy. The Republic of Rome was destroyed by another Republic, that of France. In the same year Marx launched the gospel of the religion of Socialism with the famous *Communist Manifesto*. In 1851 Napoleon III carried out his unliberal *coup d'état* and ruled over France until 1870, when he was dethroned by a popular revolt, but as a consequence of a military defeat which ranks among the most resounding that history can relate. The victor was Bismarck, who never knew the home of the religion of liberty or who were its prophets. It is symptomatic that a people of high culture like the Germans should have been completely ignorant of the religion of liberty during the whole of the nineteenth century. It was, there, no more than a parenthesis, represented by what has been called the "ridiculous Parliament of Frankfort" which lasted only a season. Germany has achieved her national unity outside the doctrines of Liberalism, against Liberalism, a doctrine which seems foreign to the German soul, a soul essentially monarchical, whilst Liberalism is the historical and logical beginning of anarchism. The stages of German unity are the three wars of 1864, 1866 and 1870, conducted by "Liberals" like Moltke and Bismarck. As for Italian unity, Liberalism has had in it a part absolutely inferior to the share of Mazzini and of Garibaldi, who were not Liberals. Without the intervention of the unliberal Napoleon we should not have gained Lombardy, and without the help of the unliberal Bismarck at Sadowa and Sedan, very probably we should not have gained Venice in 1866; and in 1870 we should not have entered Rome. From 1870–1915 there occurs the period in which the very priests of the new creed had to confess the twilight of their religion: defeated as it was by decadence in literature, by activism in practice. Activism: that is to say, Nationalism, Futurism, Fascism.

The "Liberal" century, after having accumulated an infinity of Gordian knots, tried to untie them by the hecatomb of the World War. Never before has any religion imposed such a cruel sacrifice. Were the gods of Liberalism thirsty for blood? Now Liberalism is about to close the doors of its deserted temples because the peoples feel that its agnosticism in economics, its indifferentism in politics and in morals, would lead, as they have led, the States to certain ruin. In this way one can understand why all the political experiences of the contemporary world are anti-Liberal, and it is supremely ridiculous to wish on that account to class them outside of history; as if history were a hunting ground reserved to Liberalism and its professors, as if Liberalism were the definitive and no longer surpassable message of civilization.

9] But the Fascist repudiations of Socialism, Democracy, Liberalism must not make one think that Fascism wishes to make the world return to what it was before 1789, the year which has been indicated as the year of the beginning of the liberal-democratic age. One does not go backwards. The Fascist doctrine has not chosen De Maistre as its prophet. Monarchical absolutism is a think of the past and so also is every theocracy. So also feudal privileges and division into impenetrable and isolated castes have had their day. The theory of Fascist authority has nothing to do with the police State. A party that governs a nation in a totalitarian way is a new fact in history. References and comparisons are not possible. Fascism takes over from the ruins of Liberal Socialistic democratic doctrines those elements which still have a living value. It preserves those that can be called the established facts of history, it rejects all the rest, that is to say the idea of a doctrine which holds good for all times and all peoples. If it is admitted that the nineteenth century has been the century of Socialism, Liberalism and Democracy, it does not follow that the twentieth must also be the century of Liberalism, Socialism and Democracy. Political doctrines pass; peoples remain. It is to be expected that this century may be that of authority, a century of the "Right," a Fascist century. If the nineteenth was the century of the individual (Liberalism means individualism) it may be expected that this one may be the century of "collectivism" and therefore the century of the State. That a new doctrine should use the still vital elements of other doctrines is perfectly logical. No doctrine is born quite new, shining, never before seen. No doctrine can boast of an absolute "originality." It is bound, even if only historically, to other doctrines that have been, and to develop into other doctrines that will be. Thus the scientific socialism of Marx is bound to the Utopian Socialism of the Fouriers, the Owens and the Saint-Simons; thus the Liberalism of the nineteenth century is connected with the whole "Enlightenment" of the eighteenth century. Thus the doctrines of democracy are bound to the *Encyclopédie.* Every doctrine tends to direct the activity of men towards a determined objective; but the activity of man reacts upon the doctrine, transforms it, adapts it to new necessities or transcends it. The doctrine itself, therefore, must be, not words, but an act of life. Hence, the pragmatic veins in Fascism, its will to power, its will to be, its attitude in the face of the fact of "violence" and of its own courage.

10] The keystone of Fascist doctrine is the conception of the State, of its essence, of its tasks, of its ends. For Fascism the State is an absolute before which individuals and groups are relative. Individuals and groups are "thinkable" in so far as they are within the State. The Liberal State does not direct the interplay and the material and spiritual development of the groups, but limits itself to registering the results; the Fascist State has a consciousness of its own, a will of its own, on this account it is called an "ethical" State. In 1929, at the first quinquennial assembly of the regime, I said: "For Fascism, the State is not the night-watchman who is concerned only with the personal security of the citizens; nor is it an organization for purely material ends, such as that of guaranteeing a certain degree of prosperity and a relatively peaceful social order, to achieve which a council of administration would be sufficient, nor is it a creation of mere politics with no contact with the material and complex reality of the lives of individuals and the life of peoples. The State, as conceived by Fascism and as it acts, is a spiritual and moral fact because it makes concrete the political, juridical, economic organization of the nation and such an organization is, in its origin and in its development, a manifestation of the spirit. The State is the guarantor of internal and external security, but it is also the guardian and the transmitter of the spirit of the people as it has been elaborated through the centuries in language, custom, faith. The State is not only present, it is also past, and above all future. It is the State which, transcending the brief limit of individual lives, represents the immanent conscience of the nation. The forms in which States express themselves change, but the necessity of the State remains. It is the State which educates citizens for civic virtue, makes them conscious of their mission, calls them to unity; harmonizes their interests in justice; hands on the achievements of thought in the sciences, the arts, in law, in human solidarity; it carries men from the elementary life of the tribe to the highest human expression of power which is Empire; it entrusts to the ages the names of those who died for its integrity or in obedience to its laws; it puts forward as an example and recommends to the generations that are to come the leaders who increased its territory and the men of genius who gave it glory. When the sense of the State declines and the disintegrating and centrifugal tendencies of individuals and groups prevail, national societies move to their decline."

11] From 1929 up to the present day these doctrinal positions have been strengthened by the whole economico-political evolution of the world. It is the State alone that grows in size, in power. It is the State alone that can solve the dramatic contradictions of capitalism. What is called the crisis cannot be overcome except by the State, within the State. Where are the shades of the Jules Simons who, at the dawn of liberalism, proclaimed that "the State must strive to render itself unnecessary and to prepare for its demise"; of the MacCullochs who, in the second half of the last century, affirmed that the State must abstain from too much governing? And faced with the continual, necessary and inevitable interventions of the State in economic affairs what would the Englishman Bentham now say, according to whom industry should have asked of the State only to be left in peace? Or the German Humboldt, according to whom the "idle" State must be considered the best? It is true that the second generation of liberal economists was less extremist than the first, and already Smith himself opened, even though cautiously, the door to State intervention in economics. But when one says liberalism, one says the individual; when one says Fascism, one says the State. But the Fascist State is unique; it is an original creation. It is not reactionary, but revolutionary in that it anticipates the solutions of certain universal problems. These problems are no longer seen in the same light: in the sphere of politics they are removed from party rivalries, from the supreme power of parliament, from the irresponsibility of assemblies; in the sphere of economics they are removed from the sphere of the syndicates' activities — activities that were ever widening their scope and increasing their power, both on the workers' side and on the employers' — removed from their struggles and their designs; in the moral sphere they are divorced from ideas of the need for order,

discipline and obedience, and lifted into the plane of the moral com-
mandments of the fatherland. Fascism desires the State to be strong,
organic and at the same time founded on a wide popular basis. The
Fascist State has also claimed for itself the field of economics and,
through the corporative, social and educational institutions which it
has created, the meaning of the State reaches out to and includes the
farthest off-shoots; and within the State, framed in their respective
organizations, there revolve all the political, economic and spiritual
forces of the nation. A State founded on millions of individuals who
recognize it, feel it, are ready to serve it, is not the tyrannical State
of the medieval lord. It has nothing in common with the absolutist
States that existed either before or after 1789. In the Fascist State the
individual is not suppressed, but rather multiplied, just as in a regi-
ment a soldier is not weakened but multiplied by the number of his
comrades. The Fascist State organizes the nation, but it leaves sufficient scope to individuals; it has limited useless or harmful liberties
and has preserved those that are essential. It cannot be the individual
who decides in this matter, but only the State.

12] The Fascist State does not remain indifferent to the fact of
religion in general and to that particular positive religion which is
Italian Catholicism. The State has no theology, but it has an ethic. In
the Fascist State religion is looked upon as one of the deepest manifestations of the spirit; it is, therefore, not only respected, but defended and protected. The Fascist State does not create a "God" of
its own, as Robespierre once, at the height of the Convention's foolishness, wished to do; nor does it vainly seek, like Bolshevism, to
expel religion from the minds of men; Fascism respects the God
of the ascetics, of the saints, of the heroes, and also God as seen and
prayed to by the simple and primitive heart of the people.

13] The Fascist State is a will to power and to government. In it
the tradition of Rome is an idea that has force. In the doctrine of
Fascism Empire is not only a territorial, military or mercantile expression, but spiritual or moral. One can think of an empire, that is
to say a nation that directly or indirectly leads other nations, without needing to conquer a single square kilometre of territory. For
Fascism the tendency to Empire, that is to say, to the expansion of
nations, is a manifestation of vitality; its opposite, staying at home,
is a sign of decadence: peoples who rise or re-rise are imperialist,
peoples who die are renunciatory. Fascism is the doctrine that is most
fitted to represent the aims, the states of mind, of a people, like the

Italian people, rising again after many centuries of abandonment or slavery to foreigners. But Empire calls for discipline, co-ordination of forces, duty and sacrifice; this explains many aspects of the practical working of the regime and the direction of many of the forces of the State and the necessary severity shown to those who would wish to oppose this spontaneous and destined impulse of the Italy of the twentieth century, to oppose it in the name of the superseded ideologies of the nineteenth, repudiated wherever great experiments of political and social transformation have been courageously attempted: especially where, as now, peoples thirst for authority, for leadership, for order. If every age has its own doctrine, it is apparent from a thousand signs that the doctrine of the present age is Fascism. That it is a doctrine of life is shown by the fact that it has resuscitated a faith. That this faith has conquered minds is proved by the fact that Fascism has had its dead and its martyrs.

Fascism henceforward has in the world the universality of all those doctrines which, by fulfilling themselves, have significance in the history of the human spirit.

4

Escape from Freedom: A Psychoanalytic View

IF ONE were to list the outstanding developments in our century, the word "psychology" would certainly appear near the top. Not that the twentieth century discovered the unconscious: for centuries artists, poets, and religious writers have concerned themselves with the irrational in man. But never before has mankind witnessed such self-conscious awareness of the power of the irrational, turned over to it virtually the entire world of art and literature, and formulated its experience into a highly systematic science.

In the eyes of some of its critics, the "psychological revolution" has meant yet another attack on man's dignity. Galileo, so the argument goes, turned man's divinely favored earth into a speck of cosmic dust; Darwin turned God's image, man himself, into a mere rational animal; and Freud and his followers took the next step and subordinated the rational in man to the animal. In reply, advocates of psychological theory and practice argue that not only has the new psychology disclosed hitherto unknown aspects of human thought and behavior, but has also furnished man with a powerful instrument for solving perennial problems in the life of man and society.

The selection chosen to represent this aspect of our culture is from Escape from Freedom, by Erich Fromm, a practicing psychoanalyst, teacher, and prolific author of works concerned with the many expressions of psychological disturbance in man's personal, social, and international life. This particular passage has been chosen because of its specific relevance to the preceding materials on the most horrendous explosion of the irrational in this century, Nazism.

Eric Fromm, Escape from Freedom

I COME now to the main question: What is the root of both the masochistic perversion and masochistic character traits respectively? Furthermore, what is the common root of both the masochistic *and* the sadistic strivings?

The direction in which the answer lies has already been suggested in the beginning of this chapter. Both the masochistic and sadistic strivings tend to help the individual to escape his unbearable feeling of aloneness and powerlessness. Psychoanalytic and other empirical observations of masochistic persons give ample evidence (which I cannot quote here without transcending the scope of this book) that they are filled with a terror of aloneness and insignificance. Frequently this feeling is not conscious; often it is covered by compensatory feelings of eminence and perfection. However, if one only penetrates deeply enough into the unconscious dynamics of such a person, one finds these feelings without fail. The individual finds himself "free" in the negative sense, that is, alone with his self and confronting an alienated, hostile world. In this situation, to quote a telling description of Dostoevski, in *The Brothers Karamasov*, he has "no more pressing need than the one to find somebody to whom he can surrender, as quickly as possible, that gift of freedom which he, the unfortunate creature, was born with." The frightened individual seeks for somebody or something to tie his self to; he cannot bear to be his own individual self any longer, and he tries frantically to get rid of it and to feel security again by the elimination of this burden: the self.

Masochism is one way toward this goal. The different forms which the masochistic strivings assume have one aim: *to get rid of the individual self, to lose oneself;* in other words, *to get rid of the burden of freedom.* This aim is obvious in those masochistic strivings in which the individual seeks to submit to a person or power which he feels as being overwhelmingly strong. (Incidentally, the conviction of superior strength of another person is always to be understood in relative terms. It can be based either upon the actual strength of the other person, or upon a conviction of one's own utter insignifi-

From Erich Fromm, ESCAPE FROM FREEDOM (New York, 1941), pp. 151–164. Copyright © 1941 by Erich Fromm. Reprinted by permission of Holt, Rinehart and Winston, Inc. and Routledge & Kegan Paul Ltd.

cance and powerlessness. In the latter event a mouse or a leaf can assume threatening features.) In other forms of masochistic strivings the essential aim is the same. In the masochistic feeling of smallness we find a tendency which serves to increase the original feeling of insignificance. How is this to be understood? Can we assume that by making a fear worse one is trying to remedy it? Indeed, this is what the masochistic person does. As long as I struggle between my desire to be independent and strong and my feeling of insignificance or powerlessness I am caught in a tormenting conflict. If I succeed in reducing my individual self to nothing, if I can overcome the awareness of my separateness as an individual, I may save myself from this conflict. To feel utterly small and helpless is one way toward this aim; to be overwhelmed by pain and agony another; to be overcome by the effects of intoxication still another. The phantasy of suicide is the last hope if all other means have not succeeded in bringing relief from the burden of aloneness.

Under certain conditions these masochistic strivings are relatively successful. If the individual finds cultural patterns that satisfy these masochistic strivings (like the submission under the "leader" in Fascist ideology), he gains some security by finding himself united with millions of others who share these feelings. Yet even in these cases, the masochistic "solution" is no more of a solution than neurotic manifestations ever are: the individual succeeds in eliminating the conspicuous suffering but not in removing the underlying conflict and the silent unhappiness. When the masochistic striving does not find a cultural pattern or when it quantitatively exceeds the average amount of masochism in the individual's social group, the masochistic solution does not even solve anything in relative terms. It springs from an unbearable situation, tends to overcome it, and leaves the individual caught in new suffering. If human behavior were always rational and purposeful, masochism would be as inexplicable as neurotic manifestations in general are. This, however, is what the study of emotional and mental disturbances has taught us: that human behavior can be motivated by strivings which are caused by anxiety or some other unbearable state of mind, that these strivings tend to overcome this emotional state and yet merely cover up its most visible manifestations, or not even these. Neurotic manifestations resemble the irrational behavior in a panic. Thus a man, trapped in a fire, stands at the window of his room and shouts for help, forgetting entirely that no one can hear him and that he could still escape by the staircase which will also be aflame in a few minutes. He shouts because he wants to be saved, and for the moment this behavior appears to be a step on the way to being saved — and yet it will end in complete catastrophe. In the same way the masochistic strivings are caused by the desire to get rid of the individual self with all its shortcomings, conflicts, risks, doubts, and unbearable aloneness, but they only succeed in removing the most noticeable pain or they even lead to greater suffering. The irrationality of masochism, as of all other neurotic manifestations, consists in the ultimate futility of the means adopted to selve an untenable emotional situation.

These considerations refer to an important difference between neurotic and rational activity. In the latter the *result* corresponds to the *motivation* of an activity — one acts in order to attain a certain result. In neurotic strivings one acts from a compulsion which has essentially a negative character: to escape an unbearable situation. The strivings tend in a direction which only fictitiously is a solution. Actually the result is contradictory to what the person wants to attain; the compulsion to get rid of an unbearable feeling was so strong that the person was unable to choose a line of action that could be a solution in any other but a fictitious sense.

The implication of this for masochism is that the individual is driven by an unbearable feeling of aloneness and insignificance. He then attempts to overcome it by getting rid of his self (as a psychological, not as a physiological entity); his way to achieve this is to belittle himself, to suffer, to make himself utterly insignificant. But pain and suffering are not what he wants; pain and suffering are the price he pays for an aim which he compulsively tries to attain. The price is dear. He has to pay more and more and, like a peon, he only gets into greater debts without ever getting what he has paid for: inner peace and tranquillity.

I have spoken of the masochistic perversion because it proves beyond doubt that suffering can be something sought for. However, in the masochistic perversion as little as in moral masochism suffering is not the real aim; in both cases it is the means to an aim: forgetting one's self. The difference between the perversion and masochistic character traits lies essentially in the following: In the perversion the trend to get rid of one's self is expressed through the medium of the body and linked up with sexual feelings. While in moral masochism, the masochistic trends get hold of the whole person and tend to destroy all the aims which the ego consciously tries to achieve, in the perversion the masochistic strivings are more or less restricted to the physical realm; moreover by their amalgamation with sex they participate in the release of tension occurring in the sexual sphere and thus find some direct release.

The annihilation of the individual self and the attempt to overcome thereby the unbearable feeling of powerlessness are only one side of the masochistic strivings. The other side is the attempt to become a part of a bigger and more powerful whole outside of oneself, to submerge and participate in it. This power can be a person, an institution, God, the nation, conscience, or a psychic compulsion. By becoming part of a power which is felt as unshakably strong, eternal, and glamorous, one participates in its strength and glory. One surrenders one's own self and renounces all strength and pride connected with it, one loses one's integrity as an individual and surrenders freedom; but one gains a new security and a new pride in the participation in the power in which one submerges. One gains also security against the torture of doubt. The masochistic person, whether his master is an authority outside of himself or whether he has internalized the master as conscience or a psychic compulsion, is saved from making decisions, saved from the final responsibility for the fate of his self, and thereby saved from the doubt of what decision to make. He is also saved from the doubt of what the meaning of his life is or who "he" is. These questions are answered by the relationship to the power to which he has attached himself. The meaning of his life and the identity of his self are determined by the greater whole into which the self has submerged.

The masochistic bonds are fundamentally different from the primary bonds. The latter are those that exist before the process of individuation has reached its completion. The individual is still part of "his" natural and social world, he has not yet completely emerged from his surroundings. The primary bonds give him genuine security and the knowledge of where he belongs. The masochistic bonds are escape. The individual self has emerged, but it is unable to realize his freedom; it is overwhelmed by anxiety, doubt, and a feeling of powerlessness. The self attempts to find security in "secondary bonds," as we might call the masochistic bonds, but this attempt can never be successful. The emergence of the individual self cannot be reversed; consciously the individual can feel secure and as if he "belonged," but basically he remains a powerless atom who suffers under the submergence of his self. He and the power to which he clings never become one, a basic antagonism remains and with it an impulse, even if it is not conscious at all, to overcome the masochistic dependence and to become free.

What is the essence of the sadistic drives? Again, the wish to inflict pain on others is not the essence. All the different forms of sadism which we can observe go back to one essential impulse, namely, to have complete mastery over another person, to make of him a helpless object of our will, to become the absolute ruler over him, to become his God, to do with him as one pleases. To humiliate him, to enslave him, are means to this end and the most radical aim is to make him suffer, since there is no greater power over another person than that of inflicting pain on him, to force him to undergo suffering without his being able to defend himself. The pleasure in the complete domination over another person (or other animate objects) is the very essence of the sadistic drive.[1]

It seems that this tendency to make oneself the absolute master over another person is the opposite of the masochistic tendency, and it is puzzling that these two tendencies should be so closely knitted together. No doubt with regard to its practical consequences the wish to be dependent or to suffer is the opposite of the wish to dominate and to make others suffer. Psychologically, however, both tendencies are the outcomes of one basic need, springing from the inability to bear the isolation and weakness of one's own self. I suggest calling the aim which is at the basis of both sadism and masochism: *symbiosis*. Symbiosis, in this psychological sense, means the union of one individual self with another self (or any other power outside of the own self) in such a way as to make each lose the integrity of its own self and to make them completely dependent on each other. The sadistic person needs his object just as much as the masochistic needs his. Only instead of seeking security by being swallowed, he gains it by swallowing somebody else. In both cases the integrity of the individual self is lost. In one case I dissolve myself in an outside power; I lose myself. In the other case I enlarge myself by making another being part of myself and thereby I gain the strength I lack as an independent self. It is always the inability to stand the aloneness of one's individual self that leads to the drive to enter into a symbiotic relationship with someone else. It is evident from this why masochistic and sadistic trends are always blended with each other. Although on the surface they seem contradictions, they are essentially rooted in the same basic need. People are not sadistic *or* masochistic, but there is a constant oscillation between the active and the passive side of the symbiotic complex, so that it is often difficult to determine which side of it is operating at a given moment. In both cases individuality and freedom are lost.

If we think of sadism, we usually think of the destructiveness and hostility which is so blatantly connected with it. To be sure, a greater or lesser amount of destructiveness is always to be found linked up with sadistic tendencies. But this is also true of masochism. Every analysis of masochistic traits shows this hostility. The main difference seems to be that in sadism the hostility is usually more conscious and directly expressed in action, while in masochism the hostility is mostly unconscious and finds an indirect expression. I shall try to show later on that destructiveness is the result of the thwarting of the individual's sensuous, emotional, and intellectual expansiveness; it is therefore to be expected as an outcome of the same conditions that make for the symbiotic need. The point I wish to emphasize here is that sadism is not identical with distructiveness, although it is to a great extent blended with it. The destructive person wants to destroy the object, that is, to do away with it and to get rid of it. The sadist wants to dominate his object and therefore suffers a loss if his object disappears.

Sadism, as we have used the word, can also be relatively free from destructiveness and blended with a friendly attitude towards its object. This kind of "loving" sadism has found classical expression in Balzac's *Lost Illusions,* a description which also conveys the particular quality of what we mean by the need for symbiosis. In this passage Balzac describes the relationship between young Lucien and the Bagno prisoner who poses as an Abbé. Shortly after he makes the acquaintance of the young man who has just tried to commit suicide the Abbé says: ". . . This young man has nothing in common with the poet who died just now. I have picked you up, I have given life to you, and you belong to me as the creature belongs to the creator, as — in the Orient's fairy tales — the Ifrit belongs to the spirit, as the body belongs to the soul. With powerful hands I will keep you straight on the road to power; I promise you, nevertheless, a life of pleasures, of honors, of everlasting feasts. You will never lack money, you will sparkle, you will be brilliant; whereas I, stooped down in the filth of promoting, shall secure the brilliant edifice of your success. I love power for the sake of power! I shall always enjoy your pleasures although I shall have to renounce them. Shortly: I shall be one and the same person with you. . . . I will love my creature, I will mold him, will shape him to my services, in order to love him as a father loves his child. I shall drive at your side in your Tilbury, my dear boy, I shall delight in your successes with women. I shall say: I am this handsome young man. I have created this Marquis de Rubempré and have placed him among the aristocracy; his success is my product. He is silent and he talks with my voice, he follows my advice in everything."

Frequently, and not only in the popular usage, sado-masochism is confounded with love. Masochistic phenomena, especially, are looked upon as expressions of love. An attitude of complete self-denial for the sake of another person and the surrender of one's own rights and claims to another person have been praised as examples of "great love." It seems that there is no better proof for "love" than sacrifice and readiness to give oneself up for the sake of the beloved person. Actually, in these cases, "love" is essentially a masochistic yearning and rooted in the symbiotic need of the person involved. If we mean by love the passionate affirmation and active relatedness to the essence of a particular person, if we mean by it the union with another person on the basis of the independence and integrity of the two persons involved, then masochism and love are opposites. Love is based on equality and freedom. If it is based on subordination and loss of integrity of one partner, it is masochistic dependence, regardless of how the relationship is rationalized. Sadism also appears frequently under the disguise of love. To rule over another person, if one can claim that to rule him is for that person's own sake, frequently appears as an expression of love, but the essential factor is the enjoyment of domination.

At this point a question will have arisen in the mind of many a reader: Is not sadism, as we have described it here, identical with the craving for power? The answer to this question is that although the more destructive forms of sadism, in which the aim is to hurt and torture another person, are not identical with the wish for power, the latter is the most significant expression of sadism. The problem has gained added significance in the present day. Since Hobbes, one has seen in power the basic motive of human behavior; the following centuries, however, gave increased weight to legal and moral factors which tended to curb power. With the rise of Fascism, the lust for power and the conviction of its right has reached new heights. Millions are impressed by the victories of power and take it for the sign of strength. To be sure, power over people is an expression of superior strength in a purely material sense. If I have the power over another person to kill him, I am "stronger" than he is. But in a psychological sense, *the lust for power is not rooted in strength but in weakness.* It is the expression of the inability of the individual self to stand alone and live. It is the desperate attempt to gain secondary strength where genuine strength is lacking.

The word "power" has a twofold meaning. One is the possession of power *over* somebody, the ability to dominate him; the other meaning is the possession of power to do something, to be able, to be potent. The latter meaning has nothing to do with domination; it expresses mastery in the sense of ability. If we speak of powerlessness we have this meaning in mind; we do not think of a person who is not able to dominate others, but of a person who is not able to do what he wants. Thus power can mean one of two things, *domination* or *potency.* Far from being identical, these two qualities are mutually exclusive. Impotence, using the term not only with regard to the sexual sphere but to all spheres of human potentialities, results in the sadistic striving for domination; to the extent to which an individual is potent, that is, able to realize his potentialities on the basis of freedom and integrity of his self, he does not need to dominate and is lacking the lust for power. Power, in the sense of domination, is the perversion of potency, just as sexual sadism is the perversion of sexual love.

Sadistic and masochistic traits are probably to be found in everybody. At one extreme there are individuals whose whole personality is dominated by these traits, and at the other there are those for whom these sado-masochistic traits are not characteristic. Only in discussing the former can we speak of a sado-masochistic character. The term "character" is used here in the dynamic sense in which Freud speaks of character. In this sense it refers not to the sum total of behavior patterns characteristic for one person, but to the dominant drives that motivate behavior. Since Freud assumed that the basic motivating forces are sexual ones, he arrived at concepts like "oral," "anal," or "genital" characters. If one does not share this assumption, one is forced to devise different character types. But the dynamic concept remains the same. The driving forces are not necessarily conscious as such to a person whose character is dominated by them. A person can be entirely dominated by his sadistic strivings and consciously believe that he is motivated only by his sense of duty. He may not even commit any overt sadistic acts but suppress his sadistic drives sufficiently to make him appear on the surface as a person who is not sadistic. Nevertheless, any close analysis of his behavior, his phantasies, dreams, and gestures, would show the sadistic impulses operating in deeper layers of his personality.

Although the character of persons in whom sado-masochistic drives are dominant can be characterized as sado-masochistic, such persons are not necessarily neurotic. It depends to a large extent on the particular tasks people have to fulfill in their social situation and what patterns of feelings and behavior are present in their culture whether or not a particular kind of character structure is "neurotic" or "normal." As a matter of fact, for great parts of the lower middle class in Germany and other European countries, the sado-masochistic character is typical, and, as will be shown later, it is this kind of character structure to which Nazi ideology had its strongest appeal. Since the term "sado-masochistic" is associated with ideas of perversion and neurosis, I prefer to speak of the sado-masochistic character, especially when not the neurotic but the normal person is meant, as the "*authoritarian character.*" This terminology is justifiable because the sado-masochistic person is always characterized by his attitude toward authority. He admires authority and tends to submit to it, but at the same time he wants to be an authority himself and have others submit to him. There is an additional reason for choosing this term. The Fascist system call themselves authoritarian because of the dominant role of authority in their social and political structure. By the term "authoritarian character," we imply that it represents the personality structure which is the human basis of Fascism.

NOTE

1. Marquis de Sade held the view that the quality of domination is the essence of sadism in this passage from *Juliette II* (quoted from *Marquis de Sade,* by G. Gorer, Liveright Publishing Corporation, New York, 1934): "It is not pleasure which you want to make your partner feel but impression you want to produce; that of pain is far stronger than that of pleasure . . . one realizes that; one uses it and is satisfied." Gorer in his analysis of de Sade's work defines sadism "as the pleasure felt from the observed modifica-

tions on the external world produced by the observer." This definition comes nearer to my own view of sadism than that of other psychologists. I think, however, that Gorer is wrong in identifying sadism with the pleasure in mastery or productivity. The sadistic mastery is characterized by the fact that it wants to make the object a will-less instrument in the sadist's hands, while the nonsadistic joy in influencing others respects the integrity of the other person and is based on a feeling of equality. In Gorer's definition sadism loses it specific quality and becomes identical with any kind of productivity.

5

Man Without God

For those guided by traditional religious faiths, the monstrous brutalities of our century come as no surprise. The optimistic belief in man's inherent reason and virtue, the abiding faith in progress, and the seemingly exclusive concern with secular interests and material comforts were, according to these religious critics, vast delusions and self-deceptions. Man without God, they insist, is man without good: until he is at one with God, man can be neither at one with himself nor with his fellow man. The consequences of this widespread and profound disillusionment with earlier secularist world-views have been a remarkable resurgence of traditional Western religions and a passionate search for spiritual guidance in a variety of forms of mysticism and symbolism, both of the East and of the West.

One of the most influential contributors to this spiritual renaissance was Nicolas Berdyaev. Born in Kiev, Russia, in 1874, he began his intellectual career in the 1890's as a leading exponent of Russian Marxism. By the turn of the century, along with a number of other leading Russian thinkers, he moved from Marxism to philosophical idealism and somewhat later to Christian existentialism. A bitter foe of the Bolsheviks as well as one of the most insightful historians of their movement, he left Russia in 1922 and settled in Paris in 1924. His imaginative and provocative commentaries on the "burning issues" of our time as well as his many philosophical and religious writings won him fame the world over. He died in Paris in 1948. Among his best works available in English are his autobiography Dream and Reality, The Meaning of History, The Meaning of the Creative Act, and The Beginning and the End.

Nicolas Berdyaev, The Fate of Man in the Modern World

Dehumanization]

I] THE CENTRAL theme of our epoch is that of all history — the fate of man. What is taking place in the world to-day is not a crisis of humanism (that is a topic of secondary importance), but the crisis of humanity. We face the question, is that being to whom the future belongs to be called man, as previously, or something other? We are witnessing the process of dehumanization in all phases of culture and of social life. Above all, moral consciousness is being dehumanized. Man has ceased to be the supreme value: he has ceased to have any value at all. The youth of the whole world, communist, fascist, nationalsocialist or those simply carried away by technics or sport — this youth is not only anti-humanistic in its attitudes, but often anti-human. Does this mean that we should defend the old humanism against to-day's youth? In many of my books I have called attention to the crisis in humanism, and tried to show that it inevitably develops into anti-humanism and that its final stage is a denial of man. Humanism has become powerless and must be replaced. Humanism bound up with the renaissance of antiquity is very frail; its development implies an aristocratic social order and democracy has dealt it terrible blows, with the masses and the power of technics breaking into cultural life. The machine dehumanizes human life. Man, desiring no longer to be the image of God, becomes the image of the machine. In its process of democratization, beginning with the eighteenth century, humanism goes along the line of subjecting man to society, to social ordinariness, it generalizes man — it is losing itself.

This democratized and generalized humanism has ceased to be attentive to man: it is interested in the structure of society, but not in man's inner life. This is a fatal and inevitable process. Hence humanism can never be a force capable of withstanding the process of dehumanization. From humanism, which is, after all, a sort of

From Nicolas Berdyaev, THE FATE OF MAN IN THE MODERN WORLD (Ann Arbor, 1935), pp. 25-40, 61-70. Copyright © 1935 by The University of Michigan Press. Reprinted by permission of The University of Michigan Press.

middle-of-the-road humanity, progress is possible in two directions, up or down; toward the idea of the God-man, or toward that of the beast-man. Movement toward super-humanity and the superman, toward super-human powers, all too often means nothing other than a bestialization of man. Modern anti-humanism takes the form of bestialism. It uses the tragic and unfortunate Nietzsche as a superior sort of justification for dehumanization and bestialization. Few there be who are moving toward the god-man, "god-humanism" toward the true super-humanism: many move toward bestialism, the deification of the bestial. A bestial cruelty toward man is characteristic of our age, and this is more astonishing since it is displayed at the very peak of human refinement, where modern conceptions of sympathy, it would seem, have made impossible the old, barbaric forms of cruelty. Bestialism is something quite different from the old, natural, healthy barabarism; it is barbarism within a refined civilization. Here the atavistic, barbaric instincts are filtered through the prism of civilization, and hence they have a pathological character. Bestialism is a phenomenon of the human world, but a world already civilized. It does not exist in the animal world, which belongs to a different degree of being, with its own significance and justification. The animals are something much higher than bestialized man. Hence we speak of man's fallen state. Just now bestialism is set up higher than humanism, as the next degree to which we should progress. But bestialism at all events is worse and lower than humanism, although the latter is powerless to resist it. The bestialism of our time is a continuation of the war, it has poisoned mankind with the blood of war. The morals of war-time have become those of "peaceful" life, which is actually the continuation of war, a war of all against all. According to this morality, everything is permissible: man may be used in any way desired for the attainment of inhuman or anti-human aims. Bestialism is a denial of the value of the human person, of every human personality; it is a denial of all sympathy with the fate of any man. The new humanism is closing: this is inescapable. But if the end of humanism be held to be the end of humanity, this is a moral catastrophe.

We are entering an inhuman world, a world of inhumanness, inhuman not merely in fact, but in principle as well. Inhumanity has begun to be presented as something noble, surrounded with an aureole of heroism. Over against man there rises a class or a race, a deified collective or state. Modern nationalism bears marks of bestial inhumanity. No longer is every man held to be a man, a value, the image and likeness of God. For often even Christianity is interpreted inhumanly. The "Aryan paragraph" offered to German Christians is the project for a new form of inhumanity in Christianity. But this is nothing very new. Too often in the past Christianity, that is to say Christian humanity, has been inhuman. The old bestialism, naïve, barbarian, instinctive, was not self-conscious; it was pre-conscious. But modern bestialism is conscious, deliberate, the product of reflection and civilization, self-justified. Over against the inhumanity of modern nationalism stands that of modern communism. It also refuses to consider every man as of real value, as the likeness and image of God. The class-enemy may be treated as you like. We shall return to this subject later and shall see that nationalism and racialism are worse than communism.

There may have been a time when the image of man, his truly human nature, was not yet revealed — man was in a sort of potential state. This was the case in the past. But now we face something quite different. The image of man has been shaken and has begun to disintegrate after it was revealed. This is going on now in all spheres. Dehumanization has penetrated into all phases of human creativity. In making himself God, man has unmanned himself. This is, of course, a collapse of the humanistic theory of progress. The fate of man is infinitely more complex than it was thought to be in the nineteenth century. The new world which is taking form is moved by other values than the value of man or of human personality, or the value of truth: it is moved by such values as power, technics, race-purity, nationality, the state, the class, the collective. The will to justice is overcome by the will to power. The dialectic of the process is very delicate. Man desires power, power for himself, but this leads him to put power above self, above man; it leads him to readiness to sacrifice his own humanity for the sake of power. Power is objectified and drawn away from human existence. Such values as those of technics, the state, the race or the class bestialize man: for the sake of these sorts of power, any desired treatment of the individual is permitted.

It would be a mistake to think that modern bestialism and its attendant dehumanization are based upon the triumph of base instincts and appetites and a denial of all the values ordinarily held to be idealistic. Modern bestialism and dehumanization are based upon idolatry, the worship of technics, race or class or production, and upon the adaptation of atavistic instincts to this worship. We have already noted that modern barbarism is a civilized barbarism. The war aroused ancient instincts — racial and national: the instincts of power and violence, instincts of revenge, but all these are now realized in the forms of technical civilization. In reality we are witnessing a return of the human mass to the ancient collective with which its history began; the return to a state which preceded the development of personality. But this ancient collective takes on civilized forms and uses the technical instruments of civilization. Keyserling sees this "world-revolution" as the uprising of tellurian forces, the Earth opposing the Spirit. But telluric forces are natural, cosmic, while the forces of to-day are those of technical civilization.

In modern tendencies the influence of two thinkers of the nineteenth century is very strongly felt — the influence of Marx and Nietzsche. They signify the end and the destruction of humanism. Marx and Nietzsche are in conflict for the control of the world. The influence of Nietzsche upon fascism and national-socialism is unmistakable. His influence is felt in the modern apotheosis of a powerful leader, and in the development of a cruel type of youth devoid of all sympathy with suffering. Nietzsche himself, that solitary aristocratic thinker, would turn away in horror from the social results of his preaching. Nietzsche did not like the idea of Pan-Germanism, he was not a German nationalist and would probably suffer pangs of disgust at the modern plebeian spirit, devoid of all traits of nobility.

But influence works that way, in the subterranean and subconscious sphere, and often arouses forces which it was far from the thought of the creative mind to set in motion. The historical influence of Luther, for instance, moved in quite a different direction from that which he intended. Luther never thought that protestantism would become rationalistic and moralistic. The influence of Marx on communism is apparently developing much more as he intended, but still the Russian communist revolution would doubtless greatly surprise him, since it quite contradicts or even renounces his teaching. At the moment the influence of Marx and Nietzsche is active in the direction of the dehumanization of society and culture. And this dehumanization is at the same time de-christianization. Conservative Christians rarely note how completely this is true. They are inclined to think that humanism was a de-christianization, and for some reason they do not associate dehumanization with the fact that the image of God in man is being darkened, that man is losing the sense, which Christianity revealed to him, of being a son of God.

In the cultural and ideal tendencies of our epoch dehumanization moves in two directions, toward naturalism and toward technicism. Man is subject either to cosmic forces or to technical civilization. It is not enough to say that he subjects himself: he is dissolved and disappears either in cosmic life or else in almighty technics; he takes upon himself the image, either of nature or of the machine. But in either case he loses his own image and is dissolved into his component elements. Man as a whole being, as a creature centred within himself, disappears; he ceases to be a being with a spiritual centre, retaining his inner continuity and his unity. To the fractional and partial elements of man there is offered not only the right to autonomy, but to supremacy in life. The self-assertion of these disunited elements in man, as, for instance, the non-sublimated elements of the subconscious, sexual desire, or the will to dominance and power, bear witness to the fact that the unified, whole image of man is disappearing and giving place to non-human and natural elements. Man has disappeared; there remain only certain of his functions.

This dissolution of man into certain functions is the product, first of all, of technical civilization. The process of dehumanization attains its climax in the technique of modern war, where human bravery is no longer necessary. Technical civilization demands that man shall fulfil one or another of his functions, but it does not want to reckon with man himself — it knows only his functions. This is not dissolving man in nature, but making him into a machine. When civilized man yearns for nature, he is longing to return to wholeness and unconsciousness, since consciousness has shaken his unity and made him unhappy. This is romanticism. Klages is a good example of this attitude. When man strives for complete fulfilment of his technical functions, when he tries to be like his new god, the machine, the tendency is just the opposite to that noted above: not toward wholeness, integrity, but toward greater and greater differentiation. But man disappears in both these tendencies, both dehumanize him. Man cannot be the image either of nature or of the machine. Man is the image and likeness of God. The formation of man as an integral being, as a personality, that process which began in the world of the Bible and the Greek world, was finished only in Christianity. Now we are witnessing a sort of reverse cosmic process, against not only Christianity, but against the Bible and against Greek culture. Modern neo-classicism is deadly formalism, and without life or power.

The process of dehumanization is specially notable in modern literature, particularly in the novel. If we consider two of the most prominent French novelists, Proust and André Gide, we cannot fail to remark that in their works man is decomposed, that a whole image no longer exists, that there are only elements of sensation and intellectual or rational states. First of all the heart disappears, as the central and integral organ of the human being, as the bearer of human feelings. Man mourns, even to despair, at this loss of the integral human being, but he is powerless to regain it. Occasionally he even rejoices at his own elimination. These novels no longer contain a wealth of human types, the multifarious human world, but only fragments and elements of that being which once was called man. The modern psychological novel, talented and refined, is concerned with the analysis of the subconscious, is plunged into the uncertain world of sensations, is terribly complex, from the intellectual point of view. Man is resolved into some of his component elements under the power of the subconscious and the rationalistic. Modern novelists almost completely lack creative imagination, they are either preoccupied with themselves or simply picture the evil realities with which they are burdened. This is the case, for instance, with Celine. The creative gift of transfiguration is disappearing from art.

Even the rare novelists who concern themselves with the metaphysical or the mystical, as for example Jouhandeau, are oppressed by demoniac powers such as even Dostoevsky knew not; Dostoevsky who saw in every man the image of God, who perceived light in the deepest shadow. Malraux's characters disappear beneath their sadistic instincts. In the works of Lawrence, man as an integral being is lost in the mystical elements of sex; man becomes a function of sex, instead of sex being a function of man. This is not pornography, it is a reflection of the same dehumanizing process now going on in the world, expressed with great artistic talent. Huxley pictures a varied human world, but a world in disintegration, where the true

image of man is hard to discover. Compare the modern novelist with
Dickens, for example. The distance novels have travelled since then
is surprising — it is as though some cosmic catastrophe had taken
place. In Dickens we find a richly varied human world, a world of
truly human types and images, tremendous power and great creative
imagination. Man is still himself, he retains his own image, even
when he is comic or really bad. In the genial *Pickwick Club,* which
has in it somewhat of Cervantes, the purely human world is still
intact, man's true image remains. The same surprising difference is
observed in comparing the modern novel with those of Balzac or
Leo Tolstoy. In Tolstoy we find a strong element of the cosmic, but
the integral and varied world of humanity, not yet decomposed, is
still preserved in the midst of cosmic forces and elements. Nothing
of the sort can be discovered in the novels of to-day, although the
modern novels contain much of perfect truth about man and what
is happening to him in the present age.

The process of dehumanization is evident in modern science as
well, in the sense that science reveals phases of natural life which are
not connected with the natural milieu to which man is habituated.
Physics has revealed sounds that we cannot hear and colours we
cannot see. And the technical results of modern physics place man in
a new and untried sphere, a non-humanized, cosmic milieu. Physics
takes pride in its completely ex-centric attitude toward man. The
breath-taking achievements of modern technics are connected with
the great discoveries of modern physics. That modern technics are
dehumanizing man and turning him into a mere technical function
is clear to everyone, and, as I pointed out in my article "Man and
the Machine," this is everywhere recognized.

When we turn to the question if dehumanization is philosophic
thought, we find a more complex process. This process has long
been going on in philosophy: it was evident in empiricism, in idealism, in positivism, in philosophic naturalism and materialism. But at
the same time modern creative philosophy is a reaction against these
processes. Philosophy has always sought the meaning of things — it
could never be content with meaninglessness. Hence philosophy now
puts the question, more sharply than ever before, of man and of
human existence. The so-called existential philosophy is seeking to
discover the structure of being in human existence, but even here the
integral image of man disappears. In this regard Heidegger is most

interesting. Being, as worry, fear, prosaicness, death, is being revealed in fallen and unfortunate human existence. But man himself is lost behind this fear, this care, this death. Worry turns out to be more significant than the man who worries. Man is constructed out of worries, just as human existence is built up from death. The philosophy of Heidegger is a philosophy of *nothing*. Nothing is nonexistent. This is an ontology of nothing as the final mystic secret of being, a philosophy of despair, absolute pessimism. This type of philosophy is characteristic of our times. The same motives, although in softened forms, may be seen in Jaspers. The melancholy and tragic Kirkegaard is now exerting on modern philosophy an influence toward an ontology of nihilism, which is not found in Kirkegaard himself. Immersion in human existence, instead of revealing man, shows forth his decomposition and decay. What metaphysics there is in Freud is a metaphysic of death and nothingness. The only instinct higher than that of sex, and capable of being set over against it, is the instinct of death.

But even in modern European religious and theological thought this process of dehumanization is evident, although here it has a different significance. Karl Barth with his dialectic theology is the dehumanization of Christianity. This mode of thought discovers in the creative world only sin and powerlessness. There remains a fervent faith in God, but in a God absolutely transcendent, separated by an abyss from the world and from man. The image of God in man is shattered. The Word of God is the only connection between God and creation and for man there remains only the possibility of hearkening to God's word. Here we glimpse the influence of Kirkegaard in a different direction. Just as is the case with Heidegger, Karl Barth's world and his humanity are godless, but God remains. This is a passionate reaction against humanism in Christianity which has resulted in a degradation or even a denial of man. Thomism, so powerful in the Catholic world, seeks to maintain a Latin balance and equality; it remains optimistic, and we discover in it elements of that old humanism which dates back to the medieval renaissance. In Thomism man is not denied, he is merely diminished: man is regarded as an insignificant being, possessing neither real freedom, nor creative capacities; he is a second-rate being. Thomism is also a reaction against the humanism of our modern age. It also contains elements of dehumanization hidden behind the conflict with all

modernism in religious and philosophical thought. But most powerful of all are the elements of dehumanization in the life of modern
society and the modern state.

* * *

3] Both Russian Communism and Fascism, as modern phenomena
are by-products, after-effects of the war. Fascism, besides being a war-
baby, is also a reaction against Communism, and its emotional bases
are less positive and creative than negative and reactionary. German
Fascism, National-Socialism, was born of the misfortunes and dep-
riviations of the German people. Both Communism and Fascism,
much alike in their social morphology, justly protest against the
degeneration of formal liberty which means scepticism, unbelief and
indifference to the truth. But instead of proceeding to the true freedom of man, as an integral being, a spiritual nature, as producer and
citizen, they proceed to both formal and actual denial of liberty.
From the oppression of human personality in a capitalist economy or
the a-personalism and inhumanity of the war or of the state, they
proceed to the unification of the same oppression and extend it over
the whole race. This is merely a continuation of the same process
of hehumanization and depersonalization which has been noted
above. Freedom and personality are denied, not in some special
"bourgeois" sense, as is so often claimed by modern demagogues, but
in their enternal, spiritual sense. Man is being betrayed. He has
ceased to be the supreme value: he has been replaced by values
which are really beneath him in the scale. Our epoch faces the
question of whether man shall continue to exist, or be replaced by
quite another being, produced by class and social, or racial and national training.

There is a difference between Italian Fascism and German Naziism in both style and symbolism. The Italian Fascism is based upon
the symbol and myth of the state as the higher being and the supreme value; it strives to continue the Roman tradition and is
classic in style. In fact it is much better, much less tyrannous, than
German National-Socialism, although its deification of the state is
a patent return to paganism. German National-Socialism is based
upon the symbol and myth of the race as a higher form of being
and the supreme value. It loves to talk of the spirit of the German
people, of the earth, of the mystical significance of blood: its style

is romantic. The state is only an instrument in the hands of nationality and the race. But this touches the inner being of man far more vitally than the fascist ideology of the state. The development of a pure and powerful race becomes a maniacal, pathological idea, something which demands a psycho-analysis of the whole people which has fallen into a state of collective insanity and demoniac possession.

It may be said in passing, that the other nations of Europe who consider themselves more healthy and sane, have little right to pass judgment upon the Germans, since international policies, the Treaty of Versailles, the self-seeking of each nation under the guise of the best interests of Europe — all these are much to blame for the unfortunate state of the German people to-day. It must also be noted that in spite of their thoroughly unhealthy nature, both Fascism and Naziism contain some positive values. Among such we may note the sound criticism of formal political democracy which is living through a mortal crisis, in the desire to set up a real corporative or syndical representation, truly representing the economic and professional interests of the people, in the elimination of party conflicts and even in the necessity of a powerful authority for social reform or the appeal to direct action arising from popular life, as contrasted with the indirect action presented in a fictitious party representation in the sphere of parliament. This is a transition from formal social realism. That old socialist, Mussolini, who now cannot bear the sound of the word, is nevertheless at present engaged in working out a very radical socialist programme, and will probably see it realized. The Socialism of the Nazis is much less certain, in spite of their retention of the word. This merely shows the relative use of words in modern social life. Up to the present moment Hitler has done almost nothing for social reform, and is even, to judge by appearances, compelled to rely upon financial and capitalist groups. Still there are some positive social-economic elements in the national-socialist programme.

It has become quite usual to contrast Fascism with democracy. The battle against Fascism is to be waged in the name of democratic principles. This is a very superficial attitude. Democracy may not be considered as something static; we must penetrate into the dynamic of democracy. Fascism is one of the extreme results of democracy, a revelation of its dialectic. Fascism sets itself up against a liberal-parliamentarian democracy, rather than democracy in general. In

his book on the principles of Fascism, Mussolini says definitely that
Fascism is democracy, but democracy of an authoritarian sort. This
may sound paradoxical and may shock the adepts of old forms of
democracy, still it may be affirmed that Fascism is one of the results
of J. J. Rousseau's doctrine of the sovereignty of the people. The
doctrine of popular sovereignty, which seems to be implied in the
word democracy, of itself gives no guarantee of liberty for human
personality. Rousseau believed that the common will of a sovereign
people was holy and infallible, which gave rise to the myth he
created, like that of Marx concerning the infallibility and sanctity
of the will of the proletariat.

In reality, however, a sovereign people, just like a sovereign proletariat, may abolish all liberty and completely suppress human
personality, may demand that man renounce his personal conscience.
In complete control of the state, a sovereign people may take its state
for a church and on that basis begin to organize the spirit and
spiritual life. And every "ideocracy," whose prototype is the Republic
of Plato, takes the state for a church and ascribes ecclesiastical functions to the state. In principle the Jacobin democracy is already a
tyrannical ideocracy denying the freedom of the spirit. The idea
of inalienable subjective rights for personality is of quite a different
origin, and is, of course, much more Christian than that of a sovereign
people. As Mussolini remarks, when a united people takes the state
finally into its own hands, the state actually becomes that of the
people. Then the state becomes absolute, it is subject to no limitations whatever. Against an absolute state, oppressed personality has
always struggled, the personality of subject-groups such as the bourgeoisie, the intellectuals, the workers, and they have tried to enforce
limitations upon the state. But when the struggle between castes,
classes and social groups is eliminated, when the unification of a
people has been accomplished and there are no social groups oppressed by the state, then the people and the state are equivalent, and
the state is finally deified. It is not absolutely necessary that the
people should express their will in the form of a liberal democracy
with a parliament; it may be expressed in the form of an authoritarian democracy with a leader endowed with supreme power. Thus
we may see that it is possible to have a leader with dictatorial powers
and at the same time retain the old democracy. This is the case with
Roosevelt: he is evoked by the need for radical social reforms, which

always demand a strongly individual authority, initiative and responsibility.

In essence Mussolini says the same thing as Marx. Marx teaches that the conflict between personality and society existed only because of the conflict between classes. When class disappears, when the exploiting class, and hence class conflict, has been abolished, no conflict between personality and society will remain. For Mussolini the state is the absolute, for Marx it is society. But both maintain the same principle, both deny the tragic and eternal conflict between personality and the state or society, both deny the inalienable freedom of personality. The truth is just the reverse. The conflict of class and social groups has merely disguised the eternal conflict between personality and society. And when there are no more classes, when society is socially democratized and unified, then there will be revealed in all its metaphysical depths the never-ending tragedy of the conflict between personality and society. In the same way, the moment the elementary problems of assuring the economic life of every human being is solved, there will at once appear the full sharpness of the problem of the spirit. This may be a problem for the perhaps distant future, but it now seems that human societies are destined to pass through the ordeals and temptations of ideocracy, of the absolute state, nation or society, the negation of spiritual liberty. Perhaps liberal democracy will not endure. Parliamentarianism with its regime of parties and the power of money is in decomposition. The old forms of democracy hinder the radical reform of human societies, and new forms are appearing, more mobile, more dynamic, more capable of swift action, better suited to the instincts of the mass of modern youth. Fascism is one of these evolving forms, arising out of the atmosphere of the world war and the world crisis which accompanied it.

The world evidently must pass through dictatorship which will in its turn vanish, once certain radical reforms of society are accomplished. Escape from dictatorship is possible only by moral rebirth and the application of creative spiritual forces. The old socialist parties are powerless — they have lost their enthusiasm, become bourgeois, they have been bureaucratized and are no longer capable of action. In this connection the fate of the German social-democrats is very revealing. We are entering a period of great difficulty for human personality, for freedom of the spirit, for higher culture. And the question poses itself: can these dictatorships confine themselves only to politics and economics, or is it inevitable that they also become dictatorships of world-view, of ideas, of the spirit, this is to say, the denial of all free spiritual life and work and conscience? In principle the first is possible, but what actually happens is the second, because of the decline in Christian faith. And we shall have spiritual war. It is already taking place in German Christianity, and it will spread over the whole world. We must battle against monism, for dualism, for the reality of the distinction between the spiritual and the natural-social, between the world of being and the objectivized world, between the Church and the State, between what is God's and what belongs to Cæsar.

It is surprising, as I noted above, that absolute monism, absolute ideocracy, is realizable without any real unity of belief. Such a thing as unity of belief does not exist in a single society or state to-day. An obligatory unity is attained by a sort of collective emotional demonic possession. Unity is attained by the dictatorship of a party which makes itself the equivalent of the state. From the sociological viewpoint it is very interesting that freedom is constantly diminishing in the world, not only in comparison with societies founded on liberal and democratic principles, but even in comparison with the old monarchical and aristocratic societies where, actually, there was more liberty, in spite of the fact that there was far greater unity in the matter of religious faith. In the older social forms, really great liberty was assured for fairly limited groups — liberty was an aristocratic privilege. When the circle was widened and society made uniform, instead of freedom being extended to all, it is non-freedom which becomes universal: all are equally subject to the state or to society. A socially differentiated order preserved certain liberties for an elect group. Freedom is an aristocratic rather than a democratic privilege. Tocqueville saw in democracy a danger for liberty. The same problem is posed by Marx and Mussolini as illustrated in Communism and Fascism.

The world has entered a period of the agony of the free spirit. Man is shaken to his very foundations by the process of dehumanization. The ideal of man has been eclipsed. This is a trying period, but one of transition. It may be that man must be crucified and die, that he may rise again to new life. Neither Communism nor Fascism is that new life: they are only passing forms in which elements of truth are mingled with frightful untruth and injustice. These transition-forms are born of suffering and misfortune, not of creative abundance. All old authorities have collapsed, and the world is threatened with relapse into anarchy. The world has been stunned by the new forces which have entered it so unexpectedly. They entered the world at a time when the unity of faith had been lost, when scepticism had corroded and dissolved the old society. What are these new forces?

6

Irrationalism and the World of Art

INTELLECTUAL and cultural historians who emphasize the influence of society on the arts find some of their most convincing evidence in our own century. Incessant and violent displacement of old forms and values; obsession with the irrational and the unconscious; successive social, political, and economic crises; astounding "breakthroughs" in science and technology; frenzied existence in the mechanized megalopolis — this has been the turbulent milieu for the twentieth-century artist and writer. Is it any wonder that their thoughts on aesthetics should be radically different from those of their predecessors?

No longer are they content to depict surface realities, allowing only as much selection or distortion as necessary to suggest subtler meanings and beauties. They strive instead to reveal their personal response to the turmoil and distress, the grandeur and exhilaration that surround them; to symbolize somehow their inner fears and fantasies; or simply to express or evoke pleasing or disturbing moods by patterns of forms and colors unrelated to recognizable "real" objects. The defenders of this contemporary approach to art insist that such abstract, surrealist, non-objective, and expressionist styles actually disclose deeper and more significant realities in human life than did the preceding representational art, and that they are, therefore, far more "realistic."

The following selections have been chosen to indicate something of the mood and concerns of two principal trends in contemporary art — abstract and surrealist. No one had closer associations with or more ardently defended early non-representational painting than Guillaume de Kostrowitsky Apollinaire (1880–1918). Mainly a poet, he was attracted by attempts to do in art what French poets had been for decades doing in language — re-create reality. It is from his first important published defense of the cubist painters, Les Peintres Cubistes, that his comments are taken.

Although it was Apollinaire who coined the term "surrealism," the atmosphere and intentions of this trend emerge with particular clarity in the so-called Dada movement. Jean Arp (1887–), French painter and sculptor, captures much of this atmosphere in his autobiographical and critical study On My Way, from which the second selection is drawn.

a Guillaume Apollinaire, The Cubist Painters

On painting]

THE plastic virtues: purity, unity, and truth, keep nature in subjection.

The rainbow is bent, the seasons quiver, the crowds push on to death, science undoes and remakes what already exists, whole worlds disappear forever from our understanding, our mobile images repeat themselves, or revive their vagueness, and the colors, the odors, and the sounds to which we are sensitive astonish us, then disappear from nature — all to no purpose.

This monster beauty is not eternal.

We know that our breath has had no beginning and will never cease, but our first conceptions are of the creation and the end of the world.

However too many painters still adore plants, stones, the sea, or men.

We quickly get used to the bondage of the mysterious. And servitude ends by creating real delights.

Workers are allowed to control the universe, yet gardeners have even less respect for nature than have artists.

The time has come for us to be the masters. And good will is not enough to make victory certain.

On this side of eternity dance the mortal forms of love, whose accursed discipline is summed up by the name "nature."

Flame is the symbol of painting, and the three plastic virtues burn with radiance.

Flame has a purity which tolerates nothing alien, and cruelly transforms in its image whatever it touches.

Flame has a magical unity; if it is divided, each fork will be like the single flame.

Finally it has the sublime and incontestable truth of its own light.

Good western painters of this period hold to their purity, without regard to natural forces.

FROM DOCUMENTS OF MODERN ART (New York, 1944–1951), vol. i, pp. 9–15; vol. vi, pp. 39–49. Reprinted by permission of George Wittenborn, Inc., 1018 Madison Avenue, New York, N.Y. 10021.

Purity is a forgetting after study. And for a single pure artist to die, it would be necessary for all pure artists of past ages to have never existed.

Painting purifies itself in Europe with the ideal logic which the older painters handed on to the new ones, as if giving them life.

And that is all.

This painter finds pleasure, that one, pain; one squanders his inheritance, another becomes rich, and still others have nothing but life.

And that is all.

You cannot carry around on your back the corpse of your father. You leave him with the other dead. You remember him, miss him, speak of him with admiration. And if you become a father yourself, you cannot expect one of your children to be willing to split in two for the sake of your corpse.

But in vain do our feet relinquish the soil which holds the dead.

To insist on purity is to baptize instinct, to humanize art, and to deify personality.

The root, the stem and the flower of the lily instance the development of purity to its symbolical blossoming.

All bodies stand equal before light, and their modifications are determined by this dazzling power, which molds them according to its will.

We do not know all the colors. Each of us invents new ones.

But above all, the painter must contemplate his own divinity, and the pictures which he offers to the admiration of men will confer upon them, likewise, the glory of exercising their divinity — if only for a moment. To achieve this, it is necessary to encompass in one glance the past, the present, and the future.

The canvas should present that essential unity which alone can elicit ecstasy.

Then nothing unstable will send us off half-cocked. We will not be suddenly turning back. Free spectators, we will not sacrifice our lives to our curiosity. The smugglers of appearances will not be able to get their contraband past the salt statues before our customs house of reason.

We will not go astray in the unknown future, which, severed from eternity, is but a word fated to tempt man.

We will not waste our strength on the too fugitive present; the fashionable, for the artist, can only be the mask of death.

The picture will exist ineluctably. The vision will be entire, complete, and its infinity, instead of indicating some imperfection, will simply express the relation between a newly created thing and a new creator, nothing more. Otherwise there would be no unity, and the connection which the different points of the canvas have with various dispositions, objects, and lights, would reveal only an assemblage of odds and ends, lacking all harmony.

For while an infinite number of creatures, each testifying to its creator, can exist without any one creation encroaching on the space of the others, yet it is impossible to conceive them all at once, and death results from their juxtaposition, their union, their love.

Each god creates in his own image, and so do painters. Only photographers manufacture duplicates of nature.

Neither purity nor unity count without truth, which cannot be compared to reality, since it is always the same, subsisting beyond the scope of nature, which strives to imprison us in that fatal order of things limiting us to the merely animal.

Artists are above all men who want to become inhuman.

Painfully they search for traces of inhumanity, traces which are to be found nowhere in nature.

These traces are clues to truth, aside from which there is no reality we can know.

But reality will never be discovered once and for all. Truth is always new. Otherwise truth would be a system even more wretched than nature itself.

But such pitiful truth, more distant, less distinct, less real each day, would reduce painting to a sort of plastic writing, intended simply to facilitate communication between people of the same race.

In our times, a machine to reproduce such signs would be quickly invented.

2] Many new painters limit themselves to pictures which have no real subjects. And the titles which we find in the catalogues are like proper names, which designate men without characterizing them.

There are men named Stout who are in fact quite thin, and others named White who are very dark; well now, I have seen pictures entitled *Solitude* containing many human figures.

In the cases in question, the artists even condescend at times to use vaguely explanatory words such as *Portrait, Landscape, Still-life;* however, many young painters use as a title only the very general term *Painting.*

These painters, while they still look at nature, no longer imitate it, and carefully avoid any representation of natural scenes which they may have observed, and then reconstructed from preliminary studies.

Real resemblance no longer has any importance, since everything is sacrifiecd by the artist to truth, to the necessities of a higher nature whose existence he assumes, but does not lay bare. The subject has little or no importance any more.

Generally speaking, modern art repudiates most of the techniques of pleasing devised by the great artists of the past.

While the goal of painting is today, as always, the pleasure of the eye, the art-lover is henceforth asked to expect delights other than those which looking at natural objects can easily provide.

Thus we are moving towards an entirely new art which will stand, with respect to painting as envisaged heretofore, as music stands to literature.

It will be pure painting, just as music is pure literature.

The music-lover experiences, in listening to a concert, a joy of a different order from the joy given by natural sounds, such as the murmur of the brook, the uproar of a torrent, the whistling of the wind in a forest, or the harmonies of human speech based on reason rather than on aesthetics.

In the same way the new painters will provide their admirers with artistic sensations by concentrating exclusively on the problem of creating harmony with unequal lights.

Everybody knows the story told by Pliny about Apelles and Protogenes. It clearly illustrates the aesthetic pleasure resulting solely from the contradictory harmonies referred to above.

Apelles landed, one day, on the Isle of Rhodes, and went to see the work of Protogenes, who lived there. Protogenes was not in the studio when Apelles arrived. An old woman was there, looking after a large canvas which the painter had prepared. Instead of leaving his name, Apelles drew on the canvas a line so subtle that nothing happier could be conceived.

Returning, Protogenes saw the line, recognized the hand of Apelles, and drew on the latter's line another line of another color, one even more subtle, so that it seemed as if there were three lines.

Apelles came back the next day, and again did not find his man; the subtlety of the line which he drew this time caused Protogenes to despair. The sketch aroused for many years the admiration of connoisseurs, who contemplated it with as much pleasure as if it had depicted gods and goddesses, instead of almost invisible lines.

The secret aim of the young painters of the extremist schools is to produce pure painting. Theirs is an entirely new plastic art. It is still in its beginnings, and is not yet as abstract as it would like to be. Most of the new painters depend a good deal on mathematics, without knowing it; but they have not yet abandoned nature, which they still question patiently, hoping to learn the right answers to the questions raised by life.

A man like Picasso studies an object as a surgeon dissects a cadaver.

This art of pure painting, if it succeeds in freeing itself from the art of the past, will not necessarily cause the latter to disappear; the development of music has not brought in its train the abandonment of the various genres of literature, nor has the acridity of tobacco replaced the savoriness of food.

3] The new artists have been violently attacked for their preoccupation with geometry. Yet geometrical figures are the essence of drawing. Geometry, the science of space, its dimensions and relations, has always determined the norms and rules of painting.

Until now, the three dimensions of Euclid's geometry were sufficient to the restiveness felt by great artists yearning for the infinite.

The new painters do not propose, any more than did their predecessors, to be geometers. But it may be said that geometry is to the plastic arts what grammar is to the art of the writer. Today, scientists no longer limit themselves to the three dimensions of Euclid. The painters have been led quite naturally, one might say by intuition, to preoccupy themselves with the new possibilities of spatial measurement which, in the language of the modern studios, are designated by the term: the fourth dimension.

Regarded from the plastic point of view, the fourth dimension appears to spring from the three known dimensions: it represents the immensity of space eternalizing itself in all directions at any given moment. It is space itself, the dimension of the infinite; the fourth dimension endows objects with plasticity. It gives the object its right proportions on the whole, whereas in Greek art, for instance, a somewhat mechanical rhythm constantly destroys the proportions.

Greek art had a purely human conception of beauty. It took man as the measure of perfection. But the art of the new painters takes the infinite universe as its ideal, and it is to this ideal that we owe a new norm of the perfect, one which permits the painter to proportion objects in accordance with the degree of plasticity he desires them to have.

Nietzsche divined the possibility of such an art:

"O divine Dionysius, why pull my ears?" Ariadne asks her philosophical lover in one of the celebrated dialogues on the Isle of Naxos. "I find something pleasant and delightful in your ears, Ariadne; why are they not even longer?"

Nietzsche, in relating this anecdote, puts in the mouth of Dionysius an implied condemnation of all Greek art.

Finally, I must point out that the fourth dimension — this utopian expression should be analyzed and explained, so that nothing more than historical interest may be attached to it — has come to stand for the aspirations and premonitions of the many young artists who contemplate Egyptian, negro, and oceanic sculptures, meditate on various scientific works, and live in the anticipation of a sublime art.

4] Wishing to attain the proportions of the ideal, to be no longer limited to the human, the young painters offer us works which are more cerebral than sensual. They discard more and more the old art of optical illusion and local proportion, in order to express the grandeur of metaphysical forms. This is why contemporary art, even if it does not directly stem from specific religious beliefs, nonetheless possesses some of the characteristics of great, that is to say, religious art.

5] It is the social function of great poets and artists to renew continually the appearance nature has for the eyes of men.

Without poets, without artists, men would soon weary of nature's monotony. The sublime idea men have of the universe would collapse with dizzying speed. The order which we find in nature, and which is only an effect of art, would at once vanish. Everything would break up in chaos. There would be no seasons, no civilization, no thought, no humanity; even life would give way, and the impotent void would reign everywhere.

Poets and artists plot the characteristics of their epoch, and the future docilely falls in with their desires.

The general from of an Egyptian mummy is in conformity with the figures drawn by Egyptian artists, and yet the ancient Egyptians were far from being all alike. They simply conformed to the art of their time.

To create the illusion of the typical is the social role and peculiar end of art. God knows how the pictures of Monet and Renoir were abused! Very well! But one has only to glance at some photographs of the period to see how closely people and things conformed to the pictures of them by these great painters.

Since of all the plastic products of an epoch, works of art have the most energy, this illusion seems to me quite natural. The energy of art imposes itself on men, and becomes for them the plastic standard of the period. Thus, those who mock the new painters are actually laughing at their own features, for people in the future will portray the men of today to be as they are represented in the most alive, which is to say, the newest art of our time. And do not tell me there are today various other schools of painting in whose images humanity will be able to recognize itself. All the art works of an epoch end by resembling the most energetic, the most expressive, and the most typical works of the period. Dolls belong to popular art; yet they always seem to be inspired by the great art of the same epoch. This is a truth which can easily be verified. Yet who would dare to say that the dolls which were sold at bargain counters, around 1880, were shaped by a sentiment akin to what Renoir felt when he painted his portraits? No one perceived the relationship then. But this only means that Renoir's art was sufficiently energetic to take hold of our senses, even though to the general public of the epoch in which he made his debut, his conceptions seemed absurd and foolish.

6] There has been a certain amount of suspicion, notably in the case of the most recent painters, of some collective hoax or error.

But in all the history of art there is not a single instance of such general collaboration in artistic fraud or error. There are, indeed, isolated cases of mystification and blundering. But the conventional elements of which works of art are to a great extent composed guarantee the impossibility of such instances becoming general.

If the new school of painting were indeed an exception to this rule, it would be so extraordinary as to verge on the miraculous. As readily imagine all the children of some country born without heads, legs or arms, an obvious absurdity. There are no collective errors or hoaxes in art; there are only various epochs and dissimilar schools. Even if the aims pursued by these schools are not all equally elevated or equally pure, all are equally respectable, and, according to the ideas one has of beauty, each artistic school is successively admired, despised, and admired once more.

7] The new school of painting is known as cubism, a name first applied to it in the fall of 1908 in a spirit of derision by Henri-Matisse, who had just seen a picture of some houses, whose cube-like appearance had greatly struck him.

The new aesthetics was first elaborated in the mind of André Derain, but the most important and audacious works the movement at once produced were those of a great artist, Pablo Picasso, who must also be considered one of the founders: his inventions, corroborated by the good sense of Georges Braque, who exhibited a cubist picture at the *Salon des Indépendants* as early as 1908, were envisaged in the studies of Jean Metzinger, who exhibited the first cubist portrait (a portrait of myself) at the *Salon des Indépendants* in 1910, and who in the same year managed to induce the jury of the *Salon d'Automne* to admit some cubist paintings. It was also in 1910 that pictures by Robert Delaunay, Marie Laurencin, and Le Fauconnier, who all belonged to the same school, were exhibited at the *Indépendants.*

The first group exhibition of the cubists, who were becoming more numerous, took place in 1911 at the *Indépendants;* room 41, which was devoted to their works, made a deep impression. There were the knowing and seductive works of Jean Metzinger; some landscapes, *Male Nude* and *Women with Phlox* by Albert Gleizes; *Portrait of Mme Fernande X* and *Young Girls* by Marie Laurencin; *The Tower,* by Robert Delaunay, *Abundance,* by Le Fauconnier, and *Landscape with Nudes,* by Fernand Léger.

That same year the cubists made their first appearance outside of

France, in Brussels; and in the preface to the catalogue of this exhibition, I accepted on behalf of the exhibitors the appelations: cubism and cubist.

Towards the end of 1911 the exhibition of the cubists at the *Salon d'Automne* made a considerable stir, and Gleizes (*The Hunt, Portrait of Jacques Nayral*), Metzinger (*Woman with Spoon*), and Fernand Léger were ridiculed without mercy. A new painter, Marcel Duchamp, had joined the group, as had the sculptor-architect, Duchamp-Villon.

Other group exhibitions were held in November, 1911 (at the Galerie d'Art Contemporain, *rue Tronchet, Paris), and in 1912 (at the* Salon des Indépendants; *this show was marked by the debut of Juan Gris); in May of the same year another cubist exhibition was held in Spain (Barcelona welcomed the young Frenchmen with enthusiasm); finally in June, at Rouen an exhibition was organized by the* Société des Artistes Normands (*important for presenting Francis Picabia, who had just joined the new school). (Note written in September, 1912.)*

Cubism differs from the old schools of painting in that it aims, not at an art of imitation, but at an art of conception, which tends to rise to the height of creation.

In representing conceptualized reality or creative reality, the painter can give the effect of three dimensions. He can to a certain extent cube. But not by simply rendering reality as seen, unless he indulges in *trompe-l'oeil*, in foreshortening, or in perspective, thus distorting the quality of the forms conceived or created.

I can discriminate four trends in cubism. Of these, two are pure, and along parallel lines.

Scientific cubism is one of the pure tendencies. It is the art of painting new structures out of elements borrowed not from the reality of sight, but from the reality of insight. All men have a sense of this interior reality. A man does not have to be cultivated in order to conceive, for example, of a round form.

The geometrical aspect, which made such an impression on those who saw the first canvases of the scientific cubists, came from the fact that the essential reality was rendered with great purity, while visual accidents and anecdotes had been eliminated. The painters who follow this tendency are: Picasso, whose luminous art also belongs to the other pure tendency of cubism, Georges Braque, Albert-Gleizes, Marie Laurencin, and Juan Gris.

Physical cubism is the art of painting new structures with elements borrowed, for the most part, from visual reality. This art, however, belongs in the cubist movement because of its constructive discipline. It has a great future as historical painting. Its social role is very clear, but it is not a pure art. It confuses what is properly the subject with images. The painter-physicist who created this trend is Le Fauconnier.

Orphic cubism is the other important trend of the new art school. It is the art of painting new structures out of elements which have not been borrowed from the visual sphere, but have been created entirely by the artist himself, and been endowed by him with fullness of reality. The works of the orphic artist must simultaneously give a pure aesthetic pleasure, a structure which is self-evident, and a sublime meaning, that is, a subject. This is pure art. The light in Picasso's paintings is based on this conception, to which Robert Delaunay's inventions have contributed much, and towards which Fernand Léger, Francis Picabia, and Marcel Duchamp are also addressing themselves.

Instinctive cubism, the art of painting new structures of elements which are not borrowed from visual reality, but are suggested to the artist by instinct and intuition, has long tended towards orphism. The instinctive artist lacks lucidity and an aesthetic doctrine; instinctive cubism includes a large number of artists. Born of French impressionism, this movement has now spread all over Europe.

Cézanne's last paintings and his water-colors belong to cubism, but Courbet is the father of the new painters; and André Derain, whom I propose to discuss some other time, was the eldest of his beloved sons, for we find him at the beginning of the fauvist movement, which was a kind of introduction to cubism, and also at the beginnings of this great subjective movement; but it would be too difficult today to write discerningly of a man who so willfully stands apart from everyone and everything.

The modern school of painting seems to me the most audacious that has ever appeared. It has posed the question of what is beautiful in itself.

It wants to visualize beauty disengaged from whatever charm man has for man, and until now, no European artist has dared attempt this. The new artists demand an ideal beauty, which will be, not merely the proud expression of the species, but the expression of the universe, to the degree that it has been humanized by light.

The new art clothes its creations with a grandiose and monumental appearance which surpasses anything else conceived by the artists of our time. Ardent in its search for beauty, it is noble and energetic, and the reality it brings us is marvelously clear. I love the art of today because above all else I love the light, for man loves light more than anything; it was he who invented fire.

b Jean Arp, On My Way

Dadaland]

IN Zurich in 1915, losing interest in the slaughterhouses of the world war, we turned to the Fine Arts. While the thunder of the batteries rumbled in the distance, we pasted, we recited, we versified, we sang with all our soul. We searched for an elementary art that would, we thought, save mankind from the furious folly of these times. We aspired to a new order that might restore the balance between heaven and hell. This art gradually became an object of general reprobation. Is it surprising that the "bandits" could not understand us? Their puerile mania for authoritarianism expects art itself to serve the stultification of mankind.

The Renaissance taught men the haughty exaltation of their reason. Modern times, with their science and technology turned men towards megalomania. The confusion of our epoch results from this overestimation of reason. We wanted an anonymous and collective art. Here is what I wrote on the occasion of an exhibition we put on in Zurich in 1915: "These works are constructed with lines, surfaces, forms and colors. They strive to surpass the human and achieve the infinite and the eternal. They are a negation of man's egotism. . . . The hands of our brothers, instead of serving us as our own hands, had become enemy hands. Instead of anonymity there was celebrity and the masterpiece; wisdom was dead. . . . To reproduce is to imitate, to play a comedy, to walk the tight-rope. . . ."

In 1915 Sophie Taeuber and I made in painting, embroidery and collage the first works derived from the simplest forms. These are probably the very first manifestations of this art. These pictures are Realities in themselves, without meaning or cerebral intention. We rejected everything that was copy or description, and allowed the Elementary and Spontaneous to react in full freedom. Since the disposition of planes, and the proportions and colors of these planes seemed to depend purely on chance, I declared that these works, like nature, were ordered "according to the law of chance," chance being for me merely a limited part of an unfathomable *raison d'être,* of an order inaccessible in its totality. Various Russian and Dutch artists who at that time were producing works rather close to ours in appearance, were pursuing quite different intentions. They are in fact a homage to modern life, a profession of faith in the machine and technology. Though treated in an abstract manner, they retain a base of naturalism and of "trompe l'œil."

From 1916 to 1920 Sophie Taeuber danced in Zurich. I shall quote the beautiful lines that Hugo Ball wrote about her in an essay entitled "Occultism and other things rare and beautiful": "All around her is the radiance of the sun and the miracle that replaces tradition. She is full of invention, caprice, fantasy. She danced to the 'Song of the Flying Fishes and the Hippocamps,' an onomatopoetic plaint. It was a dance full of flashes and fishbones, of dazzling lights, a dance of penetrating intensity. The lines of her body break, every gesture decomposes into a hundred precise, angular, incisive movements. The buffoonery of perspective, lighting and atmosphere is for her hypersensitive nervous system the pretext for drollery full of irony and wit. The figures of her dance are at once mysterious, grotesque and ecstatic. . . ."

I met Eggeling in Paris in 1915 at the studio of Madame Wassilieff, who in her two studios had set up canteens where artists could eat supper for very little money. Our friends on leave from the front spoke to us of the war, and when the gloom was too great a young woman with a pleasant voice sang: *En passant par la Lorraine avec mes sabots . . .* A drunken Swede accompanied her on the piano. Every night my brother and I walked several miles from Montmartre to the Gare Montparnasse, where Wassilieff's studio was located, through the darkness of Paris menaced by the Germans. Eggeling lived in a damp and sinister studio on the Boulevard Raspail. Across from him lived Modigliani, who often came to see him, to recite Dante and get drunk. He also took cocaine. One night it was decided that along with several other innocents I should be initiated into the *"paradis artificiels."* Each of us gave Modigliani several francs with which to lay in a store of the drug. We waited for hours. Finally he returned, hilarious and sniffling, having consumed the whole supply by himself. Eggeling did not paint much at that time; for hours he would discuss art. I met him again in 1917 in Zurich. He was searching for the rules of a plastic counterpoint, composing and drawing its first elements. He tormented himself almost to death. On great rolls of paper he had set down a sort of hieratic writing with the help of figures of rare proportion and beauty. These figures grew, subdivided, multiplied, moved, intertwined from one group to another, vanished and partly reappeared, organized themselves into an impressive construction with plantlike forms. He called this work a "Symphony." He died in 1922. With his friend Hans Richter he had just finished adapting his invention to the cinema.

Secretly, in his quiet little room, Janco devoted himself to a "naturalism in zigzag." I forgive him this secret vice because in one of his paintings he evoked and commemorated the "Cabaret Voltaire." On a platform in an overcrowded room, splotched with color, are seated several fantastic characters who are supposed to represent Tzara, Janco, Ball, Huelsenbeck, Madame Hennings, and your humble servant. We are putting on one of our big Sabbaths. The people around us are shouting, laughing, gesticulating. We reply with sighs of love, salvos of hiccups, poems, and the bow-wows and meows of mediaeval bruitists. Tzara makes his bottom jump like the belly of an oriental dancer. Janco plays an invisible violin and bows down to the ground. Madame Hennings with a face like a madonna attempts a split. Huelsenbeck keeps pounding on a big drum, while Ball, pale as a plaster dummy, accompanies him on the piano. The honorific title of nihilists was bestowed on us. The directors of public cretinization conferred this name on all those who did not follow in their path. The great matadors of the "Dadaist Movement" were Ball and Tzara. Ball in my opinion is one of the greatest German writers. He was a long, dry man with the face of a pater dolorosus. Tzara at that time wrote the *Vingt-Cinq Poèmes,* which belong to the best in French poetry. Later we were joined by Dr. Serner, adventurer, writer of detective stories, ballroom dancer, physician specializing in skin diseases, and gentleman burglar.

I met Tzara and Serner at the Odéon and at the Café de la Terrasse in Zurich, where we wrote a cycle of poems: *Hyperbole of the crocodile-barber and the walking cane.* This type of poem was later baptized "Automatic Poetry" by the Surrealists. *Automatic poetry* issues straight from the entrails of the poet or from any other organ that has stored up reserves. Neither the Postillion de Longjumeau nor the Alexandrine, nor grammar, nor aesthetics, nor Buddha, nor the Sixth Commandment can interfere with it in the least. It crows, curses, sighs, stammers, yodels, just as it pleases. Its poems are like nature: they stink, laugh, rhyme, like nature. It esteems foolishness, or at least what men call foolishness, as highly as sublime rhetoric, for in nature a broken twig is equal to the stars in beauty and importance, and it is men who decree what is beautiful and what is ugly.

Dada objects are formed of elements found or manufactured, simple or heteroclite. The Chinese several thousand years ago, Duchamp, Picabia in the United States, Schwitters and myself during the war of 1914, were the first to invent and disseminate these games of wisdom and clairvoyance which were to cure human beings of the raging madness of genius and return them modestly to their rightful place in nature. The natural beauty of these objects is inherent in them as in a bunch of flowers gathered by children. Several thousand years ago, an emperor of China sent his artists out to the most distant lands to search for stones of rare and fantastic forms which he collected and placed on a pedestal beside his vases and his gods. It is obvious that this game will not appeal to our modern thinkers of the go-getter school, who lie in wait for the art-lover like hotel porters waiting at the station for guests.

Are you still singing that diabolical song about the mill at Hirza-Pirza, shaking your gypsy curls with wild laughter, my dear Janco? I haven't forgotten the masks you used to make for our Dada demonstrations. They were terrifying, most of them daubed with bloody red. Out of cardboard, paper, horsehair, wire and cloth, you made your languorous foetuses, your Lesbian sardines, your ecstatic mice. In 1917 Janco did some abstract works which have grown in importance ever since. He was a passionate man with faith in the evolution of art.

Auguste Giacometti was already a success in 1916, yet he had a liking for the Dadaists and often took part in their demonstrations. He looked like a prosperous bear and, doubtless out of sympathy for the bears of his country, wore a bearskin cap. One of his friends confided to me that he had a well-garnished bankbook hidden in the lining of his cap. On the occasion of a Dada festival, he gave us a souvenir thirty yards long, painted in the colors of the rainbow and covered with sublime inscriptions. One evening we decided to give Dada a little modest private publicity. Going from one beer hall to another on the Limmatkai, he carefully opened the door, shouted in a loud precise voice: "Vive Dada!" and closed the door just as carefully. The diners gaped dropping their sausages. What could be the meaning of this mysterious cry from the mouth of a mature, respectable-looking man who didn't look at all like a charlatan or a métèque. At this period Giacometti painted stars of flowers, cosmic conflagrations, tongues of flame, fiery pits. For us the interest of his paintings lies in that they proceed from pure color and imagination. Giacometti is also the first who attempted to create a moving object; this he did with a clock metamorphosed by the addition of forms and colors. In spite of the war, it was a delightful period, and we shall look back on it as an idyll in the next world war when, transformed into hamburger steak, we shall be scattered to the four winds.

I became more and more removed from aesthetics]

I became more and more removed from aesthetics. I wanted to find another order, another value for man in nature. He was no longer to be the measure of all things, no longer to reduce everything to his own measure, but on the contrary, all things and man were to be like nature, without measure. I wanted to create new appearances, extract new forms from man. This tendency took shape in 1917 in my "objects." Alexandre Partens wrote of them in the *Almanach Dada:* "It was the distinction of Jean Arp to have at a certain moment discovered the true problem in the craft itself. This allowed him to feed it with a new, spiritual imagination. He was no longer interested in improving, formulating, specifying an aesthetic system. He wanted immediate and direct production, like a stone breaking away from a cliff, a bud bursting, an animal reproducing. He wanted objects impregnated with imagination and not museum pieces, he wanted animalesque objects with wild intensities and colors, he wanted a new body among us which would suffice unto itself, an object which would be just as well off squatting on the corners of tables as nestling in the depths of the garden or staring at us from the wall. . . . To him the frame and later the pedestal seemed to be useless crutches. . . ."

Even in my childhood, the pedestal enabling a statue to stand, the frame enclosing the picture like a window, were for me occasions for merriment and mischief, moving me to all sorts of tricks. One day I attempted to paint on a windowpane a blue sky under the houses that I saw through the window. Thus the houses seemed to hang in mid-air. Sometimes I took our pictures out of their frames and looked with pleasure at these windows hanging on the wall. Another time I hung up a frame in a little wooden shack, and sawed a hole in the wall behind the frame, disclosing a charming landscape animated by men and cattle. I asked my father for his opinion of the work I had just completed. He gave me a strange, somewhat surprised look. As a child I also took pleasure in standing on the pedestal of a statue that had collapsed and mimicking the attitude of a modest nymph.

Here are a few of the names of my Dadaist objects: Adam's Head, Articulating Comma, Parrot Imitating the Thunder, Mountain with Shirtfront of Ice, Spelling Furniture, Eggboard, Navel Bottle. The fragility of life and human works was converted with the Dadaists into black humor. No sooner is a building, a monument completed than it begins to decay, fall apart, decompose, crumble. The pyramids, temples, cathedrals, the paintings of the masters, are convincing proof of this. And the buzzing of man does not last much longer than the buzzing of the fly spiraling so enthusiastically around my *baba au rhum.*

Dada aimed to destroy the reasonable deceptions of man and recover the natural and unreasonable order. Dada wanted to replace the logical nonsense of the men of today by the illogically senseless.

That is why we pounded with all our might on the big drum of Dada and trumpeted the praises of unreason. Dada gave the Venus de Milo an enema and permitted Laocoon and his sons to relieve themselves after thousands of years of struggle with the good sausage Python. Philosophies have less value for Dada than an old abandoned toothbrush, and Dada abandons them to the great world leaders. Dada denounced the infernal ruses of the official vocabulary of wisdom. Dada is for the senseless, which does not mean nonsense. Dada is senseless like nature. Dada is for nature and against art. Dada is direct like nature. Dada is for infinite sense and definite means.

The navel bottle]

The bourgeois regarded the Dadaist as a dissolute monster, a revolutionary villain, a barbarous Asiatic, plotting against his bells, his safe-deposits, his honors. The Dadaist thought up tricks to rob the bourgeois of his sleep. He sent false reports to the newspapers of hair-raising Dada duels, in which his favorite author, the "King of Bernina," was said to be involved. The Dadaist gave the bourgeois a sense of confusion and distant, yet mighty rumbling, so that his bells began to buzz, his safes frowned, and his honors broke out in spots. "The Eggboard," a game for the upper ten thousand, in which the participants leave the arena covered with egg yolk from top to toe; "The Navel Bottle," a monstrous home furnishing in which bicycle, whale, brassière and absinthe spoon are combined; "The Glove," which can be worn in place of the old-fashioned head — were devised to show the bourgeois the unreality of his world, the nullity of his endeavors, even of his extremely profitable patrioteer- ings. This of course was a naive undertaking on our part, since actually the bourgeois has less imagination than a worm, and in place of a heart has an over-life-size corn which twitches in times of approaching storm — on the stock exchange.

Talk]

When Dada revealed its eternal wisdom to man, man laughed indulgently and went on talking. Man talks enough to make the very rats sick to their stomach. While his voracity forces him to stuff into his mouth everything that fails to evade his claws, he still manages to talk. He talks so much that the day darkens and the night pales with fright. He talks so much that the sea runs dry and the desert turns to swamp. The main thing for him is to talk, for talk is healthy ventilation. After a fine speech he feels very hungry and changes his mind. At the same time he assumes the noble attitude of rotten meat. Man declares red what he called green the day before and what in reality is black. He is forever making definitive statements on life, man and art, and he has no more idea than the mushroom what life, man and art actually are.

7

Science and Society

JUDGING from what we have seen so far in this collection, our century might well go down in history as the age of unreason. Yet, paradoxical though it seems, one could with equal warrant summarize these decades as the great age of reason. Never before in man's history has the advance of science in both the understanding and the control of nature been more spectacular. Some philosophers of history have seen in this extraordinary merger of a new age of science with a new irrationalism a strange, dialectical synthesis between the two eras that preceded our own, the medieval and the Renaissance. Others, influenced by psychological theory, see nothing strange in this merger. They argue that the very overemphasis on the rational aspects of human nature necessary for the remarkable progress in science and economic productivity causes man to repress his non-intellectual, emotional needs, which find expression and satisfaction in artistic fantasy, evangelic spiritualism, and frenzied, nihilistic outbursts.

Whether or not one fits the advance of science into some such larger pattern, the advance itself and its immense impact on our lives can hardly be denied. Two selections have been included to review this impact. The first is from Physics and Philosophy, by Werner Heisenberg, a German physicist whose work in quantum mechanics contributed significantly to advances in atomic and nuclear physics. While the focus of Heisenberg's essay is the impact of science on thought, that of the second is its most recent impact on society. Specifically, it concerns several dramatic economic, social, and psychological dislocations resulting from automation, "computerization," and related features of the new technological revolution. The author, Donald Michael, has at various times worked with UNESCO, the U.S. Department of Defense, and the National Aeronautics and Space Administration. At the time this commentary first appeared he was director of planning and programs of the Peace Research Institute.

a   Werner Heisenberg, Physics and Philosophy

The role of modern physics in the present development of human thinking]

THE PHILOSOPHICAL implications of modern physics have been discussed in the foregoing chapters in order to show that this most modern part of science touches very old trends of thought at many points, that it approaches some of the very old problems from a new direction. It is probably true quite generally that in the history of human thinking the most fruitful developments frequently take place at those points where two different lines of thought meet. These lines may have their roots in quite different parts of human culture, in different times or different cultural environments or different religious traditions; hence if they actually meet, that is, if they are at least so much related to each other that a real interaction can take place, then one may hope that new and interesting developments will follow. Atomic physics as a part of modern science does actually penetrate in our time into very different cultural traditions. It is not only taught in Europe and the Western countries, where it belongs to the traditional activity in the natural sciences, but it is also studied in the Far East, in countries like Japan and China and India, with their quite different cultural background, and in Russia, where a new way of thinking has been established in our time; a new way related both to specific scientific developments of the Europe of the nineteenth century and to other entirely different traditions from Russia itself. It can certainly not be the purpose of the following discussion to make predictions about the probable result of the encounter between the ideas of modern physics and the older traditions. But it may be possible to define the points from which the interaction between the different ideas may begin.

In considering this process of expansion of modern physics it would certainly not be possible to separate it from the general expansion of natural science, of industry and engineering, of medicine, etc., that is, quite generally of modern civilization in all parts of the world. Modern physics is just one link in a long chain of

From Werner Heisenberg, PHYSICS AND PHILOSOPHY (New York, 1958), pp. 187–206. Copyright © 1958 by Werner Heisenberg. Reprinted by permission of Harper & Row, Publishers, Inc. and Allen & Unwin Ltd.

events that started from the work of Bacon, Galileo and Kepler and from the practical application of natural science in the seventeenth and eighteenth centuries. The connection between natural science and technical science has from the beginning been that of mutual assistance: The progress in technical science, the improvement of the tools, the invention of new technical devices have provided the basis for more, and more accurate, empirical knowledge of nature; and the progress in the understanding of nature and finally the mathematical formulation of natural laws have opened the way to new applications of this knowledge in technical science. For instance, the invention of the telescope enabled the astronomers to measure the motion of the stars more accurately than before; thereby a considerable progress in astronomy and in mechanics was made possible. On the other hand, precise knowledge of the mechanical laws was of the greatest value for the improvement of mechanical tools, for the construction of engines, etc. The great expansion of this combination of natural and technical science started when one had succeeded in putting some of the forces of nature at the disposal of man. The energy stored up in coal, for instance, could then perform some of the work which formerly had to be done by man himself. The industries growing out of these new possibilities could first be considered as a natural continuation and expansion of the older trades; at many points the work of the machines still resembled the older handicraft and the work in the chemical factories could be considered as a continuation of the work in the dyehouses and the pharmacies of the older times. But later entirely new branches of industry developed which had no counterpart in the older trades; for instance, electrical engineering. The penetration of science into the more remote parts of nature enabled the engineers to use forces of nature which in former periods had scarcely been known; and the accurate knowledge of these forces in terms of a mathematical formulation of the laws governing them formed a solid basis for the construction of all kinds of machinery.

The enormous success of this combination of natural and technical science led to a strong preponderance of those nations or states or communities in which this kind of human activity flourished, and as a natural consequence this activity had to be taken up even by those nations which by tradition would not have been inclined toward natural and technical sciences. The modern means of communication and of traffic finally completed this process of expansion of technical civilization. Undoubtedly the process has fundamentally changed the conditions of life on our earth; and whether one approves of it or not, whether one calls it progress or danger, one must realize that it has gone far beyond any control through human forces. One may rather consider it as a biological process on the largest scale whereby the structures active in the human organism encroach on larger parts of matter and transform it into a state suited for the increasing human population.

Modern physics belongs to the most recent parts of this development, and its unfortunately most visible result, the invention of nuclear weapons, has shown the essence of this development in the sharpest possible light. On the one hand, it has demonstrated most clearly that the changes brought about by the combination of natural and technical sciences cannot be looked at only from the optimistic viewpoint; it has at least partly justified the views of those who had always warned against the dangers of such radical transmutation of our natural conditions of life. On the other hand, it has compelled even those nations or individuals who tried to keep apart from these dangers to pay the strongest attention to the new development, since obviously political power in the sense of military power rests upon the possession of atomic weapons. It can certainly not be the task of this volume to discuss extensively the political implications of nuclear physics. But at least a few words may be said about these problems because they always come first into the minds of people when atomic physics is mentioned.

It is obvious that the invention of the new weapons, especially of the thermonuclear weapons, has fundamentally changed the political structure of the world. Not only has the concept of independent nations or states undergone a decisive change, since any nation which is not in possession of such weapons must depend in some way on those very few nations that do produce these arms in large quantity; but also the attempt of warfare on a large scale by means of such weapons has become practically an absurd kind of suicide. Hence one frequently hears the optimistic view that therefore war has become obsolete, that it will not happen again. This view, unfortunately, is a much too optimistic oversimplification. On the contrary, the absurdity of warfare by means of thermonuclear weapons may, in a first approximation, act as an incentive for war on a small scale. Any nation or political group which is convinced of its historical or moral right to enforce some change of the present situation will feel that the use of conventional arms for this purpose will not involve any great risks; they will assume that the other side will certainly not have recourse to the nuclear weapons, since the other side being historically and morally wrong in this issue will not take the chance of war on a large scale. This situation would in turn induce the other nations to state that in case of small wars inflicted upon them by aggressors, they would actually have recourse to the nuclear weapons, and thus the danger obviously remains. It may quite well be that in about twenty or thirty years from now the world will have undergone so great changes that the danger of warfare on a large scale, of the application of all technical resources for the annihilation of the opponent, will have greatly diminished or disappeared. But the way to this new state will be full of the greatest dangers. We must as in all former times, realize that what looks historically or morally right to the one side may look wrong to the other side. The continuation of the status quo may not always be the correct solution; it may, on the contrary, be most important to find peaceful means of adjustments to new situations, and it may in many cases be extremely difficult to find any just decision at all. Therefore, it is probably not too pessimistic to say that the great war can be avoided only if all the different political groups are ready to renounce some of their apparently most obvious rights — in view of the fact that the question of right and wrong may look essentially different from the other side. This is certainly not a new point of view; it is in fact only an application of that human attitude which has been taught through many centuries by some of the great religions.

The invention of nuclear weapons has also raised entirely new problems for science and scientists. The political influence of science has become very much stronger than it was before World War II, and this fact has burdened the scientist, especially the atomic physicist, with a double responsibility. He can either take an active part in the administration of the country in connection with the importance of science for the community; then he will eventually have to face the responsibility for decisions of enormous weight which go far beyond the small circle of research and university work to which he was wont. Or he may voluntarily withdraw from any participation in political decisions; then he will still be responsible for wrong decisions which he could possibly have prevented had he not preferred the quiet life of the scientist. Obviously it is the duty of the scientists to inform their governments in detail about the unprecedented destruction that would follow from a war with thermonuclear weapons. Beyond that, scientists are frequently requested to participate in solemn resolutions in favor of world peace; but considering this latter demand I must confess that I have never been able to see any point in declarations of this kind. Such resolutions may seem a welcome proof of goodwill; but anyone who speaks in favor of peace must at once be suspected of speaking only about that kind of peace in which he and his group thrive best — which of course would be completely worthless. Any honest declaration for peace must be an enumeration of the sacrifices one is prepared to make for its preservation. But as a rule the scientists have no authority to make statements of this kind.

At the same time the scientist can do his best to promote international co-operation in his own field. The great importance that many governments attach to research in nuclear physics nowadays and the fact that the level of scientific work is still very different in different countries favors international co-operation in this work. Young scientists of many different countries may gather in research institutions in which a strong activity in the field of modern physics is going on and the common work on difficult scientific problems will foster mutual understanding. In one case, that of the Geneva organization, it has even been possible to reach an agreement between a number of different nations for building a common laboratory and for constructing by a combined effort the expensive experimental equipment for research in nuclear physics. This kind of co-operation will certainly help to establish a common attitude toward the problems of science — common even beyond the purely scientific problems — among the younger generation of scientists. Of course one does not know beforehand what will grow out of the seeds that have been sown in this way when the scientists return into their old environments and again take part in their own cultural traditions. But one can scarcely doubt that the exchange of ideas between young scientists of different countries and between the different generations in every country will help to approach without too much tension that new state of affairs in which a balance is reached between the older traditional forces and the inevitable necessities of modern life. It is especially one feature of science which makes it more than anything else suited for establishing the first strong connection between different cultural traditions. This is the fact that the ultimate decisions about the value of a special scientific work, about what is correct or wrong in the work, do not depend on any human authority. It may sometimes take many years before one knows the solution of a problem, before one can distinguish between truth and error; but finally the questions will be decided, and the decisions are made not by any group of scientists but by nature itself. Therefore, scientific ideas spread among those who are interested in science in an entirely different way from the propagation of political ideas.

While political ideas may gain a convincing influence among great masses of people just because they correspond or seem to correspond to the prevailing interests of the people, scientific ideas will spread only because they are true. There are objective and final criteria assuring the correctness of a scientific statement.

All that has here been said about international co-operation and exchange of ideas would of course be equally true for any part of modern science; it is by no means confined to atomic physics. In this respect modern physics is just one of the many branches of science, and even if its technical applications — the arms and the peaceful use of atomic energy — attach a special weight to this branch, there would be no reason for considering international co-operation in this field as far more important than in any other field. But we have now to discuss again those features of modern physics which are essentially different from the previous development of natural science, and we have for this purpose once more to go back to the European history of this development that was brought about by the combination of natural and technical sciences.

It has frequently been discussed among the historians whether the rise of natural science after the sixteenth century was in any way a natural consequence of earlier trends in human thinking. It may be argued that certain trends in Christian philosophy led to a very abstract concept of God, that they put God so far above the world that one began to consider the world without at the same time also seeing God in the world. The Cartesian partition may be called a final step in this development. Or one may point out that all the theological controversies of the sixteenth century produced a general discontent about problems that could not really be settled by reason and were exposed to the political struggles of the time; that this discontent favored interest in problems which were entirely separated from the theological disputes. Or one may simply refer to the enormous activity, the new spirit that had come into the European societies through the Renaissance. In any case during this period a new authority appeared which was completely independent of Christian religion or philosophy or of the Church, the authority of experience, of the empirical fact. One may trace this authority back into older philosophical trends, for instance, into the philosophy of Occam and Duns Scotus, but it became a vital force of human activity only from the sixteenth century onward. Galileo did not only *think* about the mechanical motions, the pendulum and the falling stone; he tried out by experiments, quantitatively, how these motions took place. This new activity was in its beginning certainly not meant as a deviation from the traditional Christian religion. On the contrary, one spoke of two kinds of revelation of God. The one was written in the Bible and the other was to be found in the book of nature. The Holy Scripture had been written by man and was therefore subject to error, while nature was the immediate expression of God's intentions.

However, the emphasis on experience was connected with a slow and gradual change in the aspect of reality. While in the Middle Ages what we nowadays call the symbolic meaning of a thing was in some way its primary reality, the aspect of reality changed toward what we can perceive with our senses. What we can see and touch became primarily real. And this new concept of reality could be connected with a new activity: we can experiment and see how things really are. It was easily seen that this new attitude meant the departure of the human mind into an immense field of new possibilities, and it can be well understood that the Church saw in the new movement the dangers rather than the hopes. The famous trial of Galileo in connection with his views on the Copernican system marked the beginning of a struggle that went on for more than a century. In this controversy the representatives of natural science could argue that experience offers an undisputable truth, that it cannot be left to any human authority to decide about what really happens in nature, and that this decision is made by nature or in this sense by God. The representatives of the traditional religion, on the other hand, could argue that by paying too much attention to the material world, to what we perceive with our senses, we lose the connection with the essential values of human life, with just that part of reality which is beyond the material world. These two arguments do not meet, and therefore the problem could not be settled by any kind of agreement or decision.

In the meantime natural science proceeded to get a clearer and wider picture of the material world. In physics this picture was to be described by means of those concepts which we nowadays call the concepts of classical physics. The world consisted of things in space and time, the things consist of matter, and matter can produce and can be acted upon by forces. The events follow from the interplay between matter and forces; every event is the result and the cause of other events. At the same time the human attitude toward nature changed from a contemplative one to the pragmatic one. One was not so much interested in nature as it is; one rather asked what one could do with it. Therefore, natural science turned into technical science; every advancement of knowledge was connected with the question as to what practical use could be derived from it. This was true not only in physics; in chemistry and biology the attitude was essentially the same, and the success of the new methods in medicine or in agriculture contributed essentially to the propagation of the new tendencies.

In this way, finally, the nineteenth century developed an extremely rigid frame for natural science which formed not only science but also the general outlook of great masses of people. This frame was supported by the fundamental concepts of classical physics, space, time, matter and causality; the concept of reality applied to the things or events that we could perceive by our senses or that could be observed by means of the refined tools that technical science had provided. Matter was the primary reality. The progress of science was pictured as a crusade of conquest into the material world. Utility was the watchword of the time.

On the other hand, this frame was so narrow and rigid that it was difficult to find a place in it for many concepts of our language that had always belonged to its very substance, for instance, the concepts of mind, of the human soul or of life. Mind could be introduced into the general picture only as a kind of mirror of the material world; and when one studied the properties of this mirror in the science of psychology, the scientists were always tempted — if I may carry the comparison further — to pay more attention to its mechanical than to its optical properties. Even there one tried to apply the concepts of classical physics, primarily that of causality. In the same way life was to be explained as a physical and chemical process, governed by natural laws, completely determined by causality. Darwin's concept of evolution provided ample evidence for this interpretation. It was especially difficult to find in this framework room for those parts of reality that had been the object of the traditional religion and seemed now more or less only imaginary. Therefore, in those European countries in which one was wont to follow the ideas up to their extreme consequences, an open hostility of science toward religion developed, and even in the other countries there was an increasing tendency toward indifference toward such questions; only the ethical values of the Christian religion were excepted from this trend, at least for the time being. Confidence in the scientific method and in rational thinking replaced all other safeguards of the human mind.

Coming back now to the contributions of modern physics, one may say that the most important change brought about by its results consists in the dissolution of this rigid frame of concepts of the nineteenth century. Of course many attempts had been made before to get away from this rigid frame which seemed obviously too narrow for an understanding of the essential parts of reality. But it had not been possible to see what could be wrong with the fundamental concepts like matter, space, time and causality that had been so extremely successful in the history of science. Only experimental research itself, carried out with all the refined equipment that technical science could offer, and its mathematical interpretation, provided the basis for a critical analysis — or, one may say, enforced the critical analysis — of these concepts, and finally resulted in the dissolution of the rigid frame.

This dissolution took place in two distant stages. The first was the discovery, through the theory of relativity, that even such fundamental concepts as space and time could be changed and in fact must be changed on account of new experience. This change did not concern the somewhat vague concepts of space and time in natural language; but it did concern their precise formulation in the scientific language of Newtonian mechanics, which has erroneously been accepted as final. The second stage was the discussion of the concept of matter enforced by the experimental results concerning the atomic structure. The idea of the reality of matter had probably been the strongest part in that rigid frame of concepts of the nineteenth century, and this idea had at least to be modified in connection with the new experience. Again the concepts so far as they belonged to the natural language remained untouched. There was no difficulty in speaking about matter or about facts or about reality when one had to describe the atomic experiments and their results. But the scientific extrapolation of these concepts into the smallest parts of matter could not be done in the simple way suggested by classical physics, though it had erroneously determined the general outlook on the problem of matter.

These new results had first of all to be considered as a serious warning against the somewhat forced application of scientific concepts in domains where they did not belong. The application of the concepts of classical physics, e.g., in chemistry, had been a mistake. Therefore, one will nowadays be less inclined to assume that the concepts of physics, even those of quantum theory, can certainly be applied everywhere in biology or other sciences. We will, on the contrary, try to keep the doors open for the entrance of new concepts even in those parts of science where the older concepts have been very useful for the understanding of the phenomena. Especially at those points where the application of the older concepts seems somewhat forced or appears not quite adequate to the problem we will try to avoid any rash conclusions.

Furthermore, one of the most important features of the development and the analysis of modern physics is the experience that the concepts of natural language, vaguely defined as they are, seem to be more stable in the expansion of knowledge than the precise terms of scientific language, derived as an idealization from only limited groups of phenomena. This is in fact not surprising since the concepts of natural language are formed by the immediate connection with reality; they represent reality. It is true that they are not very well defined and may therefore also undergo changes in the course of the centuries, just as reality itself did, but they never lose the immediate connection with reality. On the other hand, the scientific concepts are idealizations; they are derived from experience obtained by refined experimental tools, and are precisely defined through axioms and definitions. Only through these precise definitions is it possible to connect the concepts with a mathematical scheme and to derive mathematically the infinite variety of possible phenomena in this field. But through this process of idealization and precise definition the immediate connection with reality is lost. The concepts still correspond very closely to reality in that part of nature which had been the object of the research. But the correspondence may be lost in other parts containing other groups of phenomena.

Keeping in mind the intrinsic stability of the concepts of natural language in the process of scientific development, one sees that — after the experience of modern physics — our attitude toward concepts like mind or the human soul or life or God will be different from that of the nineteenth century, because these concepts belong to the natural language and have therefore immediate connection with reality. It is true that we will also realize that these concepts are not well defined in the scientific sense and that their application may lead to various contradictions, for the time being we may have to take the concepts, unanalyzed as they are; but still we know that they touch reality. It may be useful in this connection to remember that even in the most precise part of science, in mathematics, we cannot avoid using concepts that involve contradictions. For instance, it is well known that the concept of infinity leads to contradictions that have been analyzed, but it would be practically impossible to construct the main parts of mathematics without this concept.

The general trend of human thinking in the nineteenth century had been toward an increasing confidence in the scientific method and in precise rational terms, and had led to a general skepticism with regard to those concepts of natural language which do not fit into the closed frame of scientific thought — for instance, those of religion. Modern physics has in many ways increased this skepticism; but it has at the same time turned it against the overestimation of precise scientific concepts, against a too-optimistic view on progress in general, and finally against skepticism itself. The skepticism against precise scientific concepts does not mean that there should be a definite limitation for the application of rational thinking. On the contrary, one may say that the human ability to understand may be in a certain sense unlimited. But the existing scientific concepts cover always only a very limited part of reality, and the other part that has not yet been understood is infinite. Whenever we proceed from the known into the unknown we may hope to understand, but we may have to learn at the same time a new meaning of the word "understanding." We know that any understanding must be based finally upon the natural language because it is only there that we can be certain to touch reality, and hence we must be skeptical about any skepticism with regard to this natural language and its essential concepts. Therefore, we may use these concepts as they have been used at all times. In this way modern physics has perhaps opened the door to a wider outlook on the relation between the human mind and reality.

This modern science, then, penetrates in our time into other parts of the world where the cultural tradition has been entirely different from the European civilization. There the impact of the new activity in natural and technical science must make itself felt even more strongly than in Europe, since changes in the conditions of life that have taken two or three centuries in Europe will take place there within a few decades. One should expect that in many places this new activity must appear as a decline of the older culture, as a ruthless and barbarian attitude, that upsets the sensitive balance on which all human happiness rests. Such consequences cannot be avoided; they must be taken as one aspect of our time. But even there the openness of modern physics may help to some extent to reconcile the older traditions with the new trends of thought. For instance, the great scientific contribution in theoretical physics that has come from Japan since the last war may be an indication for a certain relationship between philosophical ideas in the tradition of the Far East and the philosophical substance of quantum theory. It may be easier to adapt oneself to the quantum-theoretical concept of reality when one has not gone through the naïve materialistic way of thinking that still prevailed in Europe in the first decades of this century.

Of course such remarks should not be misunderstood as an underestimation of the damage that may be done or has been done to old cultural traditions by the impact of technical progress. But since this whole development has for a long time passed far beyond any control by human forces, we have to accept it as one of the most essential features of our time and must try to connect it as much as possible with the human values that have been the aim of the older cultural and religious traditions. It may be allowed at this point to quote a story from the Hasidic religion: There was an old rabbi, a priest famous for his wisdom, to whom all people came for advice. A man visited him in despair over all the changes that went on around him, deploring all the harm done by so-called technical progress. "Isn't all this technical nuisance completely worthless," he exclaimed "if one considers the real values of life?" "This may be so," the rabbi replied, but if one has the right attitude one can learn from everything." "No," the visitor rejoined, "from such foolish things as railway or telephone or telegraph one can learn nothing whatsoever." But the rabbi answered, "You are wrong. From the railway you can learn that you may by being one instant late miss everything. From the telegraph you can learn that every word counts. And from the telephone you can learn that what we say here can be heard there." The visitor understood what the rabbi meant and went away.

Finally, modern science penetrates into those large areas of our present world in which new doctrines were established only a few decades ago as foundations for new and powerful societies. There modern science is confronted both with the content of the doctrines, which go back to European philosophical ideas of the nineteenth century (Hegel and Marx), and with the phenomenon of uncompromising belief. Since modern physics must play a great role in these countries because of its practical applicability, it can scarcely be avoided that the narrowness of the doctrines is felt by those who have really understood modern physics and its philosophical meaning. Therefore, at this point an interaction between science and the general trend of thought may take place. Of course the influence of science should not be overrated; but it might be that the openness of modern science could make it easier even for larger groups of people to see that the doctrines are possibly not so important for the society as had been assumed before. In this way the influence of modern science may favor an attitude of tolerance and thereby may prove valuable.

On the other hand, the phenomenon of uncompromising belief carries much more weight than some special philosophical notions of the nineteenth century. We cannot close our eyes to the fact that the great majority of the people can scarcely have any well-founded judgment concerning the correctness of certain important general ideas or doctrines. Therefore, the word "belief" can for this majority not mean "perceiving the truth of something" but can only be understood as "taking this as the basis for life." One can easily understand that this second kind of belief is much firmer, is much more fixed than the first one, that it can persist even against immediate contradicting experience and can therefore not be shaken by added scientific knowledge. The history of the past two decades has shown by many examples that this second kind of belief can sometimes be upheld to a point where it seems completely absurd, and that it then ends only with the death of the believer. Science and history can teach us that this kind of belief may become a great danger for those who share it. But such knowledge is of no avail, since one cannot see how it could be avoided, and therefore such belief has always belonged to the great forces in human history. From the scientific tradition of the nineteenth century one would of course be inclined to hope that all belief should be based on a rational analysis of every argument, on careful deliberation; and that this other kind of belief, in which some real or apparent truth is simply taken as the basis for life, should not exist. It is true that cautious deliberation based on purely rational arguments can save us from many errors and dangers, since it allows readjustment to new situations, and this may be a necessary condition for life. But remembering our experience in modern physics it is easy to see that there must always be a fundamental complementarity between deliberation and decision. In the practical decisions of life it will scarcely ever be possible to go through all the arguments in favor of or against one possible decision, and one will therefore always have to act on insufficient evidence. The decision finally takes place by pushing away all the arguments — both those that have been understood and others that might come up through further deliberation — and by cutting off all further pondering. The decision may be the result of deliberation, but it is at the same time complementary to deliberation; it excludes deliberation. Even the most important decisions in life must always contain this inevitable element of irrationality. The decision itself is necessary, since there must be something to rely upon, some principle to guide our actions. Without such a firm stand our own actions would lose all force. Therefore, it cannot be avoided that some real or apparent truth form the basis of life; and this fact should be acknowledged with regard to those groups of people whose basis is different from our own.

Coming now to a conclusion from all that has been said about modern science, one may perhaps state that modern physics is just one, but a very characteristic, part of a general historical process that tends toward a unification and a widening of our present world. This process would in itself lead to a diminution of those cultural and political tensions that create the great danger of our time. But it is accompanied by another process which acts in the opposite direction. The fact that great masses of people become conscious in this process of unification leads to an instigation of all forces in the existing cultural communities that try to ensure for their traditional values the largest possible role in the final state of unification. Thereby the tensions increase and the two competing processes are so closely linked with each other that every intensification of the unifying process — for instance, by means of new technical progress — intensifies also the struggle for influence in the final state, and thereby adds to the instability of the transient state. Modern physics plays perhaps only a small role in this dangerous process of unification. But it helps at two very decisive points to guide the development into a calmer kind of evolution. First, it shows that the use of arms in the process would be disastrous and, second, through its openness for all kinds of concepts it raises the hope that in the final state of unification many different cultural traditions may live together and may combine different human endeavors into a new kind of balance between thought and deed, between activity and meditation.

b *Donald N. Michael,* The Problems of Cybernation

Unemployment and employment]

Blue-Collar Adults]

In the highly automated chemical industry, the number of production jobs has fallen 3% since 1956 while output has soared 27%. Though steel capacity has increased 20% since 1955, the number of men needed to operate the industry's plants — even at full capacity — has dropped 17,000. Auto employment slid from a peak of 746,000 in boom 1955 to 614,000 in November. . . . Since the meat industry's 1956 employment peak, 28,000 workers have lost their jobs despite a production increase of 3%. Bakery jobs have been in a steady decline from 174,000 in 1954 to 163,000 last year. On the farm one man can grow enough to feed 24 people; back in 1949 he could feed only 15.

From Donald N. Michael, CYBERNATION: THE SILENT CONQUEST (*Santa Barbara, Calif.,* 1962), pp. 14-24, 29-33, 44-46. Reprinted by permission of the Center for the Study of Democratic Institutions.

◩ FURTHER insight into the problem of declining employment for the blue-collar worker comes from union statements to the effect that the number of these employees in manufacturing has been reduced by 1,500,000 in the last six years. As one example from the service industries, automatic elevators have already displaced 40,000 operators in New York.

Another disturbing aspect of the blue-collar displacement problem is its impact on employment opportunities for Negroes. There is already an increasingly lopsided Negro-to-white unemployment ratio as the dock, factory, and mine operations where Negroes have hitherto found their steadiest employment are cybernated. This, plus the handicaps of bias in hiring and lack of educational opportunity, leaves Negroes very few chances to gain new skills and new jobs. Continued widespread and disproportionate firings of Negroes, if accompanied by ineffectual reemployment methods, may well produce a situation that will increase disenchantment abroad and encourage discontent and violence here.

Service Industries]

It is commonly argued that, with the growth of population, there will always be more need for people in the service industries. The assumption is that these industries will be able to absorb the displaced, retrained blue-collar labor force; that automation will not seriously displace people who perform service functions; and that the demand for engineers and scientists will be so great as to provide employment for any number of the young people who graduate with engineering training. (Indeed, some of this demand is expected to arise from the needs of cybernetic systems themselves.)

It is all very well to speak glowingly of the coming growth in the service industries and the vast opportunities for well-paid jobs and job-upgrading that these activities will provide as blue-collar opportunities diminish. But is the future as bright and as simple as this speculation implies? In the first place, service activities will also tend to displace workers by becoming self-service, by becoming cybernated, and by being eliminated. Consider the following data: The U.S. Census Bureau was able to use fifty statisticians in 1960 to do the tabulations that required 4,100 in 1950. Even where people are not being fired, service industries can now carry on a vastly greater amount of business without hiring additional personnel; for example, a 50 per cent increase in the Bell System's volume of calls in the last ten years with only a 10 per cent increase in personnel.

Automation frequently permits the mass production of both cheap items and items of adequate to superior quality. It frequently uses methods of fabrication that make replacement of part or all of the item more efficient or less bother than repairing it. As automation results in more leisure time, certainly some of this time will be used by more and more do-it-yourselfers to replace worn-out or faulty components in home appliances that are now repaired by paid service personnel. Nor is it clear that repairing computers will be big business. Computer design is in the direction of microminiaturized components: when there is a failure in the system, the malfunctioning part is simply unplugged or pulled out, much as a drawer from a bureau, and replaced by a new unit. Routine procedures determine which component is malfunctioning, so routine that the larger computers now indicate where their own troubles are, so routine that small computers could be built to troubleshoot others. This does not mean that clever maintenance and repair people will be completely unnecessary, but it does mean that a much more careful estimate is required of the probable need for these skills in home-repair work or in computer-repair work.

Drip-dry clothes, synthetic fabrics, plus self-service dry and wet cleaning facilities, probably will outmode this type of service activity.

Identification by fingerprints, instantly checked against an up-to-date nation-wide credit rating (performed by a central computer facility), could eliminate all service activities associated with processing based on identification (for example, bank tellers). A computer that can identify fingerprints does not yet exist, but there is no reason to believe it will not be invented in the next two decades.

If people cost more than machines — either in money or because of the managerial effort involved — there will be growing incentives to replace them in one way or another in most service activities where they perform routine, predefined tasks. It is possible, of course, that eventually people will not cost more than machines, because there may be so many of them competing for jobs, including a growing number of working women. But will service people be this cheap? As union strength is weakened or threatened through reductions in blue-collar membership, unions will try, as they have already begun to do, to organize the white-collar worker and other service personnel more completely in order to help them to protect their jobs from managements willing to hire those who, having no other work to turn to, would work for less money. Former blue-collar workers who through retraining, will join the ranks of the service group may help to produce an atmosphere conducive to such unionizing. But how many service organizations will accept the complications of union negotiations, strikes, personnel services, and higher wages in preference to investing in cybernation?

It is possible that as automation and computers are applied more widely an attitude of indifference to personalized service will gradually develop. People will not demand it and organizations will not provide it. The family doctor is disappearing; clerks of all sorts in stores of all sorts are disappearing as well. For example:

> The R. H. Macy Co. is trying out its first electronic sales girl. This machine is smart enough to dispense 36 different items in 10 separate styles and sizes. It accepts one- and five-dollar bills in addition to coins and returns the correct change plus rejecting counterfeit currency.

People either get used to this or, as in the case of the self-service supermarket, seem to prefer it.

It is already the rare sales clerk who knows the "real" differences between functionally similar items; indeed, in most stores, sales clerks as such are rare. Thus, the customer is almost forced to do much of his own selecting and to know at least as much about or to be at least as casual about the differences between competing items as the clerk. As automation increases, the utility of the sales clerk will further diminish. With some products, automation will permit extensive variation in design and utility. With others, especially if our society follows its present course, automation will encourage the endless proliferation of items only marginally different from one another. In either event there is no reason to believe that the clerk or salesman will become more knowledgeable about an even larger variety of competing items. Finally, it is obvious that the remaining tasks of the clerk, such as recording the sale and insuring that the item is paid for, can be cybernated without difficulty.

The greater the indifference to personalized service by both buyers and sellers, the greater the opportunity, of course, to remove human

judgments from the system. Cybernation may well encourage acceptance of such depersonalization, and this, in turn, would encourage
further reductions in opportunities for service jobs.

Middle Management]

The blue-collar worker and the relatively menial service worker
will not be the only employment victims of cybernation.

... Broadly, our prognostications are along the following lines:
"1] Information technology should move the boundary between planning and performance upward. Just as planning was
taken from the hourly worker and given to the industrial engineer, we now expect it to be taken from a number of middle
managers and given to as yet largely nonexistent specialists:
'operation researchers,' perhaps, or 'organizational analysts.'
Jobs at today's middle-management level will become highly
structured. Much more of the work will be programmed, *i.e.,*
covered by sets of operating rules governing the day-to-day
decisions that are made.

"2] Correlatively, we predict that large industrial organizations
will recentralize, that top managers will take on an ever larger
proportion of the innovating, planning, and other 'creative'
functions than they have now.

"3] A radical reorganization of middle-management levels
should occur with *certain* classes of middle-management jobs
moving downward in status and compensation (because they
will require less autonomy and skill), while other classes move
upward into the top-management group.

"4] We suggest, too, that the line separating the top from the
middle of the organization will be drawn more clearly and im-
penetrably than ever, much like the line drawn in the last few
decades between hourly workers and first-line supervisors.

"... Information technology promises to allow fewer people to
do more work. The more it can reduce the number of middle
managers, the more top managers will be willing to try it. ...
One can imagine major psychological problems arising from the
depersonalization of relationships within management and the
greater distance between people at different levels. ... In particular, we may have to reappraise our traditional notions about
the worth of the individual as opposed to the organization, and

about the mobility rights of young men on the make. This kind of inquiry may be painfully difficult, but will be increasingly necessary.

As cybernation moves into the areas now dominated by middle management in government and in business — and this move is already beginning — growing numbers of middle managers will find themselves displaced. Perhaps the bulk of displaced members of the blue-collar and service work force might be trained "up" or "over" to other jobs with, generally speaking, little or no decline in status. But the middle manager presents a special and poignant problem. Where can he go? To firms that are not as yet assigning routine liaison, analysis, and minor executive tasks to machines? This may take care of some of the best of the displaced managers and junior executives, but if these firms are to have a future, the chances are that they will have to computerize eventually in order to compete. To the government? Again, some could join it, but the style and format of governmental operations may require readjustments that many junior executives would be unable to make. And, in any case, government too, as we have seen, is turning to computers, and it is entirely possible that much of the work of *its* middle management will also be absorbed by the computers. Up into top management? A few, of course, but necessarily only a few. Into the service end of the organization, such as sales? Some here, certainly, if they have the talent for such work. If computers and automation lead to an even greater efflorescence of marginally differentiated articles and services, there will be a correspondingly greater emphasis on sales in an effort to compete successfully. But can this be an outlet for a truly significant portion of the displaced? And at what salary? Overseas appointments in nations not yet using cybernation at the management level? Again, for a few, but only for those with the special ability to fit into a different culture at the corresponding level from which they came.

Middle management is the group in the society with the most intensive emotional drive for success and status. Their family and social life is molded by these needs, as the endless literature on life in suburbia and exurbia demonstrate. They stand to be deeply disturbed by the threat and fact of their replacement by machines. One wonders what the threat will do to the ambitions of those who will still be students and who, as followers of one of the pervasive American dreams, will have aspired to the role of middle manager "on the way up."

With the demise or downgrading of this group, changes in consumption levels and patterns can also be expected. These people, although they are not the only consumers of products of the sort advertised in *The New Yorker, Holiday,* and the like, are certainly among the largest of such consumers. They are the style-setters, the innovators, and the experimenters with new, quality products. With their loss of status and the loss of their buying power, one can imagine changes in advertising, or at least changes in the "taste" that this advertising tries to generate. It is possible that the new middle élite, the engineers, operations researchers, and systems analysts, will simply absorb the standards of the group they will have replaced. But they may be different enough in outlook and motives to have different styles in consumption.

Overworked Professionals]

There are service jobs, of course, that require judgments about people by people. (We are not including here the "personalized service" type of salesmanship.) The shortage of people with these talents is evidenced by the 60-hour and more work-weeks of many professionals. But these people are the products of special education, special motives, and special attitudes that are not shared to any great degree by those who turn to blue-collar or routine service tasks. Increasing the proportion of citizens with this sort of professional competence would require systematic changes in attitudes, motives, and levels of education, not to mention more teachers, a professional service already in short supply. Alterations of this magnitude cannot be carried out overnight or by casual advertising campaigns or minor government appropriations. It is doubtful indeed, in our present operating context, that they can be done fast enough to make a significant difference in the employment picture for professional services in the next decade or two. Values become imbedded early in life. They are subject to change, to be sure, but we are not, as a democratic society, adept at or inclined to change them deliberately and systematically.

Even if the teachers and the appropriate attitudes already existed, service needs at the professional level might not be great enough to absorb a large share of the potentially unemployed. Much of the work that now takes up the time of many professionals, such as doctors and lawyers, could be done by computers — just as much of the time of teachers is now taken up by teaching what could be done as well by machines.

The development of procedures for medical diagnosis by machine is proceeding well. A completely automatic analysis of data can produce just as good a diagnosis of brain malfunction as that done by a highly trained doctor. Cybernated diagnosis will be used in conjunction with improved multi-purpose antibiotics and with microminiaturized, highly sensitive, and accurate telemetering equipment (which can be swallowed, imbedded in the body, or affixed to it) in order to detect, perhaps at a distance, significant symptoms. All of these developments are likely to change the nature of a doctor's time-consuming tasks. In the field of law successful codification, so that searches and evaluations can be automatic, as well as changes in legal procedures, will probably make the lawyer's work substantially different from what it is today, at least in terms of how he allocates his time.

Computers probably will perform tasks like these because the shortage of professionals will be more acute at the time the computers acquire the necessary capabilities. By then, speeded-up data processing and interpretation will be necessary if professional services are to be rendered with any adequacy. Once the computers are in operation, the need for additional professional people may be only moderate, and those who are needed will have to be of very high calibre indeed. Probably only a small percentage of the population will have the natural endowments to meet such high requirements. A tour of the strongholds of science and engineering and conversations with productive scientists and engineers already lead to the conclusion that much of what now appears to be creative, barrier-breaking "research and development" is in fact routine work done by mediocre scientists and engineers. We lose sight of the fact that not everybody with dirty hands or a white coat is an Einstein or a Steinmetz. Many first-class scientists in universities will testify that one consequence of the increasingly large federal funds for research is that many more mediocre scientists doing mediocre work are being supported. No doubt for some time to come good use can be made by good professionals of battalions of mediocre professionals. But battalions are not armies. And sooner or later one general of science or engineering will be able to fight this war for knowledge more effectively with more push-buttons than with more intellectual foot-soldiers.

Untrained Adolescents]

Altogether the United States will need 13,500,000 more jobs in the Sixties merely to keep abreast of the expected growth in the labor force. This means an average of 25,000 new jobs each week, on top of those required to drain the reservoir of present unemployment and to replace jobs made superfluous by improved technology. In the last year, despite the slackness of employment opportunities, 2,500,000 more people came into the job scramble than left it through death, age, sickness or voluntary withdrawal. This was more than double the 835,000 average annual growth in the working population in the last ten years. By the end of this decade, 3,000,000 youngsters will be starting their quest for jobs each year, as against 2,000,000 now. This almost automatically guarantees trouble in getting the over-all unemployment rate down to 4 per cent because the proportion of idleness among teen-age workers is always far higher than it is among their elders.

The Labor Department estimates that 26,000,000 adolescents will seek work in the Sixties. If present performance is any indicator, in the decade ahead 30 per cent of adolescents will continue to drop out before completing high school and many who could go to college won't. The unemployment rate for such drop-outs is about 30 per cent now. Robert E. Iffert, of the Department of Health, Education, and Welfare, concluded in a 1958 study that approximately one-fourth of the students who enter college leave after their freshman year never to return. Figures compiled since then lead him to conclude that there has been no significant change, in spite of the National Defense Education Act, which was supposed to help reduce this figure.

If some figures recently given by James B. Conant turn out to be typical, at least one situation is much more serious than the average would imply. He found that in one of our largest cities, in an almost exclusively Negro slum of 125,000, 70 per cent of the boys and girls between 16 and 21 were out of school and unemployed. In another city, in an almost exclusively Negro slum, in the same age group, 48 per cent of the high school graduates were unemployed and 63 per cent of the high school drop-outs were unemployed. These adolescents would in the normal course join the untrained or poorly trained work force, a work force that will be more and more the repository of untrainable or untrained people displaced from their jobs by cybernation. These adolescents will have the following choices: they can stay in school, for which they are unsuited either by motivation or by intelligence; they can seek training that will raise them out of the untrained work force; they can compete in the growing manpower pool of those seeking relatively unskilled jobs; or they can loaf.

If they loaf, almost inevitably they are going to become delinquent. Thus, without adequate occupational outlets for these youths, cybernation may contribute substantially to further social disruption.

Threatened institutions often try forcibly to repress groups demanding changes in the *status quo*. Imagine the incentives to use force that would exist in a nation beset by national and international frustrations and bedeviled by anarchic unemployed-youth movements. Imagine, too, the incentives to use force in view of the reserves of volunteeer "police" made up of adults who can vent their own unemployment-based hostility in a socially approved way by punishing or disciplining these "children."

A constructive alternative, of course, is to provide appropriate training for these young people in tasks that are not about to be automated. But this implies an elaborate, costly program of research and planning to recruit teachers, to apply advanced teaching machine methods as a supplement to teachers, and to stimulate presently unmotivated youngsters to learn. The program would also require intensive cooperation among business, labor, education, local social service agencies, and the government. And all this must begin *now* in order for it to be ready when it will be needed.

None of this is easily met. Persuading drop-outs to stay in school will not be easy. Teachers will not be easy to recruit unless they are well paid. There is already a shortage of teachers. And let no one suggest that an easy source of teachers would be displaced workers. There is no reason to believe that they have the verbal and social facility to teach, and most of them would have nothing to teach but skills that have become obsolete. Some, of course, might be taught to teach, though this would add obvious complications to the whole effort.

Knowing what to teach will depend on knowing what types of

jobs are likely to exist when the student finishes his training. This will require knowledge about the trends and plans of local industry, if that is where the youths are to work (and if that is where industry plans to stay!), and of industries in other localities, if the youths are willing to move. Such knowledge often does not exist in a rapidly changing world or, if it exists, may not be forthcoming from businesses more concerned with competition than with the frustrated "delinquents" of their community. As of now, in the words of Dr. Conant, "unemployment of youth is literally nobody's affair."

*   *   *

Additional leisure]

It is generally recognized that sooner or later automation and computers will mean shorter working hours and greater leisure for most if not all of the American people. It is also generally, if vaguely, recognized that there probably are problems connected with the use of leisure that will take time to work out.

Two stages need to be distinguished: the state of leisure over the next decade or two, when our society will still be in transition to a way of life based on the widespread application of cybernation; and the relatively stable state some time in the future when supposedly everybody will have more leisure time than today and enough security to enjoy it. The transitional stage is our chief concern, for the end is far enough off to make more than some general speculations about it footless. At this later time people's behavior and attitudes will be conditioned as much by presently unforeseeable social and technological developments as by the character and impact of cybernation itself.

During the transition there will be four different "leisure" classes: 1) the unemployed, 2) the low-salaried employees working short hours, 3) the adequately paid to high-salaried group working short hours, and 4) those with no more leisure than they now have — which in the case of many professionals means very few hours of leisure indeed.

Leisure Class One]

Today, most of the unemployed are from low educational backgrounds where leisure has always been simply a respite from labor. No particular aspirations to or positive attitudes about the creative use of leisure characterize this group. Since their main concern is finding work and security, what they do with their leisure is a gratuitous question; whatever they do, it will hardly contribute to someone else's profits.

It is worth speculating that one thing they might do is to participate in radical organizations through which they could vent their hostility over being made insecure and useless. Another thing they could do, if so motivated and if the opportunity were available, would be to learn a skill not likely to be cybernated in the near future, although, as we have seen, the question arises of what this would be. Another thing would be to move to areas where there is still a demand for them. But breaking community ties is always difficult, especially during periods of threat when the familiar social group is the chief symbol of security. And who would pay for their move and who would guarantee a job when they got where they were going?

As cybernation expands its domain, the unemployed "leisure" class will not consist only of blue-collar workers. The displaced service worker will also swell the ranks of the unemployed, as well as the relatively well-trained white-collar workers until they can find jobs or displace from jobs the less well-trained or less presentable, like the college graduate filling-station attendant of not so many years ago. It is doubtful that during their unemployed period these people will look upon that time as "leisure" time. For the poorly educated, watching television, gossiping, and puttering around the house will be low-cost time-fillers between unemployment checks; for the better educated, efforts at systematic self-improvement, perhaps, as well as reading, television, and gossip; for many, it will be time spent in making the agonizing shift in style of living required of the unemployed. These will be more or less individual tragedies representing at any given time a small portion of the work force of the nation, statistically speaking. They will be spread over the cities and suburbs of the nation, reflecting the consequences of actions taken by particular firms. If the spirit of the day grows more statistical than individualistic, as this paper suggests later that it well might, there is a real question of our capacity to make the necessary organized effort in order to anticipate and cope with these "individual" cases.

The free time of some men will be used to care for their children while their wives, in an effort to replace lost income, work at service jobs. But this arrangement is incompatible with our image of what properly constitutes man's role and man's work. The effects of this use of "leisure" on all family members will be corrosive rather than constructive and will contribute to disruption of the family circle. "Leisure" for this group of people may well acquire a connotation that will discourage for a long time to come any real desire to achieve it or any effort to learn how to use it creatively.

One wonders, too, what women, with their growing tendency to work — to combat boredom as well as for money — will do as the barriers to work become higher, as menial white-collar jobs disappear under the impact of cybernation, and as the competition increases for the remaining jobs. If there are jobs, 6,000,000 more women are expected to be in the labor force in 1970 than were in it in 1960. Out of a total labor force of 87,000,000 at that time, 30,000,000 would be women. To the extent that women who want jobs to combat boredom will not be able to get them, there will be a growing leisure class that will be untrained for and does not want the added leisure. As for those women who have a source of adequate income but want jobs because they are bored, they will have less and less to do at home as automated procedures further routinize domestic chores.

Leisure Class Two]

A different kind of leisure problem will exist for the low-income group working shorter hours. This group will be composed of people with the attitudes and behavior traditionally associated with this class, as well as some others who will have drifted into the group as a result of having been displaced by cybernation. What evidence there is indicates that now and probably for years to come, when members of this group have leisure time as a result of fewer working hours, the tendency will be to take another job. It is reasonable to believe that the general insecurity inevitably arising from changing work arrangements and the over-all threat of automation would encourage "moonlighting" rather than the use of free time for recreation. If these people cannot find second jobs, it is hard to imagine their doing anything different with their free time from what they do now, since they will not have the money, the motives, or the knowledge to search out different activities.

If the shorter hours are of the order of four eight-hour days, potentially serious social problems will arise. For example, a father will be working fewer hours than his children do in school. What he will do "around the house" and what adjustments he, his wife, and children will have to make to each other will certainly add very real difficulties to the already inadequate, ambiguous, and frustrating personal relationships that typify much of middle-class family life.

Leisure Class Three]

Workers with good or adequate income employed for shorter hours are the group usually thought of when one talks about the positive opportunities for using extra leisure in a cybernated world. Its members for the most part will be the professional, semi-professional, or skilled workers who will contribute enough in their social role to command a good salary but who will not be so rare as to be needed for 40 hours a week. These people already value learning and learning to learn. Given knowledge about, money for, and access to new leisure-time activities, they are likely to make use of them. They could help to do various desirable social service tasks in the community, tasks for which there is not enough money to attract paid personnel of high enough quality. They could help to teach, and, by virtue of their own intimate experiences with cybernation, they would be able to pass on the attitudes and knowledge that will be needed to live effectively in a cybernated world. It is likely, too, that this group will be the chief repository of creative, skilled manual talents. In a nation living off mass-produced, automatically produced products, there may be a real if limited demand for hand-made articles. (We may become again in part a nation of small shopkeepers and craftsmen.) In general, this group of people will probably produce and consume most of its own leisure-time activities.

Leisure Class Four]

The fourth group consists of those who probably will have little or no more leisure time than they now have except to the extent permitted by additions to their ranks and by the services of cybernation. But extrapolations for the foreseeable future indicate insufficient increases in the class of presently overworked professionals and executives. Computers should be able to remove many of the more tedious aspects of their work in another few years, but for some time to come these people will continue to be overburdened. Some of this relatively small proportion of the population may manage to get down to a 40-hour week, and these lucky few should find no difficulty in using their leisure as productively and creatively as those in the third group.

Thus, during the transition period, it is the second group, the low-salaried workers who cannot or will not find another job, that presents the true leisure problem, as distinct from the unemployment problem. Here is where the multiple problems connected with private and public make-play efforts may prove very difficult indeed. We have some knowledge about relatively low-income workers who become voluntarily interested in adult education and adult play sessions, but we have had no real experience with the problems of how to stimulate the interests and change the attitudes of a large population that is forced to work shorter hours but is used to equating work and security, that will be bombarded with an advertising *geist* praising consumption and glamorous leisure, that will be bounded closely on one side by the unemployed and on the other by a relatively well-to-do community to which it cannot hope to aspire. Boredom may drive these people to seek new leisure-time activities if they are provided and do not cost much. But boredom combined with other factors may also make for frustration and aggression and all the social and political problems these qualities imply.

*   *   *

After the take-over]

In twenty years, other things being equal, most of the routine blue-collar and white-collar tasks that can be done by cybernation will be. Our schools will probably be turning out a larger proportion of the population better educated than they are today, but most of our citizens will be unable to understand the cybernated world in which they live. Perhaps they will understand the rudiments of calculus, biology, nuclear physics, and the humanities. But the research realm of scientists, the problems of government, and the interplay between them will be beyond the ken even of our college graduates. Besides, most people will have had to recognize that, when it comes to logic, the machines by and large can think better than they, for in that time reasonably good thinking computers should be operating on a large scale.

There will be a small, almost separate, society of people in rapport with the advanced computers. These cyberneticians will have established a relationship with their machines that cannot be shared with the average man any more than the average man today can understand the problems of molecular biology, nuclear physics, or neuropsychiatry. Indeed, many scholars will not have the capacity to share their knowledge or feeling about this new man-machine relationship. Those with the talent for the work probably will have to develop it from childhood and will be trained as intensively as the classical ballerina.

Some of the remaining population will be productively engaged in human-to-human or human-to-machine activities requiring judgment and a high level of intelligence and training. But the rest, whose innate intelligence or training is not of the highest, what will they do? We can foresee a nation with a large portion of its people doing, directly or indirectly, the endless public tasks that the welfare state needs and that the government will not allow to be cybernated because of the serious unemployment that would result. These people will work short hours, with much time for the pursuit of leisure activities.

Even with a college education, what will they do all their long lives, day after day, four-day week-end after week-end, vacation after vacation, in a more and more crowded world? (There is a population explosion to face in another ten to thirty years.) What will they believe in and aspire to as they work their shorter hours and, on the outside, pursue their "self-fulfilling" activities, whatever they may be? No one has ever seriously envisioned what characteristics these activities might have in order to be able to engross most men and women most of their adult lives. What will be the relationship of these people to government, to the "upper intellectuals," to the rest of the world, to themselves?

Obviously, attitudes toward work, play, and social responsibility will have changed greatly. Somehow we shall have had to cope emotionally with the vast gap in living standards that will then typify the difference between us and the have-not nations. We shall presumably have found some way to give meaning to the consumption of mass leisure. It would seem that a life oriented to private recreation might carry with it an attitude of relative indifference to public responsibility. This indifference, plus the centralization of authority, would seem to imply a governing élite and a popular acceptance of such an élite.

If this world is to exist as a coherent society, it will have to have its own "logic," so that it will make sense to its inhabitants. Today, for most of our population, our society makes sense, even though some other eyes hardly see us as logical in the formal sense of the word and the eyes of some of our own people look on us as a more or less pointless society. We make and solve our problems chiefly by other than mathematical-logical standards, and so must the cybernated generations. What these standards might be, we do not know. But if they are inadequate, the frustration and pointlessness that they produce may well evoke, in turn, a war of desperation — ostensibly against some external enemy but, in fact, a war to make the world safe for human beings by destroying most of society's sophisticated technological base. One thing is clear: if the new "logic" is to resolve the problems raised here, it will have to generate beliefs, behavior, and goals far different from those which we have held until now and which are driving us more and more inexorably into a contradictory world run by (and for?) ever more intelligent, ever more versatile slaves.

8

The Challenge of Population

NOT VERY long ago, it was intellectually fashionable to scoff at the pessimistic population theories of late-eighteenth-century economist Thomas Malthus. The usual argument against him was that science would certainly find ways to make the production of food keep pace with man's own reproduction. Few scoff today. By far the greater part of the world's population faces fearful dangers because science has done wonders in reducing child mortality in the lesser developed areas of the world, while it has yet to provide adequate subsistence for those it helped to save. Advances in economic growth achieved at great cost are often literally eaten up by a population that grows even more rapidly. Revealing a somewhat different side of the general problem, even advanced, highly industrialized, Western nations have felt with intensified severity the pressure of too many people on too few sources of income.

As a result, various national and international organizations are giving ever-increasing attention to these problems, and a vast literature has accumulated. Julian Huxley is a name frequently encountered in this literature. In addition to his work in England on biology and zoology, he has long participated in various British and international organizations devoted to the problem of overpopulation and related problems of man's struggle with his environment.

Julian Huxley, Too Many People!

OVERPOPULATION is the most serious threat to human happiness and progress in this very critical period in the history of the world. It is not so acute as the threat of atomic warfare, but is graver, since it springs from our own nature.

Thanks to the new vision which we have attained through the knowledge explosion, which has gone on parallel with the population explosion in the last half-century, we have a new vision of our

From Fairfield Osborn (ed.), OUR CROWDED PLANET (New York, 1962), pp. 223–233. Copyright © 1962 by Fairfield Osborn. Reprinted by permission of Doubleday & Company, Inc. and Allen & Unwin Ltd.

destiny. We may say that today evolution in the person of man is becoming conscious of itself.

I do not want to amplify this at great length. I would remind you, however, that all reality is, in a perfectly genuine sense, evolution; that biological evolution on this planet has been going on for nearly three billion years, and that in the course of that period life has advanced (not only increased in variety, but advanced in organization) so that its highest forms, from submicroscopic pre-cellular units, became cellular, then multicellular, then through hundreds of millions of years grew larger and more powerful with greater control over their environment and greater independence of its changes, culminating in land vertebrates and eventually in the latest dominant type, now spread over the whole world — man.

And man is now, whether he likes it or not, and indeed whether he knows it or not (but it is important that he is beginning to know it), the sole agent for the evolutionary process on earth. He is responsible for the future of this planet.

Before we make up our minds what we ought to do in the present crisis we must try to find what our ultimate aim is as agent or guide of evolution.

Surely, it isn't just power. Surely, it isn't just to eat, drink, and be merry, and say, "Well, what's posterity done for us? To hell with posterity!" It isn't just mere quantity of possessions or mere quantity of people. Nor is it just preparation for some rather shadowy afterlife. I would assert that it must be to conserve and to develop the resources of the earth and the resources of our own nature. And so our aim should be to increase the richness of life and enhance its quality.

"Fulfillment" is probably the embracing word; more fulfillment and less frustration for more human beings through greater realization of possibilities. We want more varied and fuller achievement in human societies. We want more variety and less drabness and monotony. We want more enjoyment and less suffering. We want more beauty and less ugliness. We want more adventure and disciplined freedom, as against routine and slavishness. We want more knowledge, more interest, more wonder, as against ignorance and apathy. We want more sense of participation in something enduring and in worthwhile projects, as against a series of competitive rat races, whether with the Russians or our neighbors on the next street.

In the most general terms, we want more transcendence of self in the fruitful development of personality. We want a greater flowering of human dignity and significance, not only as against human degradation, but as against further self-imprisonment in the human ego, and as against mere escapism.

Man has been overexploiting the natural resources of this planet. He has been misusing its soils and polluting its waters. He has wasted enormous amounts of resources which he ought to have conserved. Almost everywhere (though mainly in underdeveloped and overpopulated countries), more and more marginal land is being taken into cultivation, more forests are being cut down, more soil erosion is taking place. Everywhere (but in this case especially in the most "developed" countries) high-grade raw materials are being used up at a frightening rate, and lower-grade sources are having to be used. Almost everywhere the supplies of water are becoming insufficient. We are well on the way to ruining our habitat.

Furthermore, not content with destroying or squandering our material resources, we are beginning to destroy our resources of true enjoyment — spiritual, aesthetic, intellectual, emotional. We are spreading great masses of human habitation over the face of the land, neither cities nor suburbs nor towns nor villages, just a vast mass of urban sprawl or subtopia. And to escape from this, people are spilling out farther and farther into the wilder parts and so destroying them. And we are making our cities so big as to be monstrous. They are growing to an impossible size. Just as there is a maximum possible size for an efficient land animal — a land animal more than about twice as large as an elephant could not exist — so there is a maximum possible efficient size for a city. Cities like London, New York, and Tokyo have already got beyond that size.

Looking at the crisis more specifically, mankind is not only proliferating excessively, but increasingly so. In A.D. 1600 the total number of people in the world was only about half a billion. It first reached 1 billion at about the end of the nineteenth century. By 1950 it had passed 2 billion. Today it is 2¾ billion, and increasing by nearly 50 million a year. Every twenty-four hours it increases by over 140,000 — the equivalent of a good-sized town; and every minute by about 100 — the equivalent of ten baseball teams complete with coaches.

What is more, the *rate* of increase is itself increasing. Before the discovery of agriculture it must have been below one tenth of one percent per annum; it reached one percent only at the beginning of the present century, but by now stands at over 1½ percent, and is still going up.

Still worse, the increase is very unevenly distributed over the world. By far the highest increase is in the underdeveloped countries with the lowest standard of life, notably in Asia and Latin America. This is bad for several reasons. In the first place, it makes their development much more difficult. To develop an underdeveloped country to an industrial and social level where it can hold its own in the modern world and give its people a reasonable standard of life, needs a great deal of capital, technical skill, and trained manpower. If too many babies are born, too much of that capital and skill and manpower will be used up in providing food, housing, education, health, and other services for them, and will not be available for economic and technological development. Coale and Hoover, in their careful study of the problem, concluded that if India did not reduce its birth rate by about 50 percent in the next thirty-five or forty years it would never be able to break through from its state of underdevelopment and underemployment to a developed and developing industrially based economy; on the contrary, it would reach a point of no return, after which living standards would go down instead of up. And the same general conclusion applies to other countries, such as Pakistan or Indonesia with a high density of population at a low economic standard of life.

Then there is, as everyone knows, a great gap between the average standard of life in developed and underdeveloped areas — between the haves and have-nots. Thus the average real income of the 200 million people of North America is nearly twenty-five times as high as that of the over 1600 million people of Asia, and the disparity in energy available to an inhabitant of the United States and of India is even higher. The existence of this huge gap produces jealousy and unrest, and has generated what has been called the Revolution of Expectation in the have-not countries — an expectation of aid which must at all costs be satisfied.

The bridging of this gap is linked with the population problem. To take the Indian example again, at the moment, though the production of food is just keeping up with the production of people, it will not be able to go on doing so unless the rate of population increase slows down. Furthermore, a large proportion — about three quarters, according to the Food and Agriculture Organization — of the people in underdeveloped countries is undernourished — in plain words, not getting enough of the right food to eat — and increased food production must aim at satisfying this deficiency too. And about the same proportion is grossly undereducated — in plain words, illiterate. Finally, the economic gap is widening instead of narrowing — the rich countries are getting richer, the poor countries getting poorer.

Attempts to bridge the gap by aid and assistance to underdeveloped nations are eminently desirable, and indeed necessary, if we are to have a peaceful and prosperous world. However, as I have just pointed out, all the science and goodwill in the world cannot find a way of successfully industrializing a densely populated and underdeveloped country if its increase rate is too high.

In the long run the key to the problem is the reduction of the human birth rate. In the present century medical science, in conjunction with improved conditions of life, has markedly reduced the world death rate, but without any appreciable reduction in the birth rate. It has brought about what we may call "death control" on a world scale: the contemporary population explosion is the result. It is now necessary to supplement worldwide death control with worldwide birth control. Population control, by some form of birth control, is a prerequisite for anything that can be called progress or advance in human evolution, even in the immediate future. One major contribution that science can make is the discovery of better and simpler methods of birth control. The time has now come for the world and all its nations to think seriously about population policy.

When I say that we need a population policy, I do not mean that any national or international body is going to tell every woman how many children she may have, any more than the adoption of an economic policy will mean telling the individual businessman how much money he is allowed to make, and how he should set about it. Nationally it means that we recognize population as a major problem of national life, that we have a general aim in regard to it, and that we try to devise methods for realizing this aim. And the adoption of an international population policy does not mean dictating to underdeveloped countries or laying down the size of a nation's population. It means the recognition that population increase is a world problem, affecting every nation in many ways, and the determination to try to control it in the most helpful way. Among other things, it implies the right of the people of every nation to the best scientific information about birth control, and the duty of the UN, supported by the technologically developed nations, to carry out research on human reproduction and its control, and to provide the fullest information on the subject.

Already a few countries have an official or unofficial policy of population control — India, Pakistan, Fiji, Japan, Singapore, Barbados, Puerto Rico — but they need world encouragement and their policies should be integrated into a general and official world policy.

Public opinion is ready for this. In the last few years the barriers of prudery and religious opposition have been largely broken down, the population explosion has become news, and its resultant problems are widely discussed. But ideology, religion, and power politics are still inhibiting the UN in this matter. Owing to Roman Catholic pressure, the World Health Organization has not been allowed even to consider population density as a factor in world health. Roman Catholicism is barring the adoption of a birth-control policy in many countries, like those of Latin America, where it is most urgently needed, and is making it difficult for the United States and other Western powers to give open or effective support to birth-control measures. The USSR calls birth control Malthusianism and opposes it on ideological grounds. China has professed to regard the addition of 12 million to its population every year as a desirable source of strength (though I would prophesy that they will reverse their attitude within the next few years). Many emergent African states seem to regard any suggestion of population control as a white man's trick designed to keep the black races down.

All I can do here is to make a few personal suggestions. In the first place, a group including both underdeveloped and developed nations — say, India and Pakistan (this is a subject on which they could and should cooperate), Norway and Australia — should introduce a resolution into the UN Assembly calling for concerted thought and action on world population. At the same time a resolution authorizing and requiring the World Health Organization to consider the effects of population density on health should of course also be introduced, the International Labor Organization should report on the effects of rapid population increase on employment, and UNESCO should be made to give serious thought to the impossibility of coping with world undereducation, of providing adequate classrooms, teachers, and textbooks for the education of the world's children, so long as too many children continue to be born.

This would imply some radical changes in assistance and aid programs. For one thing, scientifically advanced countries like those of North America and western Europe would be encouraged and expected to do much more research on birth-control programs on request. Then it is most important that every request for aid or technical assistance by an underdeveloped country should be considered in the light of its demographic situation, especially its rate of population increase. No grants or loans for development should be made unless the country was willing to frame and stand by a rational population policy aimed at limiting the growth of its population, and some of the aid would be allocated to help it implement any such policy. Otherwise, as I pointed out earlier, the aid is all too likely to be useless, washed down the drain of history by the flood of new babies: some grants may even be worse than useless, for, if their possible demographic effects on population growth are not taken into account at the time, they may provoke a new excess of multiplication. A commercial bank, if approached for a loan, has the right to ask for some guarantee of financial solvency from its clients. The World Bank and other loan-making and grant-giving agencies have not only the right but the duty to ask for some guarantee of demographic solvency from their national clients.

The essential point is that overpopulation is a world problem so serious as to override all other world problems, such as soil erosion, poverty, malnutrition, raw material shortages, illiteracy, even disarmament. The future of the whole human species is at stake. If nothing is done about it, in the next hundred years man will cease to have any claims to be the Lord of Creation or the controller of his own destiny, and will have become the cancer of his planet, uselessly devouring its resources and negating his own possibilities in a spate of overmultiplication. If we do nothing about overpopulation now, our children and grandchildren now living will have a much more difficult task when they grow up, as well as a much harder, more frustrated, and often more miserable existence.

The time is ripe for action. The population problem is being passionately discussed everywhere. To change the metaphor, it is waiting in the wings of the world's international stage, ready to come on into the central limelight. But who is to bring it onto that stage? The Iron Curtain countries still pretend that the problem does not exist, or even that it has been invented by bourgeois economists. The leading Western countries seem inhibited by overconservative caution and religious opposition. The first move is up to those nations which are suffering from too many people — underdeveloped but overpopulated countries like India, Egypt, the West Indies, Indonesia, Pakistan. Let them take concerted action to ensure that the population problem ceases to be regarded as an unmentionable and horrific specter, but is considered and dealt with frankly, scientifically, and practically in the center of the international stage. Let them continue to demand UN action. Let them insist that it is not only their problem, but a world problem.

Meanwhile, of course, let them give proof of their willingness to do all they can to cope with it themselves — let them arouse their own public opinion, integrate national birth-control campaigns within their health services, train doctors and village nurses in preparation for the campaigns, do research, launch pilot projects. And let them publicize their efforts and bring their plight to the notice of world opinion. Only so shall we get what is so necessary — a world population policy.

We must look at the question of population increase in the light of the new vision of human destiny which human science and learning has revealed to us. We must look at it in the light of the glorious possibilities that are still latent in man, not merely in the light of the obvious fact that the world could be made a little better than it is. We must also look at it in the light of the appalling possibilities for evil and misery that still remain for human life in the future.

I would say that this vision, of the possibilities of wonder and more fruitful fulfillment on the one hand as against frustration and increasing misery and regimentation on the other, are the twentieth-century equivalents of the traditional Christian view of salvation as against damnation. And I would indeed say that this new vision that we are gaining, the vision of evolutionary humanism, is essentially a religious one, and that we can and should devote ourselves with truly religious devotion to the cause of ensuring greater fulfillment for the human race in its future destiny. And this serious and concerted attack on the problem of population; for the control of population is, I am quite certain, a prerequisite for any radical improvement in the human lot.

9

Containment of Communism

THE DETERMINATION of the Western nations to halt Communist expansion was expressed centrally in the Truman Doctrine and the Marshall Plan. The speeches by President Truman and Secretary of State Marshall setting forth this principle are reprinted here.

a The Truman Doctrine—March 12, 1947

THE GRAVITY of the situation which confronts the world today necessitates my appearance before a joint session of the Congress.

The foreign policy and the national security of this country are involved.

One aspect of the present situation, which I wish to present to you at this time for your consideration and decision, concerns Greece and Turkey.

The United States has received from the Greek government an urgent appeal for financial and economic assistance. Preliminary reports from the American economic mission now in Greece and reports from the American Ambassador in Greece corroborate the statement of the Greek government that assistance is imperative if Greece is to survive as a free nation.

I do not believe that the American people and the Congress wish to turn a deaf ear to the appeal of the Greek government.

Greece is not a rich country. Lack of sufficient resources has always forced the Greek people to work hard to make both ends meet. Since 1940 this industrious and peace-loving country has suffered invasion, four years of cruel enemy occupation and bitter internal strife.

When forces of liberation entered Greece they found that the re-

From THE CONGRESSIONAL RECORD (Washington, 1947), vol. 92, pp. 1999–2000.

treating Germans had destroyed virtually all the railways, roads, port facilities, communications and merchant marine. More than a thousand villages had been burned. Eighty-five per cent of the children were tubercular. Livestock, poultry and draft animals had almost disappeared. Inflation had wiped out practically all savings.

As a result of these tragic conditions, a militant minority, exploiting human want and misery, was able to create political chaos, which, until now, has made economic recovery impossible. Greece is today without funds to finance the importation of those goods which are essential to bare subsistence. Under these circumstances the people of Greece cannot make progress in solving their problems of reconstruction. Greece is in desperate need of financial and economic assistance to enable it to resume purchases of food, clothing, fuel and seeds. These are indispensable for subsistence of its people and are obtainable only from abroad. Greece must have help to import the goods necessary to restore internal order and security so essential for economic and political recovery.

The Greek government has also asked for the assistance of experienced American administrators, economists and technicians to insure that the financial and other aid given Greece shall be used effectively in creating a stable and self-sustaining economy and in improving its public administration.

The very existence of the Greek state is today threatened by the terrorist activities of several thousand armed men, led by Communists, who defy the government's authority at a number of points, particularly along the northern boundaries. A commission appointed by the United Nations Security Council is at present investigating disturbed conditions in northern Greece on the one hand and Albania, Bulgaria and Yugoslavia on the other.

Meanwhile, the Greek government is unable to cope with the situation. The Greek army is small and poorly equipped. It needs supplies and equipment if it is to restore the authority of the government throughout Greek territory.

Greece must have assistance if it is to become a self-supporting and self-respecting democracy.

The United States must supply that assistance. We have already extended to Greece certain types of relief and economic aid but they are inadequate.

There is no other country to which democratic Greece can turn.

No other nation is willing and able to provide the necessary support for a democratic Greek government.

The British government, which has been helping Greece, can give no further financial or economic aid after March 31. Great Britain finds itself under the necessity of reducing or liquidating its commitments in several parts of the world, including Greece.

We have considered how the United Nations might assist in this crisis. But the situation is an urgent one requiring immediate action, and the United Nations and its related organizations are not in a position to extend help of the kind that is required.

It is important to note that the Greek government has asked for our aid in utilizing effectively the financial and other assistance we may give to Greece, and in improving its public administration. It is of the utmost importance that we supervise the use of any funds made available to Greece, in such a manner that each dollar spent will count toward making Greece self-supporting, and will help to build an economy in which a healthy democracy can flourish.

No government is perfect. One of the chief virtues of a democracy, however, is that its defects are always visible and under democratic processes can be pointed out and corrected. The government of Greece is not perfect. Nevertheless it represents 80 per cent of the members of the Greek Parliament who were chosen in an election last year. Foreign observers, including 692 Americans, considered this election to be a fair expression of the views of the Greek people.

The Greek government has been operating in an atmosphere of chaos and extremism. It has made mistakes. The extension of aid by this country does not mean that the United States condones everything that the Greek government has done or will do. We have condemned in the past, and we condemn now, extremist measures of the Right or the Left. We have in the past advised tolerance, and we advise tolerance now.

Greece's neighbor, Turkey, also deserves our attention.

The future of Turkey as an independent and economically sound state is clearly no less important to the freedom-loving people of the world than the future of Greece. The circumstances in which Turkey finds itself today are considerably different from those of Greece. Turkey has been spared the disasters that have beset Greece. And during the war the United States and Great Britain furnished Turkey with material aid. Nevertheless, Turkey now needs our support.

Since the war, Turkey has sought financial assistance from Great Britain and the United States for the purpose of effecting that modernization necessary for the maintenance of its national integrity.

That integrity is essential for the preservation of order in the Middle East.

The British government has informed us that, owing to its own difficulties, it can no longer extend financial or economic aid to Turkey.

As in the case of Greece, if Turkey is to have the assistance it needs, the United States must supply it. We are the only country that can supply that help.

I am fully aware of the broad implications involved if the United States extends assistance to Greece and Turkey, and I shall discuss these implications with you at this time.

One of the primary objectives of the foreign policy of the United States is the creation of conditions in which we and other nations of the world will be able to work out a way of life free from coercion. This was a fundamental issue in the war with Germany and Japan. Our victory was won over countries which sought to impose their will, and their way of life, upon other nations.

To ensure the peaceful development of nations, free from coercion, the United States has taken a leading part in establishing the United Nations. The United Nations is designed to make possible lasting freedom and independence for all its members. We shall not realize our objectives, however, unless we are willing to help free people to maintain their free institutions and their national integrity against aggressive movements that seek to impose upon them totalitarian regimes. This is no more than a frank recognition that totalitarian regimes imposed on free peoples, by direct or indirect aggression, undermine the foundations of international peace and hence the security of the United States.

The peoples of a number of countries of the world have recently had totalitarian regimes forced upon them against their will. The government of the United States has made frequent protests against coercion and intimidation, in violation of the Yalta agreement, in Poland, Rumania and Bulgaria. I must also state that in a number of other countries there have been similar developments.

At the present moment in world history nearly every nation must choose between alternative ways of life. The choice is too often not a free one.

One way of life is based upon the will of the majority, and is distinguished by free institutions, representative government, free elections, guaranties of individual liberty, freedom of speech and religion and freedom from political oppression.

The second way of life is based upon the will of a minority forcibly imposed upon the majority. It relies upon terror and oppression, a controlled press and radio, fixed elections and the suppression of personal freedom.

I believe that it must be the policy of the United States to support peoples who are resisting attempted subjugation by armed minorities or by outside pressures.

I believe that we must assist free peoples to work out their own destinies in their own way.

I believe that our help should be primarily through economic and financial aid which is essential to economic stability and orderly political processes.

The world is not static, and the status quo is not sacred. But we cannot allow change in the status quo in violation of the charter of the United Nations by such methods as coercion, or by such subterfuges as political infiltration. In helping free and independent nations to maintain their freedom, the United States will be giving effect to the principles of the charter of the United Nations.

It is necessary only to glance at a map to realize that the survival and integrity of the Greek nation are of grave importance in a much wider situation. If Greece should fall under the control of an armed minority, the effect upon its neighbor, Turkey, would be immediate and serious. Confusion and disorder might well spread throughout the entire Middle East.

Moreover, the disappearance of Greece as an independent state would have a profound effect upon those countries in Europe whose people are struggling against great difficulties to maintain their freedoms and their independence while they repair the damages of war.

It would be an unspeakable tragedy if these countries, which have struggled so long against overwhelming odds, should lose that victory for which they have sacrificed so much. Collapse of free institutions and loss of independence would be disastrous not only for them but for the world. Discouragement and possibly failure would quickly be the lot of neighboring peoples striving to maintain their freedom and independence.

Should we fail to aid Greece and Turkey in this fateful hour, the effect will be far-reaching to the West as well as to the East.

I therefore ask the Congress to provide authority for assistance to Greece and Turkey in the amount of $400,000,000 for the period ending June 3, 1948. In requesting these funds, I have taken into consideration the maximum amount of relief assistance which would be furnished to Greece out of the $350,000,000 which I recently requested that the Congress authorize for the prevention of starvation and suffering in countries devastated by the war.

In addition to funds, I ask the Congress to authorize the detail of American civilian and military personnel to Greece and Turkey, at the request of those countries, to assist in the tasks of reconstruction, and for the purpose of supervising the use of such financial and material assistance as may be furnished. I recommend that authority be provided for the instruction and training of selected Greek and Turkish personnel.

Finally, I ask that the Congress provide authority which will permit the speediest and most effective use, in terms of needed commodities, supplies and equipment, of such funds as may be authorized.

If further funds, or further authority, should be needed for purposes indicated in this message, I shall not hesitate to bring the situation before Congress. On this subject the executive and legislative branches of the government must work together.

This is a serious course upon which we embark.

I would not recommend it except that the alternative is much more serious.

The United States contributed $341,000,000,000 toward winning World War II. This is an investment in world freedom and world peace.

The assistance that I am recommending for Greece and Turkey amounts to little more than one-tenth of 1 per cent of this investment. It is only common sense that we should safeguard this investment and make sure that it was not in vain.

The seeds of totalitarian regimes are nurtured by misery and want. They spread and grow in the evil soil of poverty and strife. They reach their full growth when the hope of a people for a better life has died.

We must keep that hope alive.

The free peoples of the world look to us for support in maintaining their freedoms.

If we falter in our leadership, we may endanger the peace of the world — and we shall surely endanger the welfare of our own nation.

Great responsibilities have been placed upon us by the swift movement of events.

I am confident that the Congress will face these responsibilities squarely.

b The Marshall Plan—June 5, 1947

I NEED NOT tell you, gentlemen, that the world situation is very serious. That must be apparent to all intelligent people. I think one difficulty is that the problem is one of such enormous complexity that the very mass of facts presented to the public by press and radio make it exceedingly difficult for the man in the street to reach a clear appraisement of the situation. Furthermore, the people of this country are distant from the troubled areas of the earth and it is hard for them to comprehend the plight and consequent reactions on their governments in connection with our efforts to promote peace in the world.

In considering the requirements for the rehabilitation of Europe the physical loss of life, the visible destruction of cities, factories, mines and railroads was correctly estimated, but it has become obvious during recent months that this visible destruction was probably less serious than the dislocation of the entire fabric of European economy. For the past ten years conditions have been highly abnormal.

The feverish preparation for war and the more feverish maintenance of the war effort engulfed all aspects of national economies. Machinery has fallen into disrepair or is entirely obsolete. Under the arbitrary and destructive Nazi rule, virtually every possible enterprise was geared into the German war machine. Long-standing commercial ties, private institutions, banks, insurance companies and shipping companies disappeared, through loss of capital, absorption through nationalization or by simple destruction.

In many countries, confidence in the local currency has been

From THE NEW YORK TIMES, June 6, 1947. Reprinted by permission of The New York Times.

severely shaken. The breakdown of the business structure of Europe during the war was complete. Recovery has been seriously retarded by the fact that two years after the close of hostilities a peace agreement with Germany and Austria has not been agreed upon. But even given a more prompt solution of these difficult problems, the rehabilitation of the economic structure of Europe quite evidently will require a much longer time and greater effort than had been foreseen.

There is a phase of this matter which is both interesting and serious. The farmer has always produced the foodstuffs to exchange with the city dweller for the other necessities of life. The division of labor is the basis of modern civilization. At the present time it is threatened with breakdown. The town and city industries are not producing adequate goods to exchange with the food-producing farmer. Raw materials and fuel are in short supply. Machinery is lacking or worn out.

The farmer or the peasant cannot find the goods for sale which he desires to purchase. So the sale of his farm produce for money which he cannot use, seems to him an unprofitable transaction. He, therefore, has withdrawn many fields from crop cultivation and is using them for grazing. He feeds more grain to stock and finds for himself and his family an ample supply of food, however short he may be on clothing and the other ordinary gadgets of civilization. Meanwhile, people in the cities are short of food and fuel. So the governments are forced to use their foreign money and credits to procure these necessities abroad. This process exhausts funds which are urgently needed for reconstruction. Thus a very serious situation is rapidly developing which bodes no good for the world. The modern system of the division of labor upon which the exchange of products is based is in danger of breaking down.

The truth of the matter is that Europe's requirements for the next three or four years of foreign food and other essential products — principally from America — are so much greater than her present ability to pay that she must have substantial additional help, or face economic, social and political deterioration of a very grave character.

The remedy lies in breaking the vicious circle and restoring the confidence of the European people in the economic future of their own countries and of Europe as a whole. The manufacturer and the farmer throughout wide areas must be able and willing to exchange their products for currencies, the continuing value of which is not open to question.

Aside from the demoralizing effect on the world at large and the possibilities of disturbances arising as a result of the desperation of the people concerned, the consequences to the economy of the United States should be apparent to all. It is logical that the United States should do whatever it is able to do to assist in the return of normal economic health to the world, without which there can be no political stability and no assured peace.

Our policy is directed not against any country or doctrine but against hunger, poverty, desperation and chaos. Its purpose should be the revival of a working economy in the world so as to permit the emergence of political and social conditions in which free institutions can exist. Such assistance, I am convinced, must not be on a piecemeal basis as various crises develop. Any assistance that this government may develop in the future should provide a cure rather than a mere palliative.

Any government that is willing to assist in the task of recovery will find full cooperation, I am sure, on the part of the United States Government. Any government which maneuvers to block the recovery of other countries cannot expect help from us. Furthermore, governments, political parties or groups which seek to perpetuate human misery in order to profit therefrom politically or otherwise will encounter the opposition of the United States.

It is already evident that, before the United States Government can proceed much further in its efforts to alleviate the situation and help start the European world on its way to recovery, there must be some agreement among the countries of Europe as to the requirements of the situation and the part those countries themselves will take in order to give proper effect to whatever action might be undertaken by this Government. It would be neither fitting nor efficacious for this Government to undertake to draw up unilaterally a program designed to place Europe on its feet economically. This is the business of the Europeans. The initiative, I think, must come from Europe. The role of this country should consist of friendly aid in the drafting of a European program and of later support of such a program so far as it may be practical for us to do so. The program should be a joint one, agreed to by a number, if not all European nations.

An essential part of any successful action on the part of the United States is an understanding on the part of the people of America of the character of the problem and the remedies to be applied. Political passion and prejudice should have no part. With foresight, and a willingness on the part of our people to face up to the vast responsibility which history has clearly placed upon our country, the difficulties I have outlined can and will be overcome.

10

Quest for World Justice

DESPITE the deep division of contemporary society into hostile power blocs, a consensus of judgment is emerging on some vital issues. This may be seen particularly in the work of the agencies of the United Nations. The following documents illustrate the nature and content of this consensus, though not its limits. The first, the Universal Declaration of Human Rights, was approved by the General Assembly on December 10, 1948, and the second, the Draft Covenant on Economic, Social and Cultural Rights was presented at the 18th session of the United Nations Economic and Social Council.

a Universal Declaration of Human Rights

Preamble]

Whereas recognition of the inherent dignity and of the equal and inalienable rights of all members of the human family is the foundation of freedom, justice and peace in the world,

Whereas disregard and contempt for human rights have resulted in barbarous acts which have outraged the conscience of mankind, and the advent of a world in which human beings shall enjoy freedom of speech and belief and freedom from fear and want has been proclaimed as the highest aspiration of the common people,

Whereas it is essential, if man is not to be compelled to have recourse, as a last resort, to rebellion against tyranny and oppression, that human rights should be protected by the rule of law,

Whereas it is essential to promote the development of friendly relations between nations,

Whereas the peoples of the United Nations have in the Charter reaffirmed their faith in fundamental human rights, in the dignity and worth of the human person and in the equal rights of men and

From U.N. General Assembly, Third Session, First Part, OFFICIAL RECORDS, "Resolutions" (New York, 1948), pp. 71–77.

women and have determined to promote social progress and better standards of life in larger freedom,

Whereas Member States have pledged themselves to achieve, in co-operation with the United Nations, the promotion of universal respect for and observance of human rights and fundamental freedoms,

Whereas a common understanding of these rights and freedoms is of the greatest importance for the full realization of this pledge,

Now, therefore,

The General Assembly

Proclaims this Universal Declaration of Human Rights as a common standard of achievement for all peoples and all nations, to the end that every individual and every organ of society, keeping this Declaration constantly in mind, shall strive by teaching and education to promote respect for these rights and freedoms and by progressive measures, national and international, to secure their universal and effective recognition and observance, both among the peoples of Member States themselves and among the peoples of territories under their jurisdiction.

Article 1]

All human beings are born free and equal in dignity and rights. They are endowed with reason and conscience and should act towards one another in a spirit of brotherhood.

Article 2]

Everyone is entitled to all the rights and freedoms set forth in this Declaration, without distinction of any kind, such as race, colour, sex, language, religion, political or other opinion, national or social origin, property, birth or other status.

Furthermore, no distinction shall be made on the basis of the political, jurisdictional or international status of the country or territory to which a person belongs, whether it be independent, trust, non-self-governing or under any other limitation of sovereignty.

Article 3]

Everyone has the right to life, liberty and the security of person.

Article 4]

No one shall be held in slavery or servitude; slavery and the slave trade shall be prohibited in all their forms.

Article 5]

No one shall be subjected to torture or to cruel, inhuman or degrading treatment or punishment.

Article 6]

Everyone has the right to recognition everywhere as a person before the law.

Article 7]

All are equal before the law and are entitled without any discrimination to equal protection of the law. All are entitled to equal protection against any discrimination in violation of this Declaration and against any incitement to such discrimination.

Article 8]

Everyone has the right to an effective remedy by the competent national tribunals for acts violating the fundamental rights granted him by the constitution or by law.

Article 9]

No one shall be subjected to arbitrary arrest, detention or exile.

Article 10]

Everyone is entitled in full equality to a fair and public hearing by an independent and impartial tribunal, in the determination of his rights and obligations and of any criminal charge against him.

Article 11]

1] Everyone charged with a penal offense has the right to be presumed innocent until proved guilty according to law in a public trial at which he has had all the guarantees necessary for his defence.
2] No one shall be held guilty of any penal offence on account of any act or omission which did not constitute a penal offence, under national or international law, at the time when it was committed. Nor shall a heavier penalty be imposed than the one that was applicable at the time the penal offence was committed.

Article 12]

No one shall be subjected to arbitrary interference with his privacy, family, home or correspondence, nor to attacks upon his honour and reputation. Everyone has the right to the protection of the law against such interference or attacks.

Article 13]

1] Everyone has the right to freedom of movement and residence within the borders of each State.
2] Everyone has the right to leave any country, including his own, and to return to his country.

Article 14]

1] Everyone has the right to seek and to enjoy in other countries asylum from persecution.
2] This right may not be invoked in the case of prosecutions genuinely arising from nonpolitical crimes or from acts contrary to the purposes and principles of the United Nations.

Article 15]

1] Everyone has the right to a nationality.
2] No one shall be arbitrarily deprived of his nationality nor denied the right to change his nationality.

Article 16]

1] Men and women of full age, without any limitation due to race, nationality or religion, have the right to marry and to found a family. They are entitled to equal rights as to marriage, during marriage and at its dissolution.
2] Marriage shall be entered into only with the free and full consent of the intending spouses.
3] The family is the natural and fundamental group unit of society and is entitled to protection by society and the State.

Article 17]

1] Everyone has the right to own property alone as well as in association with others.
2] No one shall be arbitrarily deprived of his property.

Article 18]

Everyone has the right to freedom of thought, conscience and religion; this right includes freedom to change his religion or belief, and freedom, either alone or in community with others and in public or private, to manifest his religion or belief in teaching, practice, worship and observance.

Article 19]

Everyone has the right to freedom of opinion and expression; this right includes freedom to hold opinions without interference and to seek, receive and impart information and ideas through any media and regardless of frontiers.

Article 20]

1] Everyone has the right to freedom of peaceful assembly and association.

2] No one may be compelled to belong to an association.

Article 21]

1] Everyone has the right to take part in the government of his country, directly or through freely chosen representatives.

2] Everyone has the right of equal access to public service in his country.

3] The will of the people shall be the basis of the authority of government; this will shall be expressed in periodic and genuine elections which shall be by universal and equal suffrage and shall be held by secret vote or by equivalent free voting procedures.

Article 22]

Everyone, as a member of society, has the right to social security and is entitled to realization, through national effort and international co-operation and in accordance with the organization and resources of each state, of the economic, social and cultural rights indispensable for his dignity and the free development of his personality.

Article 23]

1] Everyone has the right to work, to free choice of employment, to just and favourable conditions of work and to protection against unemployment.

2] Everyone, without any discrimination, has the right to equal pay for equal work.

3] Everyone who works has the right to just and favorable remuneration ensuring for himself and his family an existence worthy of human dignity, and supplemented, if necessary, by other means of social protection.

4] Everyone has the right to form and to join trade unions for the protection of his interests.

Article 24]

Everyone has the right to rest and leisure, including reasonable limitation of working hours and periodic holidays with pay.

Article 25]

1] Everyone has the right to a standard of living adequate for the health and well-being of himself and of his family, including food, clothing, housing and medical care and necessary social services, and the right to security in the event of unemployment, sickness, disability, widowhood, old age or other lack of livelihood in circumstances beyond his control.

2] Motherhood and childhood are entitled to special care and assistance. All children, whether born in or out of wedlock, shall enjoy the same social protection.

Article 26]

1] Everyone has the right to education. Education shall be free, at least in the elementary and fundamental stages. Elementary education shall be compulsory. Technical and professional education shall be made generally available and higher education shall be equally accessible to all on the basis of merit.

2] Education shall be directed to the full development of the human personality and to the strengthening of respect for human rights and fundamental freedoms. It shall promote understanding, tolerance and friendship among all nations, racial or religious groups, and shall further the activities of the United Nations for the maintenance of peace.

3] Parents have a prior right to choose the kind of education that shall be given to their children.

Article 27]

1] Everyone has the right freely to participate in the cultural life of the community, to enjoy the arts and to share in scientific advancement and its benefits.

2] Everyone has the right to the protection of the moral and material interests resulting from any scientific, literary or artistic production of which he is the author.

Article 28]

Everyone is entitled to a social and international order in which the rights and freedoms set forth in this Declaration can be fully realized.

Article 29]

1] Everyone has duties to the community in which alone the free and full development of his personality is possible.

2] In the exercise of his rights and freedoms, everyone shall be subject only to such limitations as are determined by law solely for the purpose of securing due recognition and respect for the rights and freedoms of others and of meeting the just requirements of morality, public order and the general welfare in a democratic society.

3] These rights and freedoms may in no case be exercised contrary to the purposes and principles of the United Nations.

Article 30]

Nothing in this Declaration may be interpreted as implying for any State, group or person any right to engage in any activity or to perform any act aimed at the destruction of any of the rights and freedoms set forth herein.

b *Draft Covenant on Economic, Social and Cultural Rights*

The States Parties hereto,

Considering that, in accordance with the principles proclaimed in the Charter of the United Nations, recognition of the inherent dignity and of the equal and inalienable rights of all members of the human family is the foundation of freedom, justice and peace in the world,

From U.N. Economic and Social Council, Eighteenth Session [Supplement no. 7], OFFICIAL RECORDS (New York, 1948), pp. 62–65.

Recognizing that these rights derive from the inherent dignity of the human person,

Recognizing that, in accordance with the Universal Declaration of Human Rights, the ideal of free men enjoying freedom from fear and want can only be achieved if conditions are created whereby everyone may enjoy his economic, social and cultural rights, as well as his civil and political rights,

Considering the obligation of States under the Charter of the United Nations to promote universal respect for, and observance of, human rights and freedoms,

Realizing that the individual, having duties to other individuals and to the community to which he belongs, is under responsibility to strive for the promotion and observance of the rights recognized in this Covenant,

Agree upon the following articles:

Part I

Article 1]

1] All peoples and all nations shall have the right of self-determination, namely, the right freely to determine their political economic, social and cultural status.

2] All States, including those having responsibility for the administration of Non-Self-Governing and Trust Territories and those controlling in whatsoever manner the exercise of that right by another people, shall promote the realization of that right in all their territories, and shall respect the maintenance of that right in other States, in conformity with the provisions of the United Nations Charter.

3] The right of peoples to self-determination shall also include permanent sovereignty over their natural wealth and resources. In no case may a people be deprived of its own means of subsistence on the grounds of any rights that may be claimed by other States.

Part II

Article 2]

1] Each State Party hereto undertakes to take steps, individually and through international co-operation, to the maximum of its available resources, with a view to achieving progressively the full realization of the rights recognized in this Covenant by legislative as well as by other means.

2] The State Parties hereto undertake to guarantee that the rights enunciated in this Covenant will be exercised without distinction of any kind, such as race, colour, language, religion, political or other opinion, national or social origin, property, birth or other status.

Article 3]

The States Parties to the Covenant undertake to ensure the equal right of men and women to the enjoyment of all economic, social and cultural rights set forth in this Covenant.

Article 4]

The State Parties to this Covenant recognize that in the enjoyment of those rights provided by the State in conformity with this Covenant, the State may subject such rights only to such limitations as are determined by law only in so far as this may be compatible with the nature of these rights and solely for the purpose of promoting the general welfare in a democratic society.

Article 5]

1] Nothing in this Covenant may be interpreted as implying for any State, group or person, any right to engage in any activity or to perform any act aimed at the destruction of any of the rights or freedoms recognized herein, or at their limitation to a greater extent than is provided for in this Covenant.

2] No restriction upon or derogation from any of the fundamental human rights recognized or existing in any country in virtue of law, conventions, regulations or custom shall be admitted on the pretext that the present Covenant does not recognize such rights or that it recognizes them to a lesser extent.

Part III

Article 6]

1] Work being at the basis of all human endeavour, the States Parties to the Covenant recognize the right to work, that is to say, the fundamental right of everyone to the opportunity, if he so desires, to gain his living by work which he freely accepts.

2] The steps to be taken by a State Party to this Covenant to achieve the full realization of this right shall include programmes, policies and techniques to achieve steady economic development and full and productive employment under conditions safeguarding fundamental political and economic freedoms to the individual.

Article 7]

The States Parties to the Covenant recognize the right of everyone to just and favourable conditions of work, including:

(*a*) Safe and healthy working conditions;

(*b*) Remuneration which provides all workers as a minimum with:

(*i*) Fair wages and equal remuneration for work of equal value without distinction of any kind, in particular, women being guaranteed conditions of work not inferior to those enjoyed by men, with equal pay for equal work; and

(*ii*) A decent living for themselves and their families; and

(*c*) Rest, leisure and reasonable limitation of working hours and periodic holidays with pay.

Article 8]

The States Parties to the Covenant undertake to ensure the free exercise of the right of everyone to form and join local, national and international trade unions of his choice for the protection of his economic and social interests.

Article 9]

The States Parties to the Covenant recognize the right of everyone to social security.

Article 10]

The States Parties to the Covenant recognize that:

1] Special protection should be accorded to motherhood and particularly to maternity during reasonable periods before and after childbirth; and

2] Special measures of protection, to be applied in all appropriate cases, within and with the help of the family, should be taken on behalf of children and young persons, and in particular they should not be required to do work likely to hamper their normal development. To protect children from exploitation, the unlawful use of

child labour and the employment of young persons in work harmful to health or dangerous to life should be made legally actionable; and
3] The family, which is the basis of society, is entitled to the widest possible protection. It is based on marriage, which must be entered into with the free consent of the intending spouses.

Article 11]

The States Parties to the Covenant recognize the right of everyone to adequate food, clothing and housing.

Article 12]

The States Parties to the Covenant recognize the right of everyone to an adequate standard of living and the continuous improvement of living conditions.

Article 13]

1] The States Parties to the Covenant, realizing that health is a state of complete physical, mental and social well-being, and not merely the absence of disease or infirmity, recognize the right of everyone to the enjoyment of the highest attainable standard of health.
2] The steps to be taken by the States Parties to the Covenant to achieve the full realization of this right shall include those necessary for:

(*a*) The reduction of infant mortality and the provision for healthy development of the child;

(*b*) The improvement of nutrition, housing, sanitation, recreation, economic and working conditions and other aspects of environmental hygiene;

(*c*) The prevention, treatment and control of epidemic, endemic and other diseases;

(*d*) The creation of conditions which would assure to all medical service and medical attention in the event of sickness.

Article 14]

1] The States Parties to the Covenant recognize the right of everyone to education, and recognize that education shall encourage the full development of the human personality, the strengthening of respect for human rights and fundamental freedoms and the suppression of all incitement to racial and other hatred. It shall promote understanding, tolerance and friendship among all nations, racial, ethnic or religious groups, and shall further the activities of the United Nations for the maintenance of peace and enable all persons to participate effectively in a free society.

2] It is understood:

(*a*) That primary education shall be compulsory and available free to all;

(*b*) That secondary education, in its different forms, including technical and professional secondary education, shall be generally available and shall be made progressively free;

(*c*) That higher education shall be equally accessible to all on the basis of merit and shall be made progressively free;

(*d*) That fundamental education for those persons who have not received or completed the whole period of their primary education shall be encouraged as far as possible.

3] In the exercise of any functions which they assume in the field of education, the States Parties to the Covenant undertake to have respect for the liberty of parents and, when applicable, legal guardians, to choose for their children schools other than those established by the public authorities which conform to such minimum educational standards as may be laid down or approved by the State and to ensure the religious education of their children in conformity with their own convictions.

Article 15]

Each State Party to the Covenant which, at the time of becoming a party to this Covenant, has not been able to secure in its metropolitan territory or other territories under its jurisdiction compulsory primary education, free of charge, undertakes, within two years, to work out and adopt a detailed plan of action for the progressive implementation, within a reasonable number of years, to be fixed in the plan, of the principle of compulsory primary education free of charge for all.

Article 16]

1] The States Parties to the Covenant recognize the right of everyone:

(*a*) To take part in cultural life;

(*b*) To enjoy the benefits of scientific progress and its applications.

2] The steps to be taken by the States Parties to this Covenant to achieve the full realization of this right shall include those necessary for the conservation, the development and the diffusion of science and culture.

3] The States Parties to the Covenant undertake to respect the freedom indispensable for scientific research and creative activity.

Part IV

1] The States Parties to this Covenant undertake to submit in conformity with this part of the Covenant reports concerning the progress made in achieving the observance of the rights recognized herein.

2] (*a*) All reports shall be submitted to the Secretary-General of the United Nations for the Economic and Social Council.

(*b*) Any State Party which is also a member of a specialized agency shall at the same time transmit, in respect of matters falling within the purview of that agency, a copy of its report, or relevant extracts therefrom, as appropriate, to that agency.

1] The States Parties shall furnish their reports in stages, in accordance with a programme to be established by the Economic and Social Council after consultation with the States Parties to this Covenant and the specialized agencies concerned.

2] Reports may indicate factors and difficulties affecting the degree of fulfilment of obligations under this Covenant.

3] Where relevant information has already previously been furnished to the United Nations or to any specialized agency by any State Party it will not be necessary to reproduce that information but a precise reference to the information so furnished will suffice.

Pursuant to its responsibilities under the Charter in the field of human rights, the Economic and Social Council may make arrangements with the specialized agencies in respect of their reporting to it on the progress made in achieving the observance of the provisions of this Covenant falling within the scope of their activities. These reports may include particulars of decisions and recommendations on such implementation adopted by their competent organs.

Article 20]

The Economic and Social Council may transmit to the Commission on Human Rights for study and general recommendation or as appropriate for information the reports concerning human rights submitted by States, and those concerning human rights submitted by the specialized agencies.

Article 21]

The States Parties directly concerned and the specialized agencies may submit comments to the Economic and Social Council on any general recommendation under article 20 or reference to such general recommendation in any report of the Commission or any documentation referred to therein.

Article 22]

The Economic and Social Council may submit from time to time to the General Assembly, with its own reports, reports summarizing the information made available by the States Parties to the Covenant directly to the Secretary-General and by the specialized agencies under Article . . . indicating the progress made in achieving general observance of these rights.

Article 23]

The Economic and Social Council may bring to the attention of the international organs concerned with technical assistance or of any other appropriate international organ any matters arising out of the reports referred to in this part of the Covenant which may assist such organs in deciding each within its competence, on the advisability of international measures likely to contribute to the progressive implementation of this Covenant.

Article 24]

The States Parties to the Covenant agree that international action for the achievement of these rights includes such methods as conventions, recommendations, technical assistance, regional meetings and technical meetings and studies with governments.

Article 25]

Nothing in this Covenant shall be interpreted as impairing the provisions of the Charter of the United Nations and of the constitutions of the specialized agencies, which define the respective responsibilities of the various organs of the United Nations and of the specialized agencies in regard to the matters dealt with in this Covenant.

Part V

Article 26]

1] This Covenant shall be open for signature and ratification or accession on behalf of any State Member of the United Nations or of any non-member State to which an invitation has been extended by the General Assembly.

2] Ratification of or accession to this Covenant shall be effected by the deposit of an instrument of ratification or accession with the Secretary-General of the United Nations, and as soon as twenty States have deposited such instruments, the Covenant shall come into force among them. As regards any State which ratifies or accedes thereafter the Covenant shall come into force on the date of the deposit of its instrument of ratification or accession.

3] The Secretary-General of the United Nations shall inform all Members of the United Nations, and other States which have signed or acceded, of the deposit of each instrument of ratification or accession.

Article 27]

The provisions of the Covenant shall extend to all parts of federal States without any limitations or exceptions.

Article 28]

The provisions of the present Covenant shall extend to or be applicable equally to a signatory metropolitan State and to all the territories, be they Non-Self-Governing, Trust, or Colonial Territories, which are being administered or governed by such metropolitan State.

1] Any State Party to the Covenant may propose an amendment and file it with the Secretary-General of the United Nations. The Secretary-General shall thereupon communicate the proposed amendments to the States Parties to the Covenant with a request that they notify him whether they favour a conference of States Parties for the purpose of considering and voting upon the proposal. In the event that at least one-third of the States favours such a conference the Secretary-General shall convene the conference under the auspices of the United Nations. Any amendment adopted by a majority of States present and voting at the conference shall be submitted to the General Assembly of the United Nations for approval.

2] Such amendments shall come into force when they have been approved by the General Assembly and accepted by a two-thirds majority of the States Parties to the Covenant in accordance with their respective constitutional processes.

3] When such amendments come into force they shall be binding on those Parties which have accepted them, other Parties being still bound by the provisions of the Covenant and any earlier amendment which they have accepted.

11

Democratic Socialism

WHILE MANY in the United States find it difficult to distinguish between socialism and Communism, the socialist parties in Europe consider themselves among the most persistent and forceful opponents of international Communism. The essential issue that divides socialists and Communists is the socialists' belief that socialist economic policies can be put into effect without undermining democratic political institutions or basic civil rights and liberties. The following statement of British socialist goals was written by C. A. R. Crosland for the socialist symposium, New Fabian Essays. Organized at the end of the nineteenth century and including such illustrious authors as George Bernard Shaw, Sidney Webb, and the sociologist Graham Wallas, the Fabian Society has advocated a nonviolent, gradual evolution toward socialism.

C. A. R. Crosland, The Transition from Capitalism

The post-capitalist society]

I PROPOSE to list eight essential features of this new society, choosing those which distinguish it from capitalism.

1] Individual property rights no longer constitute the essential basis of economic and social power. Under capitalism, it was the owners of the means of production who were the obvious ruling class. To-day, with active ownership converted into passive shareholding, control has passed elsewhere, and much of the traditional socialist-capitalist dispute is now irrelevant. The ownership of property is still germane, naturally, to all questions of the distribution of wealth, but (as the Nazi revolution had already shown) it is no longer true that property relationships determine the distribution of economic power.

From R. H. S. Crossman, NEW FABIAN ESSAYS (London and New York 1952), pp. 33–45, 57–68. Reprinted by permission of Phoenix House Ltd. and Frederick A. Praeger, Inc.

2] The power previously wielded by the owners of property has now largely, though not entirely, passed to the class of managers — working directors, managing directors, and the higher grades of salaried executives. The significant fact about this class is that it neither (a) itself draws its main income from property, nor (b) predominantly owns the businesses which it controls; and it is this, combined with the abdication of control by the now passive owners, which justifies one in speaking of a transfer of power from ownership to management.

This transfer of power does not, by itself, constitute the major revolution that some writers (Burnham, Drucker, et al.) have supposed. The new managers largely have the same social origins and social attitudes as the entrepreneurs whom they replace. But the curtailment in the rights of property is significant in two respects. Especially in the larger firms, there is less tenderness towards the demands of shareholders, and higher dividends are certainly not the main incentive to expansion. (This is very relevant to Government economic policy.) As a corollary, the attitude to the State is much less hostile. Co-operation comes more easily to the new managers than the old; they are, no doubt, suspicious still, but there is little of the violent hostility which would have been apparent in the vigorous days of free capitalism. Indeed, it has been a subject for comment that the removal of Government controls is often greeted with much less than unanimous enthusiasm by the industry concerned.

3] The power of the State has enormously increased, and it is now an independent intermediate power, dominating the economic life of the country. The forms that state intervention takes are primarily three: direct state operation of certain limited sectors of industry, physical controls over the remaining private sectors, and the use of budgetary policy to determine the total level of income, the distribution of that income, and (occasionally) the distribution of resources between different uses. Another essential feature of capitalism has thus disappeared — the absolute autonomy of economic life. This one change alone would justify the statement that the capitalist era has now passed into history.

4] The level of social services is now so high that our present society is often called the Welfare State. This has far-reaching consequences. It removes the insecurity which made so strongly for social discontent; it involves (since it is financed partly by high taxation of the rich) more equality than would be the case in a low-tax *laisser-faire* economy: and it makes inevitable (owing to the level of taxation involved) a high degree of governmental intervention in economic affairs.

5] The trend of employment is towards a high level, and a recurrence of chronic mass unemployment is most unlikely. The Keynesian techniques are now well understood, and there is no reason to fear a repetition of the New Deal experience of a government with the will to spend its way out of depression, but frustrated in so doing by faulty knowledge. The political pressure for full employment is stronger than ever before; the experience of the inter-war years bit so deeply into the political psychology of the nation that full employment, if threatened, would always constitute the dominant issue at any election, and no right-wing party could now survive a year in office if it permitted the figures of unemployment which were previously quite normal.

Certain characteristic features of the post-capitalist society will also help to sustain employment as compared with the position under capitalism. Generous social services and a more equal division of income will diminish the volume of savings and provide a permanent cushion of demand. The increased economic activity of the state means that over a large part of industry investment will remain steady instead of fluctuating cyclically in response to changing profit-expectations, and this in turn will exert a steadying effect on the private sector.

The strength of reforming tendencies will ensure a high level of social investment in housing, education, new towns, etc. And the needs of colonial development, combined with permanently worsened terms of trade, will make for buoyant exports in place of the chronic export-trade depression which was always dragging the economy down before the war.

It is not likely, therefore, that we shall experience in the new economy anything like the 14% average of unemployment which characterised inter-war Britain. That is not to say, of course, that every Conservative government will keep employment at the level of the last few years; such a government would have far more scruple about using the available techniques, and no doubt would be slow to do so. But it does mean that the underlying trend will be healthier than under free capitalism, and that such fluctuations as persist will take place round a much higher average level.

This is not, after all, a very surprising conclusion. Most economists would agree that an uncontrolled but highly capitalised society not only had no natural automatic tendency to rest at a full employment level, but actually had a positive bias towards instability. It was the combination of complete *laisser-faire* with consequent instability, and a very high savings ratio due to the unequal division of wealth, which led to low and fluctuating employment levels under capitalism. But in the post-capitalist society both these factors are drastically modified. The Welfare State calls for higher and more redistributive taxation, and thus increases spending at the expense of saving; while the enlarged economic activity of the state ensures a high and steady level of public or state-induced demand. *Laisser-faire* gives way to what Hansen has called the dual-production and dual-consumption economy, i.e. an economy in which both production and consumption decisions are shared between a public and a private sector. Such an economy is far more likely to give rise to chronic inflation than chronic deflation.

6] The trend of production, and therefore of the standard of living, is strongly upward. Previous sections have made it clear that even the depressions of free capitalism were not sufficient to arrest the continued rise in real income. There is still less reason to expect it to be arrested in the post-capitalist world: indeed, the opposite is much more likely. Economic depression of the inter-war kind, even though impotent to counteract entirely the forces making for expansion, quite certainly damps down the rate of expansion. Because profit-expectations are low, the level of capital expenditure is also low, and productivity rises less than it otherwise would. Both sides of industry, in a search for security and a reaction against the cut-throat competition which depression initially breeds, take eagerly to restrictive practices, and cartel arrangements flourish.

But under a high level of employment, investment is held high, and restrictive practices decline as they become less necessary; moreover, as labour is both scarce and dear, more economical methods of production are encouraged. Certainly the once popular view that full employment, though obviously desirable on short-term welfare grounds, might exact a high price in the long run through its effects on incentives, finds no support from the productivity figures in post-war Britain. It is falling markets which encourage restrictionism and go-slow, while high demand and buoyant markets induce an atmosphere more favourable to innovation and expansion. Under the higher employment provided by the mixed economy it will be surprising if the national income does not rise annually by more than the 1½% which was the norm before the war.

7] The class structure of society is more than ever variegated, and the classical outlines characteristic of early capitalism give way to a baroque profusion of detail. The (to Marx very unexpected) rise of the technical and professional middle class is largely responsible. This is likely to continue. Increased mechanisation constantly reduces the size of the strict factory working class; a higher standard of life creates a continuously-increasing demand for services as opposed to goods; and in any case middle-class psychology and standards are steadily spreading far outside the bounds of that class itself. Thus a vast amorphous cushion of intermediate classes is interposed between the top and bottom strata, and softens the struggle between them.

8] Ideologically, the dominant emphasis ceases to be on the rights of property, private initiative, competition, and the profit-motive; and is transferred to the duties of the state, social and economic security, and the virtues of co-operative action.

It can readily be seen from this list of features that the new society is quite different in kind from the capitalism which it succeeds — and also that it is very similar to post-war British or Scandinavian society after several years of Labour government. Even in pre-war Britain the transformation had begun, and right-wing governments could only delay and not resist it altogether. Under the post-war Labour administration the tempo of change was enormously accelerated, and by 1951 Britain had, in all the essentials, ceased to be a capitalist country. In Sweden also the change was virtually complete.

What should the new society be called? All manner of names suggest themselves or are suggested: the Welfare State, the Mixed Economy, the Managerial State, Progressive Capitalism, Fair Deal-ism, State Capitalism, the First Stage of Socialism, the New Society being born in the Womb of the Old, and so on to the limits of one's verbal imagination. Differences of opinion about the right nomen-clature will partly reflect merely ideological differences; because different people want to see in the new society a likeness to the system they themselves support (whether socialism or capitalism), they choose a name which is from this point of view persuasive.

But there is a genuine difficulty about classifying this form of society because it is so essentially a mixed one so far as the traditional categories are concerned. It is capitalist to the extent that private ownership of industry predominates, that most production is for the market, and that many of the old class divisions persist. It is non-capitalist to the extent that market influences are subordinated to central planning, not over the whole detailed field of labour and production, but in certain strategically decisive sectors; that the power of the state is much greater than that of any one particular class; and that the distribution of the national income is consciously a matter of political decision and not the automatic consequence of market forces. It is managerial to the extent that the control of industry has largely passed (subject to state controls) into the hands of the managerial class, which has usurped the position of the old capitalist class. It is socialist in that the distribution of income is far more egalitarian, that much economic power and parts of industry are socialised, that a national minimum and a welfare cushion exist, and that planning is largely directed to traditional socialist ends. It is, in fact, economically and socially, a pluralist society.

For all these difficulties, some name must be found, and the best that I can suggest is Statism. The name is ugly, and has too unfavourable a ring. But the most fundamental change from capitalism is the change from *laisser-faire* to state control, and it is as well to have a name which spotlights this crucial change.

Statism, then, is the form of society which, in Britain at least, is in process of succeeding to capitalism. It represents, without doubt, an impressive advance as judged by Socialist standards. Its more effective control over the level of employment, and the consequent gain in stability and output, make it if not immune from, at least much less vulnerable to, the strains and stresses inherent in any industrial society. The higher employment, generous social services, less flagrant inequalities of wealth and opportunity — in all these ways the new society is infinitely more humane and decent than the old. Most of the unbearable social tensions which afflicted capitalism will have disappeared; there will be no repetition of Jarrow and Ebbw Vale, dole queues and hunger-marches, to inspire violent feelings and actions in the working class, whose relative gains are, indeed, significantly large. Both the area, and the bitterness, of social conflict are much reduced.

An additional reason for expecting greater social peace is that power in the new society will be very widely diffused. Economic power, in the Marxist sense of control over the means of production, is distributed amongst the old capitalists (in smaller-scale industry), the new managers, the State machine, the shareholders, the executives of the public boards, and (very important) the organized workers (especially with the inevitable trend towards more workers' control in industry). With this dispersion of control, no one class can lever itself, as the capitalist class for so long did, into a dominantly possessive relationship to the means of production.

The corollary of this in the social field is that in contrast to the classical Marxist picture of two tightly-knit homogeneous social classes ranged clearly against each other, we find a very complicated class structure with an increasing proliferation of middle groups. And since political power also will be evenly balanced, and alternate between left and right, there will, in my view, be no uniquely delineated ruling class, nor clearly defined class struggle. Given this equilibrium in the balance of forces, the less violent pressure for change, and the reversion, after a brief abnormal spell of *laisser-faire,* to the normal historical pattern (both in the ancient and the modern world) of conscious control over social and economic life, the new society may prove to be a very enduring one.

*   *   *

But none of these issues is fundamental to the long-term question, or gives any guidance as to how far and in what direction socialists should wish to advance beyond the present achievement.

The answer clearly depends on how socialism is defined. One now popular type of definition provides an immediate answer. A representative example — though there are many others — is the Frankfurt declaration of the reborn Socialist International in 1951, in which (after a preamble, so vague as to be almost meaningless, about an end to 'the exploitation of man by man') the whole emphasis is placed on democratic planning, which is regarded as the basic condition of socialism. Now what is significant about this declaration is that socialism, as here defined, already largely obtains under statism. The worker can no longer be said to be exploited, and the declared objects of planning (defined in the manifesto as 'full employment, higher production, a rising standard of life, social security and a fair distribution of income and property') are (at least if one omits the one word 'property') in process of achievement. The name may still be Socialism, but the features look uncommonly like those of the Welfare State.

This type of definition represents a natural enough tendency. The planned full-employment Welfare State is the outcome of the first successful spells of majority Labour government anywhere, and it is tempting to assume that its achievement must constitute the final goal for socialists everywhere. It is, all are agreed, a great advance on pre-war capitalism, and to socialist parties which have never been in power it seems to promise gains of overwhelming significance when measured against conditions in their own countries. And at least such definitions represent a welcome advance in realism when compared with the chosen phrases from Marx or Kautsky which have so far served to define the goals of socialist action.

But to accept this approach involves maintaining that socialism was to all intents and purposes achieved (apart from certain temporary difficulties connected with rearmament) in the Britain of 1951 — or at least that it would have been achieved after a few more years of progress along the same lines. There are those on the right of the Party (and in Scandinavia also) who would maintain precisely this, especially amongst the many liberal-minded people who joined the Party in horror at the unemployment and industrial poverty of the nineteen-thirties. The Labour Party would then become essentially a party for the defence of the 1951 position, with perhaps a few more minor reforms thrown in to sweeten the temper of the rank and file.

Nobody can argue that such an attitude is *wrong*, since it is based on a normative judgment, and is therefore not open to logical disproof. But it is safe to say that it does not represent the view of the majority of socialists, and, since it does not concur with my own view either, I shall assume that socialism still means a society different in kind, not only from capitalism, but also from the statism of 1951.

I shall rule two definitions out as commanding no support — the Marxist 'nationalisation of the means of production, distribution and exchange,' and the early Fabian emphasis on collectivism — and shall choose, as probably the highest common factor of agreement, a definition by Professor Cole in 1935:

> By socialism I mean a form of society in which men and women are not divided into opposing economic classes, but live

together under conditions of approximate social and economic equality, using in common the means that lie to their hands of promoting social welfare.

And two of the riders which Professor Cole added were:

a human fellowship which denies and expels distinctions of class, and a social system in which no one is so much richer or poorer than his neighbours as to be unable to mix with them on equal terms.

Not all the phrases in this passage are entirely unambiguous, but the general emphasis is clear — it is on the 'classless society.' As Professor Arthur Lewis has put it succinctly, 'Socialism is about equality.' And by equality is meant not simply equality of opportunity on the American model, but equality of status in the widest sense — subjective as well as objective.

Once accept this definition, and the differences between statism and socialism come sharply into focus. It is true that in the Britain of 1951 great strides towards equality had been made. Current incomes had been equalised to a quite remarkable extent, and opportunities also were more equal. But Britain still did not begin to approach the ideal of a classless or egalitarian society. For all the redistribution of taxable income, there was still too great a spread in actual standards of life. The equalising intentions of fiscal policy could still be frustrated either by spending out of capital or by recourse to expense accounts, and they were widely frustrated in this way. The gap between the mode of life of the factory worker and of the regular *habitué* of the Four Hundred could scarcely be justified by socialist standards.

Much also remained to be done to equalise opportunities for entry to the professions and promotion in industry, and certainly no one could call Britain a society in which all had an equal chance.

But perhaps even more disturbing than this residue of objectively measurable social inequality was the persistence of a deep-seated *sense* of an unequal society. How deep this goes in Britain can be seen by a comparison with other countries whose actual degree of achieved equality is no greater (or is even less) than our own, but whose consciousness of equality and social solidarity is infinitely larger. To take two very different examples, both Sweden and the U.S.A. offer highly pertinent and disturbing comparisons in this respect.

Class feeling, and general social *malaise,* still persist in England to a deplorable extent. The feeling among workers of an eternal and irreconcilable conflict between wages and profits, capital and labour: their feeling too of non-participation in the control of the firm for which they work, and so of non-responsibility for its well-being: the acute sense of class that goes with different accents: the knowledge that differentials in education mean differentials in opportunity — these are all signs that Britain still is, and feels itself to be, a class society.

The purpose of socialism is quite simply to eradicate this sense of class, and to create in its place a sense of common interest and equal status. This will require not only more measures on the economic plane, directed to the greater equalisation of living standards and opportunities, but also measures on the socio-psychological plane. It is here that the essential difference between statism and socialism lies, and it is in this direction that socialists must look for the main advance.

*   *   *

First, the ownership of wealth. The still gross maldistribution of property enables the upper classes, by spending out of capital, to live at a standard of luxury which their post-tax income would never alone permit. The degree of actual social inequality is thus much greater than the inequality of incomes, with corresponding results in respect of opportunity.

Secondly, the educational system. Nothing more amazes visitors from genuinely egalitarian countries (such as Sweden or New Zealand) than the existence in Britain of a social hierarchy of schools. Probably no other single factor is so influential in the propagation of class feeling.

Thirdly, the sphere of industry, whose right organisation constitutes the central problem of our time.

The crucial problem here is not that of social control. Those controls which are needed for planning purposes, and to correct the obvious deficiencies of a free price-mechanism, were already largely established under Labour rule (although they may require resuscitation after periods of Tory decontrol).

Nor is it the problem of consumer control, of ensuring that those goods are produced which the consumer most wants. This is a problem of creating sufficiently lively competition in the private sector;

and in the nationalised sector of operating the correct price-rules under Ministerial and consumer council supervision.

Nor again is it mainly a problem of the distribution of the product. It is argued that shareholders, as the residuary legatees in industry, continuously earn a larger reward than is justified by the degree of risk involved. This may be so, but at present levels of taxation the point is not quantitatively important. The magnitudes involved are not such that great riches would accrue to the mass of the population from any reform, and the importance of this point lies really in the psychological field, and merges into the next question to be considered.

The crucial problem is the psychology of industrial relations, and the general tone and atmosphere in industry. Statism has provided negative economic satisfactions of the highest importance — full employment, high wages, security — and it has also strengthened the worker's bargaining position against his employer. But it has not given him a new social status, nor cured the basic class hostility which stems from his total exclusion from either rights or participation. Sole rights still belong to the functionless shareholder, and this knowledge still breeds frustration and annoyance among the workers.

Socialism requires that this hostility in industry should give way to a feeling of participation in a joint endeavour. How is this to be achieved? The most direct and easily exploitable line of advance is in the direction of joint consultation. Much fruitful work has been done in this sphere, and it is now clear that something more is needed than joint production committees on the present model — some more radical effort to give the worker a sense of participation in the making of decisions. A few progressive firms have already made bold advances, and the results are encouraging.

But this may not be enough as long as the workers know that the shareholders alone, though passive and (in the large firms) bearing little risk, have the only legal claim on a product which is jointly due to workers, managers and capital. Indeed, the legal framework of industry, considered logically or morally, is farcical in the contrast it presents between the sole ownership and rights of shareholders, and the essentially co-operative nature of the operations. If hostility to profits and dividends is not to bedevil industrial relations for all time, some resolution of this conflict must be found.

This question can only be solved by very radical measures of which three suggest themselves. The first would be a large-scale extension of nationalisation. This eliminates the control of private owners, and reduces the return on capital to a fixed interest payment. Over the long run it must certainly be part of the answer — not so much for the traditional reasons (to facilitate planning, deal with monopolies, increase efficiency, etc.) — as in order gradually to substitute public rights for shareholders' rights, with beneficial effects both on the distribution of income and the psychology of industrial relations. But it would be foolish to pretend that this can provide a rapid solution while so many unsolved problems remain in the existing nationalised industries.

A second approach would be by statutory dividend limitation, not in the form of a rigid dividend 'freeze,' but in some more flexible form (such as restricting dividends to a permitted percentage of total earnings, with exceptions for new or small businesses). This deserves much hard thought. Norwegian experience shows that it would not have the disastrous effects on enterprise that are sometimes prophesied, and it might play an important part in making a wages policy practicable. It would need to be accompanied by a new policy for undistributed profits. Since there would always be the chance of a Tory reaction, the large accumulation of company reserves might lead to a constant appreciation of share-values, which would partially frustrate the object of the scheme. Consideration must be given to the possibility of altering the legal ownership of company reserves, perhaps by the compulsory payment of bonus issues to the workers in the industry. A third possibility is so to alter the legal structure of company ownership as to substitute for shareholders' sole control a constitution which explicitly defines the responsibilities of the firm to worker, consumer and community; workers would become members of the company, and have their representatives on the board of directors.

I do not pretend to know which of these lines of attack will turn out to be the right one. Far more thought and study is required. But I am certain that some unorthodox and revolutionary scheme is needed, even though its exact nature is not yet clear, if the workers — and they are the majority of the population — are to have a sense of partnership in, and responsibility for, the industry in which they work. And without this sense we shall remain a class society for all time.

Even a bare recital of these desiderata of socialism is enough to show what a long revolution still lies ahead. Statism cured the worst social evils of the previous society, but its achievement was in a sense a negative one, confined to the elimination of abuses. It still remains to create the new society of which socialists have always dreamed, a society which is not bedevilled by the consciousness of class.

No one should think that this will be a short or an easy task. The easy and spectacular things have all been done, those that remain will need a prolonged and difficult effort of will. The pace will be limited, not only by the need to preserve the necessary minimum of social peace and cohesion, but also by the difficulty of engendering enthusiasm for further change in a population largely employed and enjoying rising standards every year. There will be no revival of the angry dynamic of revolt against the obvious miseries and injustices of capitalism. The temper of the people will be more contented and therefore more conservative, and public opinion will take time to acclimatise itself to the prospect of each further radical advance. These difficulties make it the more urgent that we should have a clear vision of where we want, as socialists, to go.

12

In Defense of Individualism

OPPONENTS of socialism not only doubt the compatibility of a socialist economic system and political and civil freedom, but also deny the feasibility of economic planning. One of the most influential representatives of this point of view is Friedrich A. Hayek. Born in Vienna in 1899, Hayek first studied natural sciences and law, but later turned his attention to economics. His principal works, written while he was a Professor at the London School of Economics, concern problems of trade and exchange and those relating to socialism and planning. In 1950 he joined the faculty of the University of Chicago. Among his works on socialism are Individualism and Economic Order, Collectivist Economic Planning (with Ludwig von Mises, Enrico Baron, and others), Capitalism and the Historians, The Constitution of Liberty, and The Road to Serfdom.

Friedrich A. Hayek, The Road to Serfdom

Planning and democracy]

The statesman who should attempt to direct private people in what manner they ought to employ their capitals, would not only load himself with a most unnecessary attention, but assume an authority which could safely be trusted to no council and senate whatever, and which would nowhere be so dangerous as in the hands of a man who had folly and presumption enough to fancy himself fit to exercise it. — ADAM SMITH.

THE COMMON features of all collectivist systems may be described, in a phrase ever dear to socialists of all schools, as the deliberate organization of the labors of society for a definite social goal. That our present society lacks such "conscious" direction

From Friedrich A. Hayek, THE ROAD TO SERFDOM (Chicago, 1944), pp. 56–71, 119–133. Copyright © 1944 by The University of Chicago Press.

toward a single aim, that its activities are guided by the whims and fancies of irresponsible individuals, has always been one of the main complaints of its socialist critics.

In many ways this puts the basic issue very clearly. And it directs us at once to the point where the conflict arises between individual freedom and collectivism. The various kinds of collectivism, communism, fascism, etc., differ among themselves in the nature of the goal toward which they want to direct the efforts of society. But they all differ from liberalism and individualism in wanting to organize the whole of society and all its resources for this unitary end and in refusing to recognize autonomous spheres in which the ends of the individuals are supreme. In short, they are totalitarian in the true sense of this new word which we have adopted to describe the unexpected but nevertheless inseparable manifestations of what in theory we call collectivism.

The "social goal," or "common purpose," for which society is to be organized is usually vaguely described as the "common good," the "general welfare," or the "general interest." It does not need much reflection to see that these terms have no sufficiently definite meaning to determine a particular course of action. The welfare and the happiness of millions cannot be measured on a single scale of less and more. The welfare of a people, like the happiness of a man, depends on a great many things that can be provided in an infinite variety of combinations. It cannot be adequately expressed as a single end, but only as a hierarchy of ends, a comprehensive scale of values in which every need of every person is given its place. To direct all our activities according to a single plan presupposes that every one of our needs is given its rank in an order of values which must be complete enough to make it possible to decide among all the different courses which the planner has to choose. It presupposes, in short, the existence of a complete ethical code in which all the different human values are allotted their due place.

The conception of a complete ethical code in unfamiliar, and it requires some effort of imagination to see what it involves. We are not in the habit of thinking of moral codes as more or less complete. The fact that we are constantly choosing between different values without a social code prescribing how we ought to choose does not surprise us and does not suggest to us that our moral code is incomplete. In our society there is neither occasion nor reason why people should develop common views about what should be done in such situations. But where all the means to be used are the property of society and are to be used in the name of society according to a unitary plan, a "social" view about what ought to be done must guide all decisions. In such a world we should soon find that our moral code is full of gaps.

We are not concerned here with the question whether it would be desirable to have such a complete ethical code. It may merely be pointed out that up to the present the growth of civilization has been accompanied by a steady diminution of the sphere in which individual actions are bound by fixed rules. The rules of which our common moral code consists have progressively become fewer and more general in character. From the primitive man, who was bound by an elaborate ritual in almost every one of his daily activities, who was limited by innumerable taboos, and who could scarcely conceive of doing things in a way different from his fellows, morals have more and more tended to become merely limits circumscribing the sphere within which the individual could behave as he liked. The adoption of a common ethical code comprehensive enough to determine a unitary economic plan would mean a complete reversal of this tendency.

The essential point for us is that no such complete ethical code exists. The attempt to direct all economic activity according to a single plan would raise innumerable questions to which the answer could be provided only by a moral rule, but to which existing morals have no answer and where there exists no agreed view on what ought to be done. People will have either no definite views or conflicting views on such questions, because in the free society in which we have lived there has been no occasion to think about them and still less to form common opinions about them.

Not only do we not possess such an all-inclusive scale of values: it would be impossible for any mind to comprehend the infinite variety of different needs of different people which compete for the available resources and to attach a definite weight to each. For our problem it is of minor importance whether the ends for which any person cares comprehend only his own individual needs, or whether they include the needs of his closer or even those of his more distant fellows — that is, whether he is egoistic or altruistic in the ordinary senses of these words. The point which is so important is the basic fact that it is impossible for any man to survey more than a limited field, to be aware of the urgency of more than a limited number of needs. Whether his interests center round his own physical needs, or whether he takes a warm interest in the welfare of every human being he knows, the ends about which he can be concerned will always be only an infinitesimal fraction of the needs of all men.

This is the fundamental fact on which the whole philosophy of individualism is based. It does not assume, as is often asserted, that man is egoistic or selfish or ought to be. It merely starts from the indisputable fact that the limits of our powers of imagination make it impossible to include in our scale of values more than a sector of the needs of the whole society, and that, since, strictly speaking, scales of value can exist only in individual minds, nothing but partial scales of values exist — scales which are inevitably different and often inconsistent with each other. From this the individualist concludes that the individuals should be allowed, within defined limits, to follow their own values and preferences rather than somebody else's; that within these spheres the individual's system of ends should be supreme and not subject to any dictation by others. It is this recognition of the individual as the ultimate judge of his ends, the belief that as far as possible his own views ought to govern his actions, that forms the essence of the individualist position.

This view does not, of course, exclude the recognition of social ends, or rather of a coincidence of individual ends which makes it advisable for men to combine for their pursuit. But it limits such common action to the instances where individual views coincide; what are called "social ends" are for it merely identical ends of many individuals — or ends to the achievement of which individuals are willing to contribute in return for the assistance they receive in the satisfaction of their own desires. Common action is thus limited to the fields where people agree on common ends. Very frequently these common ends will not be ultimate ends to the individuals but means which different persons can use for different purposes. In fact, people are most likely to agree on common action where the common end is not an ultimate end to them but a means capable of serving a great variety of purposes.

When individuals combine in a joint effort to realize ends they have in common, the organizations, like the state, that they form for this purpose are given their own system of ends and their own means. But any organization thus formed remains one "person" among others, in the case of the state much more powerful than any of the others, it is true, yet still with its separate and limited sphere in which alone its ends are supreme. The limits of this sphere are determined by the extent to which the individuals agree on particular ends; and the probability that they will agree on a particular course of action necessarily decreases as the scope of such action extends. There are certain functions of the state on the exercise of which there will be practical unanimity among its citizens; there will be others on which there will be agreement of a substantial majority; and so on, until we come to fields where, although each individual might wish the state to act in some way, there will be almost as many views about what the government should do as there are different people.

We can rely on voluntary agreement to guide the action of the state only so long as it is confined to spheres where agreement exists. But not only when the state undertakes direct control in fields where there is no such agreement is it bound to suppress individual freedom. We can unfortunately not indefinitely extend the sphere of common action and still leave the individual free in his own sphere. Once the communal sector, in which the state controls all the means, exceeds a certain proportion of the whole, the effects of its actions dominate the whole system. Although the state controls directly the use of only a large part of the available resources, the effects of its decisions on the remaining part of the economic system become so great that indirectly it controls almost everything. Where, as was, for example, true in Germany as early as 1928, the central and local authorities directly control the use of more than half the national income (according to an official German estimate then, 53 per cent), they control indirectly almost the whole economic life of the nation. There is, then, scarcely an individual end which is not dependent for its achievement on the action of the state, and the "social scale of values" which guides the state's action must embrace practically all individual ends.

*   *   *

Security and freedom]

The whole of society will have become a single office and a single factory with equality of work and equality of pay. — NIKOLAI LENIN (1917).

In a country where the sole employer is the State, opposition means death by slow starvation. The old principle: who does not work shall not

eat, has been replaced by a new one: who does not obey shall not eat.
—LEON TROTSKY (1937).

Like the spurious "economic freedom," and with more justice, economic security is often represented as an indispensable condition of real liberty. In a sense this is both true and important. Independence of mind or strength of character is rarely found among those who cannot be confident that they will make their way by their own effort. Yet the idea of economic security is no less vague and ambiguous than most other terms in this field; and because of this the general approval given to the demand for security may become a danger to liberty. Indeed, when security is understood in too absolute a sense, the general striving for it, far from increasing the chances of freedom, becomes the gravest threat to it.

It will be well to contrast at the outset the two kinds of security: the limited one, which can be achieved for all, and which is therefore no privilege but a legitimate object of desire; and absolute security, which in a free society cannot be achieved for all and which ought not to be given as a privilege — except in a few special instances such as that of the judges, whose complete independence is of paramount importance. These two kinds of security are, first, security against severe physical privation, the certainty of a given minimum of sustenance for all; and, second, the security of a given standard of life, or of the relative position which one person or group enjoys compared with others; or, as we may put it briefly, the security of a minimum income and the security of the particular income a person is thought to deserve. We shall presently see that this distinction largely coincides with the distinction between the security which can be provided for all outside of and supplementary to the market system and the security which can be provided only for some and only by controlling or abolishing the market.

There is no reason why in a society which has reached the general level of wealth which ours has attained the first kind of security should not be guaranteed to all without endangering general freedom. There are difficult questions about the precise standard which should thus be assured; there is particularly the important question whether those who thus rely on the community should indefinitely enjoy all the same liberties as the rest.[1] An incautious handling of these questions might well cause serious and perhaps even dangerous political problems; but there can be no doubt that some minimum of food, shelter, and clothing, sufficient to preserve health and the capacity to work, can be assured to everybody. Indeed, for a considerable part of the population of England this sort of security has long been achieved.

Nor is there any reason why the state should not assist the individuals in providing for those common hazards of life against which, because of their uncertainty, few individuals can make adequate provision. Where, as in the case of sickness and accident, neither the desire to avoid such calamities nor the efforts to overcome their consequences are as a rule weakened by the provision of assistance — where, in short, we deal with genuinely insurable risks — the case for the state's helping to organize a comprehensive system of social insurance is very strong. There are many points of detail where those wishing to preserve the competitive system and those wishing to supersede it by something different will disagree on the details of such schemes; and it is possible under the name of social insurance to introduce measures which tend to make competition more or less ineffective. But there is no incompatibility in principle between the state's providing greater security in this way and the preservation of individual freedom. To the same category belongs also the increase of security through the state's rendering assistance to the victims of such "acts of God" as earthquakes and floods. Wherever communal action can mitigate disasters against which the individual can neither attempt to guard himself nor make provision for the consequences, such communal action should undoubtedly be taken.

There is, finally, the supremely important problem of combating general fluctuations of economic activity and the recurrent waves of large-scale unemployment which accompany them. This is, of course, one of the gravest and most pressing problems of our time. But, though its solution will require much planning in the good sense, it does not — or at least need not — require that special kind of planning which according to its advocates is to replace the market. Many economists hope, indeed, that the ultimate remedy may be found in the field of monetary policy, which would involve nothing incompatible even with nineteenth-century liberalism. Others, it is true, believe that real success can be expected only from the skilful timing of public works undertaken on a very large scale. This might lead to much more serious restrictions of the competitive sphere, and, in experimenting in this direction, we shall have carefully to watch our step if we are to avoid making all economic activity progressively more dependent on the direction and volume of government expenditure. But this is neither the only nor, in my opinion, the most promising way of meeting the gravest threat to economic security. In any case, the very necessary efforts to secure protection against these fluctuations do not lead to the kind of planning which constitutes such a threat to our freedom.

The planning for security which has such an insidious effect on liberty is that for security of a different kind. It is planning designed to protect individuals or groups against diminutions of their income, which although in no way deserved yet in a competitive society occur daily, against losses imposing severe hardships having no moral justification yet inseparable from the competitive system. This demand for security is thus another form of the demand for a just remuneration — a remuneration commensurate with the subjective merits and not with the objective results of a man's efforts. This kind of security or justice seems irreconcilable with freedom to choose one's employment.

In any system which for the distribution of men between the different trades and occupations relies on their own choice it is necessary that the remuneration in these trades should correspond to their usefulness to the other members of society, even if this should stand in no relation to subjective merit. Although the results achieved will often be commensurate with efforts and intentions, this cannot always be true in any form of society. It will particularly not be true in the many instances where the usefulness of some trade or special skill is changed by circumstances which could not be foreseen. We all know the tragic plight of the highly trained man whose hard-learned skill has suddenly lost its value because of some invention which greatly benefits the rest of society. The history of the last hundred years is full of instances of this kind, some of them affecting hundreds of thousands of people at a time.

That anyone should suffer a great diminution of his income and bitter disappointment of all his hopes through no fault of his own, and despite hard work and exceptional skill, undoubtedly offends our sense of justice. The demands of those who suffer in this way, for state interference on their behalf to safeguard their legitimate expectations, are certain to receive popular sympathy and support. The general approval of these demands has had the effect that governments everywhere have taken action, not merely to protect the people so threatened from severe hardship and privation, but to

secure to them the continued receipt of their former income and to
shelter them from the vicissitudes of the market.[2]

Certainty of a given income can, however, not be given to all if
any freedom in the choice of one's occupation is to be allowed. And,
if it is provided for some, it becomes a privilege at the expense of
others whose security is thereby necessarily diminished. That security
of an invariable income can be provided for all only by the abolition
of all freedom in the choice of one's employment is easily shown.
Yet, although such a general guaranty of legitimate expectation is
often regarded as the ideal to be aimed at, it is not a thing which
is seriously attempted. What is constantly being done is to grant this
kind of security piecemeal, to this group and to that, with the result
that for those who are left out in the cold the insecurity constantly
increases. No wonder that in consequence the value attached to the
privilege of security constantly increases, the demand for it becomes
more and more urgent, until in the end no price, not even that of
liberty, appears too high.

If those who usefulness is reduced by circumstances which they
could neither foresee nor control were to be protected against unde-
served loss, and those whose usefulness has been increased in the
same way were prevented from making an unmerited gain, remuneration would soon cease to have any relation to actual usefulness. It
would depend on the views held by some authority about what a
person ought to have done, what he ought to have foreseen, and how
good or bad his intentions were. Such decisions could not but be to
a large extent arbitrary. The application of this principle would
necessarily bring it about that people doing the same work would
receive different remuneration. The differences in remuneration
would then no longer present an adequate inducement to people to
make the changes which are socially desirable, and it would not even
be possible for the individuals affected to judge whether a particular
change is worth the trouble it causes.

But if the changes in the distribution of men between different
employments, which are constantly necessary in any society, can no
longer be brought about by pecuniary "rewards" and "penalties"
(which have no necessary connection with subjective merit), they
must be brought about by direct orders. When a person's income is
guaranteed, he can neither be allowed to stay in his job merely because he likes it nor to choose what other work he would like to do.
As it is not he who makes the gain or suffers the loss dependent on

his moving or not moving, the choice must be made for him by those who control the distribution of the available income.

The problem of adequate incentives which arises here is commonly discussed as if it were a problem mainly of the willingness of people to do their best. But this, although important, is not the whole, nor even the most important, aspect of the problem. It is not merely that if we want people to give their best we must make it worth while for them. What is more important is that if we want to leave them the choice, if they are to be able to judge what they ought to do, they must be given some readily intelligible yardstick by which to measure the social importance of the different occupations. Even with the best will in the world it would be impossible for anyone intelligently to choose between various alternatives if the advantages they offered him stood in no relation to their usefulness to society. To know whether as the result of a change a man ought to leave a trade and an environment which he has come to like, and exchange it for another, it is necessary that the changed relative value of these occupations to society should find expression in the remunerations they offer.

The problem is, of course, even more important because in the world as it is men are, in fact, not likely to give their best for long periods unless their own interests are directly involved. At least for great numbers some external pressure is needed if they are to give their best. The problem of incentives in this sense is a very real one, both in the sphere of ordinary labor and in those of the managerial activities. The application of the engineering technique to a whole nation — and this is what planning means — "raises problems of discipline which are hard to solve," as has been well described by an American engineer with great experience in government planning, who has clearly seen the problem.

"In order to do an engineering job," he explains, "there ought to be surrounding the work a comparatively large area of unplanned economic action. There should be a place from which workers can be drawn, and when a worker is fired he should vanish from the job and from the pay-roll. In the absence of such a free reservoir discipline cannot be maintained without corporal punishment, as with slave labor.[3]

In the sphere of executive work the problem of sanctions for negligence arises in a different but no less serious form. It has been well said that, while the last resort of a competitive economy is the bailiff, the ultimate sanction of a planned economy is the hangman.[4] The powers the manager of any plant will have to be given will still be considerable. But no more than in the case of the worker can the manager's position and income in a planned system be made to depend merely on the success or failure of the work under his direction. As neither the risk nor the gain is his, it cannot be his personal judgment, but whether he does what he ought to have done according to some established rule, which must decide. A mistake he "ought" to have avoided is not his own affair; it is a crime against the community and must be treated as such. While so long as he keeps to the safe path of objectively ascertainable duty he may be surer of his income than the capitalist entrepreneur, the danger which threatens him in case of real failure is worse than bankruptcy. He may be economically secure so long as he satisfies his superiors, but this security is bought at the price of the safety of freedom and life.

The conflict with which we have to deal is, indeed, a quite fundamental one between two irreconcilable types of social organization, which, from the most characteristic forms in which they appear, have often been described as the commercial and the military type of society. The terms were, perhaps, unfortunate, because they direct attention to unessentials and make it difficult to see that we face a real alternative and that there is no third possibility. Either both the choice and the risk rest with the individual or he is relieved of both. The army does, indeed, in many ways represent the closest approach familiar to us to the second type of organization, where work and worker alike are allotted by authority and where, if the available means are scanty, everybody is alike put on short-commons. This is the only system in which the individual can be conceded full economic security and through the extension of which to the whole of society it can be achieved for all its members. This security is, however, inseparable from the restrictions on liberty and the hierarchical order of military life — it is the security of the barracks.

It is possible, of course, to organize sections of an otherwise free society on this principle, and there is no reason why this form of life, with its necessary restrictions on individual liberty, should not be open to those who prefer it. Indeed, some voluntary labor service on military lines might well be the best form for the state to provide the certainty of an opportunity for work and a minimum income for all. That proposals of this sort have in the past proved so little acceptable is due to the fact that those who are willing to surrender their freedom for security have always demanded that if they give up their full freedom it should also be taken from those not prepared to do so. For this claim it is difficult to find a justification.

The military type of organization as we know it gives us, however, only a very inadequate picture of what it would be like if it were extended to the whole of society. So long as only a part of society is organized on military lines, the unfreedom of the members of the military organization is mitigated by the fact that there is still a free sphere to which they can move if the restrictions become too irksome. If we want to form a picture of what society would be like if, according to the ideal which has seduced so many socialists, it was organized as a single great factory, we have to look to ancient Sparta, or to contemporary Germany, which, after moving for two or three generations in this direction, has now so nearly reached it.

In a society used to freedom it is unlikely that many people would be ready deliberately to purchase security at this price. But the policies which are now followed everywhere, which hand out the privilege of security, now to this group and now to that, are nevertheless rapidly creating conditions in which the striving for security tends to become stronger than the love of freedom. The reason for this is that with every grant of complete security to one group the insecurity of the rest necessarily increases. If you guarantee to some a fixed part of a variable cake, the share left to the rest is bound to fluctuate proportionally more than the size of the whole. And the essential element of security which the competitive system offers, the great variety of opportunities, is more and more reduced.

Within the market system, security can be granted to particular groups only by the kind of planning known as restrictionism (which includes, however, almost all the planning which is actually practiced!). "Control," i.e., limitation of output so that prices will secure an "adequate" return, is the only way in which in a market economy producers can be guaranteed a certain income. But this necessarily involves a reduction of opportunities open to others. If the producer, be he entrepreneur or worker, is to be protected against underbidding by outsiders, it means that others who are worse off are precluded from sharing in the relatively greater prosperity of the controlled industries. Every restriction on the freedom of entry into a trade reduces the security of all those outside it. And, as the number of those whose income is secured in this manner increases, the field of alternative opportunities which are open to anyone who suffers a loss of income is restricted; and for those unfavorably affected by any change the chance of avoiding a fatal diminution of their income is correspondingly diminished. And if, as has become increasingly true, in each trade in which conditions improve, the members are allowed to exclude others in order to secure to themselves the full gain in the form of higher wages or profits, those in the trades where demand has fallen have nowhere to go, and every change becomes the cause of large unemployment. There can be little doubt that it is largely a consequence of the striving for security by these means in the last decades that unemployment and thus insecurity for large sections of the population has so much increased.

In England and America such restrictions, especially those affecting the intermediate strata of society, have assumed important dimensions only in comparatively recent times, and we have scarcely yet realized their full consequences. The utter hopelessness of the position of those who, in a society which has thus grown rigid, are left outside the range of sheltered occupation, and the magnitude of the gulf which separates them from the fortunate possessors of jobs for whom protection against competition has made it unnecessary to budge ever so little to make room for those without, can be appreciated only by those who have experienced it. It is not a question of the fortunate ones' giving up their places, but merely that they should share in the common misfortune by some reduction of their incomes, or frequently even merely by some sacrifice of their prospects of improvement. The protection of their "standard of life," of the "fair price," or the "professional income" to which they regard themselves as entitled, and in the protection of which they receive the support of the state, precludes this. In consequence, instead of prices, wages, and individual incomes, it is now employment and production which have become subject to violent fluctuations. There has never been a worse and more cruel exploitation of one class by another than that of the weaker or less fortunate members of a group of producers by the well-established which has been made possible by the "regulation" of competition. Few catchwords have done so much harm as the ideal of a "stabilization" of particular prices (or wages), which, while securing the income of some, makes the position of the rest more and more precarious.

Thus, the more we try to provide full security by interfering with the market system, the greater the insecurity becomes; and, what is worse, the greater becomes the contrast between the security of those to whom it is granted as a privilege and the ever increasing insecurity of the underprivileged. And the more security becomes a privilege, and the greater the danger to those excluded from it, the higher will security be prized. As the number of the privileged increases and the difference between their security and the insecurity of the others increases, a completely new set of social values gradually arises. It is no longer independence but security which gives rank and status, the certain right to a pension more than confidence in his making good which makes a young man eligible for marriage, while insecurity becomes the dreaded state of the pariah in which those who in their youth have been refused admission to the haven of a salaried position remain for life.

The general endeavor to achieve security by restrictive measures, tolerated or supported by the state, has in the course of time produced a progressive transformation of society — a transformation in which, as in so many other ways, Germany has led and the other countries have followed. This development has been hastened by another effect of socialist teaching, the deliberate disparagement of all activities involving economic risk and the moral opporbrium cast on the gains which make risks worth taking but which only few can win. We cannot blame our young men when they prefer the safe, salaried position to the risk of enterprise after they have heard from their earliest youth the former described as the superior, more unselfish and disinterested occupation. The younger generation of today has grown up in a world in which in school and press the spirit of commercial enterprise has been represented as disreputable and the making of profit as immoral, where to employ a hundred people is represented as exploitation but to command the same number as honorable. Older people may regard this as an exaggeration of the present state of affairs, but the daily experience of the university teacher leaves little doubt that, as a result of anticapitalist propaganda, values have already altered far in advance of the change in institutions which has so far taken place. The question is whether, by changing our institutions to satisfy the new demands, we shall not unwittingly destroy values which we still rate higher.

The change in the structure of society involved in the victory of the ideal of security over that of independence cannot be better illustrated than by a comparison of what ten or twenty years ago could still be regarded as the English and the German type of society. However great the influence of the army may have been in the latter country, it is a grave mistake to ascribe what the Englishman regarded as the "military" character of German society mainly to that influence. The difference went much deeper than could be explained on that ground, and the peculiar attributes of German society existed no less in circles in which the properly military influence was negligible than in those in which it was strong. It was not so much that at almost all times a larger part of the German people was organized for war than was true in other countries, but that the same type of organization was employed for so many other purposes, which gave German society its peculiar character. It was that a larger part of the civil life of Germany than of any other country was deliberately organized from the top, that so large a proportion of her people did not regard themselves as independent but as appointed functionaries, which gave her social structure its peculiar character. Germany had, as the Germans themselves boasted, for long been a *Beamtenstaat* [bureaucratic state] in which not only in the civil service proper but in almost all spheres of life income and status were assigned and guaranteed by some authority.

While it is doubtful whether the spirit of freedom can anywhere be extirpated by force, it is not certain that any people would successfully withstand the process by which it was slowly smothered in Germany. Where distinction and rank are achieved almost exclusively by becoming a salaried servant of the state, where to do one's assigned duty is regarded as more laudable than to choose one's own field of usefulness, where all pursuits that do not give a recognized place in the official hierarchy or a claim to a fixed income are regarded as inferior and even somewhat disreputable, it is too much to expect that many will long prefer freedom to security. And where the alternative to security in a dependent position is a most precarious position, in which one is despised alike for success and for failure, only few will resist the temptation of safety at the price of freedom. Once things have gone so far, liberty indeed becomes almost a mockery, since it can be purchased only by the sacrifice of most of the good things of this earth. In this state it is little surprising that more and more people should come to feel that without economic security liberty is "not worth having" and that they are willing to sacrifice their liberty for security. But it is disquieting to find Professor Harold Laski employing the very same argument which has perhaps done more than any other to induce the German people to sacrifice their liberty.[5]

There can be no question that adequate security against severe privation, and the reduction of the avoidable causes of misdirected effort and consequent disappointment, will have to be one of the main goals of policy. But if these endeavors are to be successful and are not to destroy individual freedom, security must be provided outside the market and competition be left to function unobstructed. Some security is essential if freedom is to be preserved, because most men are willing to bear the risk which freedom inevitably involves only so long as that risk is not too great. But while this is a truth of which we must never lose sight, nothing is more fatal than the present fashion among intellectual leaders of extolling security at the expense of freedom. It is essential that we should re-learn frankly to face the fact that freedom can be had only at a price and that as individuals we must be prepared to make severe material sacrifices to preserve our liberty. If we want to retain this, we must regain the conviction on which the rule of liberty in the Anglo-Saxon countries has been based and which Benjamin Franklin expressed in a phrase applicable to us in our lives as individuals no less than as nations: "Those who would give up essential liberty to purchase a little temporary safety deserve neither liberty nor safety."

HAYEK'S NOTES

1. There are also serious problems of international relations which arise if mere citizenship of a country confers the right to a standard of living higher than elsewhere and which ought not to be dismissed too lightly.

2. Very interesting suggestions of how these hardships might be mitigated within a liberal society have been put forward by Professor W. H. Hutt in a book which will repay careful study (*Plan for Reconstruction* [1942]).

3. D. C. Coyle, "The Twilight of National Planning," *Harper's Magazine*, October, 1935, p. 558.

4. W. Roepke, *Die Gesellschaftskrisis der Gegenwart* (Zurich, 1942), p. 172.

5. H. J. Laski, *Liberty in the Modern State* (Pelican ed., 1937), p. 51: "Those who know the normal life of the poor, its haunting sense of impending disaster, its fitful search for beauty which perpetually eludes, will realise well enough that, without economic security, liberty is not worth having."

13

The New Nations Speak

A HISTORIAN viewing the whole course of Western civilization may well consider the emergence of the underdeveloped areas of Asia and Africa as one of the most significant events of our century. The West has repeatedly made its influence felt in the East since the time of the Crusades, reversing the previous direction of cultural influence which had for centuries moved from East to West. Notwithstanding the difficulties involved in these cultural crosscurrents, they have been fruitful of rich cultural achievements. At the 1955 Asian-African Conference in Bandung, Indonesia, leaders of these new nations met to declare their common hopes and beliefs. The opening speech by Sukarno [Soekarno], President of the Republic of Indonesia, provides a good summary of these views, in which the interplay of West and East may be seen.

Speech by President Soekarno at the Opening of the Asian-African Conference—April 18, 1955

 YOUR EXCELLENCIES, Ladies and Gentlemen. Sisters and Brothers!

It is my great honour and privilege on this historic day to bid you welcome to Indonesia. On behalf of the people and Government of Indonesia — your hosts — I beg your understanding and forebearance if some circumstances in our country do not meet your expectation. We have, I assure you, done our best to make your stay amongst us memorable for both our guests and your hosts. We hope that the warmth of our welcome will compensate for whatever material shortcomings there may be.

From Republic of Indonesia, Ministry of Foreign Affairs, "Let a New Asia and a New Africa Be Born!" (Bandung, 1955), in George M. Kahin, THE ASIA-AFRICAN CONFERENCE, BANDUNG, INDONESIA, 1955 (Ithaca, N.Y., 1956), Appendix, pp. 39-51.

As I survey this hall and the distinguished guests gathered here, my heart is filled with emotion. This is the first intercontinental conference of coloured peoples in the history of mankind! I am proud that my country is your host. I am happy that you were able to accept the invitations extended by the five Sponsoring Countries. But also I cannot restrain feelings of sadness when I recall the tribulations through which many of our peoples have so recently passed, tribulations which have exacted a heavy toll in life, in material things, and in the things of the spirit.

I recognise that we are gathered here today as a result of sacrifices. Sacrifices made by our forefathers and by the people of our own and younger generations. For me, this hall is filled not only by the leaders of the nations of Asia and Africa; it also contains within its walls the undying, the indomitable, the invincible spirit of those who went before us. Their struggle and sacrifice paved the way for this meeting of the highest representatives of independent and sovereign nations from two of the biggest continents of the globe.

It is a new departure in the history of the world that leaders of Asian and African peoples can meet together in their own countries to discuss and deliberate upon matters of common concern. Only a few decades ago it was frequently necessary to travel to other countries and even other continents before the spokesmen of our peoples could confer.

I recall in this connection the Conference of the "League Against Imperialism and Colonialism" which was held in Brussels almost thirty years ago. At that Conference many distinguished Delegates who are present here today met each other and found new strength in their fight for independence.

But that was a meeting place thousands of miles away, amidst foreign people, in a foreign country, in a foreign continent. It was not assembled there by choice, but by necessity.

Today the contrast is great. Our nations and countries are colonies no more. Now we are free, sovereign and independent. We are again masters in our own house. We do not need to go to other continents to confer.

Already there have been important meetings of Asian States in Asia itself.

If we look for the forerunner of this our great gathering, we must look to Colombo, capital of independent Çri Lanka, [Ceylon] and to the Conference of the five Prime Ministers which was held there in 1954. And the Bogor Conference in December 1954 showed that the road ahead was clear for Asian-African solidarity, and the Conference to which I have the honour of welcoming you today is the realisation of that solidarity.

Indeed, I am proud that my country is your host.

But my thoughts are not wholly of the honour which is Indonesia's today. No. My mind is for a part darkened by other considerations.

You have not gathered together in a world of peace and unity and co-operation. Great chasms yawn between nations and groups of nations. Our unhappy world is torn and tortured, and the peoples of all countries walk in fear lest, through no fault of theirs, the dogs of war are unchained once again.

And if, in spite of all that the peoples may do, this should happen, what then? What of our newly-recovered independence then? What of our culture, what of our spiritual heritage, what of our ancient civilisation? What of our children and our parents?

The burden of the delegates to this Conference is not a light one, for I know that these questions — which are questions of the life or death of humanity itself — must be on your minds, as they are on mine. And the nations of Asia and Africa cannot, even if they wish to, avoid their part in finding solutions to these problems.

For that is part of the duties of independence itself. That is part of the price we gladly pay for our independence. For many generations our peoples have been the voiceless ones in the world. We have been the un-regarded, the peoples for whom decisions were made by others whose interests were paramount, the peoples who lived in poverty and humiliation. Then our nations demanded, nay fought for independence, and achieved independence, and with that independence came responsibility. We have heavy responsibilities to ourselves, and to the world, and to the yet unborn generations. But we do not regret them.

In 1945, the first year of our national revolution, we of Indonesia were confronted with the question of what we were going to do with our independence when it was finally attained and secured — we never questioned that it would be attained and secured. We knew how to oppose and destroy. Then we were suddenly confronted with the necessity of giving content and meaning to our independence. Not material content and meaning only, but also ethical and moral content, for independence without ethics and without morality would be indeed a poor imitation of what we sought. The responsibilities and burdens, the rights and duties and privileges of independence must be seen as part of the ethical and moral content of independence.

Indeed, we *welcome* the change which places new burdens upon us, and we are all resolved to exert all our strength and courage in carrying these burdens.

Sisters and Brothers, how terrificly dynamic is our time! I recall that, several years ago, I had occasion to make a public analysis of colonialism, and that I then drew attention to what I called the "Life-line of imperialism." This line runs from the Straits of Gibraltar, through the Mediterranean, the Suez Canal, the Red Sea, the Indian Ocean, the South China Sea and the Sea of Japan. For most of that enormous distance, the territories on both sides of this life-line were colonies, the peoples were unfree, their futures mortgaged to an alien system. Along that life-line, that main artery of imperialism, there was pumped the life-blood of colonialism.

And today in this hall are gathered together the leaders of those same peoples. They are no longer the victims of colonialism. They are no longer the tools of others and the playthings of forces they cannot influence. Today, you are representatives of free peoples, peoples of a different stature and standing in the world.

Yes, there has indeed been a "Sturm über Asien" — and over Africa too. The last few years have seen enormous changes. Nations, States, have awoken from a sleep of centuries. The passive peoples have gone, the outward tranquillity has made place for struggle and activity. Irresistible forces have swept the two continents. The mental, spiritual and political face of the whole world has been changed, and the process is still not complete. There are new conditions, new concepts, new problems, new ideals abroad in the world. Hurricanes of national awakening and reawakening have swept over the land, shaking it, changing it, changing it for the better.

This twentieth century has been a period of terrific dynamism. Perhaps the last fifty years have seen more developments and more material progress than the previous five hundred years. Man has learned to control many of the scourges which once threatened him. He has learned to consume distance. He has learned to project his voice and his picture across oceans and continents. He has probed deep into the secrets of nature and learned how to make the desert bloom and the plants of the earth increase their bounty. He has learned how to release the immense forces locked in the smallest particles of matter.

But has man's political skill marched hand-in-hand with his technical and scientific skill? Man can chain lightning to his command — can he control the society in which he lives? The answer is No! The political skill of man has been far outstripped by his technical skill, and what he has made he cannot be sure of controlling.

The result of this is fear. And man gasps for safety and morality.

Perhaps now more than at any other moment in the history of the world, society, government and statesmanship need to be based upon the highest code of morality and ethics. And in political terms, what is the highest code of morality? It is the subordination of everything to the well-being of mankind. But today we are faced with a situation where the well-being of mankind is not always the primary consideration. Many who are in places of high power think, rather, of controlling the world.

Yes, we are living in a world of fear. The life of man today is corroded and made bitter by fear. Fear of the future, fear of the hydrogen bomb, fear of ideologies. Perhaps this fear is a greater danger than the danger itself, because it is fear which drives men to act foolishly, to act thoughtlessly, to act dangerously.

In your deliberations, Sisters and Brothers, I beg of you, do not be guided by these fears, because fear is an acid which etches man's actions into curious patterns. Be guided by hopes and determination, be guided by ideals, and, yes, be guided by dreams!

We are of many different nations, we are of many different social backgrounds and cultural patterns. Our ways of life are different. Our national characters, or colours or motifs — call it what you will — are different. Our racial stock is different, and even the colour of our skin is different. But what does that matter? Mankind is united or divided by considerations other than these. Conflict comes not from variety of skins, nor from variety of religion, but from variety of desires.

All of us, I am certain, are united by more important things than those which superficially divide us. We are united, for instance, by a common detestation of colonialism in whatever form it appears. We are united by a common detestation of racialism. And we are united by a common determination to preserve and stabilise peace in the world. Are not these aims mentioned in the letter of invitation to which you responded?

I freely confess it — in these aims I am not disinterested or driven by purely impersonal motives.

How is it possible to be disinterested about colonialism? For us, colonialism is not something far and distant. We have known it in all its ruthlessness. We have seen the immense human wastage it causes, the poverty it causes, and the heritage it leaves behind when, eventually and reluctantly, it is driven out by the inevitable march of history. My people, and the peoples of many nations of Asia and Africa know these things, for we have experienced them.

Indeed, we cannot yet say that all parts of our countries are free already. Some parts still labour under the lash. And some parts of Asia and Africa which are not represented here still suffer from the same condition.

Yes, some parts of our nations are not yet free. That is why all of us cannot yet feel that journey's end has been reached. No people can feel themselves free, so long as part of their motherland is unfree. Like peace, freedom is indivisible. There is no such thing as being half free, as there is no such thing as being half alive.

We are often told "Colonialism is dead." Let us not be deceived or even soothed by that. I say to you, colonialism is not yet dead. How can we say it is dead, so long as vast areas of Asia and Africa are unfree.

And, I beg of you, do not think of colonialism only in the classic form which we of Indonesia, and our brothers in different parts of Asia and Africa, knew. Colonialism has also its modern dress, in the form of economic control, intellectual control, actual physical control by a small but alien community within a nation. It is a skilful and determined enemy, and it appears in many guises. It does not give up its loot easily. Wherever, whenever, and however it appears, colonialism is an evil thing, and one which must be eradicated from the earth.

The battle against colonialism has been a long one, and do you know that today is a famous anniversary in that battle? On the eighteenth day of April, one thousand seven hundred and seventy five, just one hundred and eighty years ago, Paul Revere rode at midnight through the New England countryside, warning of the

approach of British troops and of the opening of the American War
of Independence, the first successful anti-colonial war in history.
About this midnight ride the poet Longfellow wrote:

> A cry of defiance and not of fear,
> A voice in the darkness, a knock at the door,
> And a word that shall echo for evermore. . . .

Yes, it shall echo for evermore, just as the other anti-colonial
words which gave us comfort and reassurance during the darkest
days of our struggle shall echo for evermore. But remember, that
battle which began 180 years ago is not yet completely won, and it
will not have been completely won until we can survey this our
own world, and can say that colonialism is dead.

So, I am not disinterested when I speak of the fight against
colonialism.

Nor am I disinterested when I speak of the battle for peace. How
can any of us be disinterested about peace?

Not so very long ago we argued that peace was necessary for us
because an outbreak of fighting in our part of the world would
imperil our precious independence, so recently won at such great
cost.

Today, the picture is more black. War would not only mean a
threat to our independence, it may mean the end of civilisation and
even of human life. There is a force loose in the world whose poten-
tiality for evil no man truly knows. Even in practice and rehearsal
for war the effects may well be building up into something of unknown horror.

Not so long ago it was possible to take some little comfort from
the idea that the clash, if it came, could perhaps be settled by what
were called "conventional weapons" — bombs, tanks, cannon and
men. Today that little grain of comfort is denied us, for it has been
made clear that the weapons of ultimate horror will certainly be
used, and the military planning of nations is on that basis. The
unconventional has become the conventional, and who knows what
other examples of misguided and diabolical scientific skill have been
discovered as a plague on humanity.

And do not think that the oceans and the seas will protect us. The
food that we eat, the water that we drink, yes, even the very air that
we breathe can be contaminated by poisons originating from thousands of miles away. And it could be that, even if we ourselves

escaped lightly, the unborn generations of our children would bear on their distorted bodies the marks of our failure to control the forces which have been released on the world.

No task is more urgent than that of preserving peace. Without peace our independence means little. The rehabilitation and up-building of our countries will have little meaning. Our revolutions will not be allowed to run their course.

What can we do? The peoples of Asia and Africa wield little physical power. Even their economic strength is dispersed and slight. We cannot indulge in power politics. Diplomacy for us is not a matter of the big stick. Our statesmen, by and large, are not backed up with serried ranks of jet bombers.

What can we do? We can do much! We can inject the voice of reason into world affairs. We can mobilise all the spiritual, all the moral, all the political strength of Asia and Africa on the side of peace. Yes, we! We, the peoples of Asia and Africa, 1,400,000,000 strong, far more than half the human population of the world, we can mobilise what I have called the *Moral Violence of Nations* in favour of peace. We can demonstrate to the minority of the world which lives on the other continents that we, the majority, are for peace, not for war, and that whatever strength we have will always be thrown on to the side of peace.

In this struggle, some success has already been scored. I think it is generally recognised that the activity of the Prime Ministers of the Sponsoring Countries which invited you here had a not unimportant role to play in ending the fighting in Indo-China.

Look, the peoples of Asia raised their voices, and the world listened. It was no small victory and no negligible precedent! The five Prime Ministers did not make threats. They issued no ultimatum, they mobilised no troops. Instead they consulted together, discussed the issues, pooled their ideas, added together their individual political skills and came forward with sound and reasoned suggestions which formed the basis for a settlement of the long struggle in Indo-China.

I have often since then asked myself why these five were success-ful when others, with long records of diplomacy, were unsuccessful, and, in fact, had allowed a bad situation to get worse, so that there was a danger of the conflict spreading. Was it because they were Asians? Maybe that is part of the answer, for the conflagration was on their doorstep, and any extension of it would have presented an immediate threat to their own houses. But I think that the answer really lies in the fact that those five Prime Ministers brought a *fresh approach* to bear on the problem. They were not seeking advantage for their own countries. They had no axe of power-politics to grind. They had but one interest — how to end the fighting in such a way that the chances of continuing peace and stability were enhanced.

That, my Sisters and Brothers, was an historic occasion. Some countries of free Asia spoke, and the world listened. They spoke on a subject of immediate concern to Asia, and in doing so made it quite clear that the affairs of Asia are the concern of the Asian peoples themselves. The days are now long past when the future of Asia can be settled by other and distant peoples.

However, we cannot, we dare not, confine our interests to the affairs of our own continents. The States of the world today depend one upon the other and no nation can be an island unto itself. Splendid isolation may once have been possible; it is so no longer. The affairs of all the world are our affairs, and our future depends upon the solutions found to all international problems, however far or distant they may seem.

As I survey this hall, my thoughts go back to another Conference of Asian peoples. In the beginning of 1949 — historically speaking only a moment ago — my country was for the second time since our Proclamation of Independence engaged in a life and death struggle. Our nation was besieged and beleaguered, much of our territory occupied, a great part of our leaders imprisoned or exiled, our existence as a State threatened.

Issues were being decided, not in the conference chamber, but on the battlefield. Our envoys then were rifles, and cannon, and bombs, and grenades, and bamboo-spears. We were blockaded, physically and intellectually.

It was at that sad but glorious moment in our national history that our good neighbour India convened a Conference of Asian and African Nations in New Delhi, to protest against the injustice committed against Indonesia and to give support to our struggle. The intellectual blockade was broken! Our Delegates flew to New Delhi and learned at first hand of the massive support which was being given to our struggle for national existence. Never before in the history of mankind has such a solidarity of Asian and African peoples been shown for the rescue of a fellow Asian Nation in danger. The diplomats and statesmen, the Press and the common men of our Asian and African neighbours were all supporting us. We were given fresh courage to press our struggle onwards to its final successful conclusion. We again realised to the full the truth of Desmoulin's statement: "Have no doubt of the omnipotence of a free people."

Perhaps in some ways the Conference which has assembled here today has some roots in that manifestation of Asian-African solidarity six years ago.

However that may be, the fact remains that everyone of you bears a heavy responsibility, and I pray to God that the responsibility will be discharged with courage and wisdom.

I pray to God that this Asian-African Conference succeeds in doing its job.

Ah, Sisters and Brothers, let this Conference be a great success! In spite of diversity that exists among its participants, — let this Conference be a great success!

Yes, there is diversity among us. Who denies it? Small and great nations are represented here, with people professing almost every religion under the sun, — Buddhism, Islam, Christianity, Confucianism, Hinduism, Jainism, Sikhism, Zoroastrianism, Shintoism, and others. Almost every political faith we encounter here — Democracy, Monarchism, Theocracy, with innumerable variants. And practically every economic doctrine has its representative in this hall — Marhaenism, Socialism, Capitalism, Communism, in all their manifold variations and combinations.

But what harm is in diversity, when there is unity in desire? This Conference is not to oppose each other, it is a conference of brotherhood. It is not an Islam-Conference, nor a Christian Conference, nor a Buddhist Conference. It is not a meeting of Malayans, nor one of Arabs, nor one of Indo-Aryan stock. It is not an exclusive club either, nor a bloc which seeks to oppose any other bloc. Rather it is a body of enlightened, tolerant opinion which seeks to impress on the world that all men and all countries have their place under the sun — to impress on the world that it is possible to live together, meet together, speak to each other, without losing one's individual identity; and yet to contribute to the general understanding of matters of common concern, and to develop a true consciousness of the interdependence of men and nations for their wellbeing and survival on earth.

I know that in Asia and Africa there is greater diversity of religions, faiths, and beliefs, than in the other continents of the world. But that is only natural! Asia and Africa are the classic birthplaces of faiths and ideas, which have spread all over the world. Therefore, it behooves us to take particular care to ensure that the principle which is usually called the "Live and let live" principle — mark, I do not say the principle of "Laissez faire, laissez passer" of Liberalism which is obsolete — is first of all applied by us most completely within our own Asian and African frontiers. Then only can it be fully extended to our relations with our neighbouring countries, and to others more distant.

Religion is of dominating importance particularly in this part of the world. There are perhaps more religions here than in other regions of this globe. But, again, our countries were the birthplaces of religions. Must we be divided by the multiformity of our religious life? It is true, each religion has its own history, its own individuality, its own "raison d'être," its special pride in its own beliefs, its own mission, its special truths which it desires to propagate. But unless we realise that all great religions are one in their message of tolerance and in their insistence on the observance of the principle of "Live and let live," unless the followers of each religion are prepared to give the same consideration to the rights of others everywhere, unless every State does its duty to ensure that the same rights are given to the followers of all faiths — unless these things are done, religion is debased, and its true purpose perverted. Unless Asian-African countries realise their responsibilities in this matter and take steps jointly to fulfill them, the very strength of religious beliefs, which should be a source of unity and a bulwark against foreign interference, will cause its disruption, and may result in destroying the hard-won freedom which large parts of Asia and Africa have achieved by acting together.

Sisters and Brothers, Indonesia is Asia-Africa in small. It is a country with many religions and many faiths. We have in Indonesia Moslims, we have Christians, we have Civa-Buddhists, we have peoples with other creeds. Moreover, we have many ethnic units, such as Achenese, Bataks, Central-Sumatrans, Sudanese, Central-Javanese, Madurese, Toradjas, Balinese, etc. But thank God, we have our will to unity. We have our Pancha Sila. We practise the "Live and let live" principle, we are tolerant to each other. *Bhinneka Tunggal Ika — Unity in Diversity —* is the motto of the Indonesian State. We are one nation.

So, let this Asian-African Conference be a great success! Make the "Live and let live" principle and the "Unity in Diversity" motto the unifying force which brings us all together — to seek in friendly, uninhibited discussion, ways and means by which each of us can live his own life, and let others live their own lives, in their own way, in harmony, and in peace.

If we succeed in doing so, the effect of it for the freedom, independence and the welfare of man will be great on the world at large. The Light of Understanding has again been lit, the Pillar of Co-operation again erected. The likelihood of success of this Conference is proved already by the very presence of you all here today. It is for us to give it strength, to give it the power of inspiration — to spread its message all over the World.

Failure will mean that the Light of Understanding which seemed to have dawned in the East — the Light towards which looked all the great religions born here in the past — has again been obscured by an unfriendly cloud before man could benefit from its warm radiance.

But let us be full of hope and full of confidence. We have so much in common.

Relatively speaking, all of us gathered here today are neighbours. Almost all of us have ties of common experience, the experience of colonialism. Many of us have a common religion. Many of us have common cultural roots. Many of us, the so-called "underdeveloped" nations, have more or less similar economic problems, so that each can profit from the others' experience and help. And I think I may say that we all hold dear the ideals of national independence and freedom. Yes, we have so much in common. And yet we know so little of each other.

If this Conference succeeds in making the peoples of the East whose representatives are gathered here understand each other a little more, appreciate each other a little more, sympathise with each other's problems a little more — if those things happen, then this Conference, of course, will have been worthwhile, whatever else it may achieve. But I hope that this Conference will give *more* than understanding only and goodwill only — I hope that it will falsify and give the lie to the saying of one diplomat from far abroad: "We will turn this Asian-African Conference into an afternoon-tea meeting." I hope that it will give evidence of the fact that we Asian and African leaders understand that Asia and Africa can prosper only when they are united, and that even the safety of the World at large can not be safeguarded without a united Asia-Africa. I hope that this Conference will give *guidance* to mankind, will point out to mankind the way which it must take to attain safety and peace. I hope that it will give evidence that Asia and Africa have been reborn, nay, that a *New Asia* and a *New Africa* have been born!

Our task is first to seek an understanding of each other, and out of that understanding will come a greater appreciation of each other, and out of that appreciation will come collective action. Bear in mind the words of one of Asia's greatest sons: "To speak is easy. To act is hard. To understand is hardest. Once one understands, action is easy."

I have come to the end. Under God, may your deliberations be fruitful, and may your wisdom strike sparks of light from the hard flints of today's circumstances.

Let us not be bitter about the past, but let us keep our eyes firmly on the future. Let us remember that no blessing of God is so sweet as life and liberty. Let us remember that the stature of all mankind is diminished so long as nations or parts of nations are still unfree. Let us remember that the highest purpose of man is the liberation of man from his bonds of fear, his bonds of human degradation, his bonds of poverty — the liberation of man from the physical, spiritual and intellectual bonds which have for too long stunted the development of humanity's majority.

And let us remember, Sisters and Brothers, that for the sake of all that, we Asians and Africans must be united.

As President of the Republic of Indonesia, and on behalf of the eighty million people of Indonesia, I bid you welcome to this country. I declare the Asian-African Conference opened, and I pray that the Blessing of God will be upon it, and that its discussions will be profitable to the peoples of Asia and Africa, and to the peoples of all nations!

Bismillah!

God speed!

14

The Great Fear

THOSE AWARE of realities will not doubt that the most urgent issue facing mankind today is the avoidance of nuclear war. Some believe that the only solution lies in the destruction of nuclear arms, even unilaterally by the West if Russia refuses to do so. Others argue that any such action would lead inevitably to an evil even greater than war, Communist conquest of the world. Still others believe that the "balance of terror" can and will continue without the dreaded holocaust. They hold that eventually changes both in international relations and within each of the principal countries involved will reduce tensions to a point where nuclear arsenals can be eliminated. To illustrate the intensity of emotions provoked by this issue, we reprint here the advocacy of a "unilateralist" policy, together with a brief reply arguing the more prevalent position.

a Philip Toynbee, Thoughts on Nuclear Warfare and a Policy to Avoid It

POSSIBILITIES which are much spoken of are often very little apprehended, and there are few people in England who have really contemplated nuclear warfare. Perhaps it is an event which is beyond the powers of the human mind to contemplate, and furthest of all beyond the power of English minds. Opening any newspaper we are within a culture which is so familiar to us and so apparently stable that the possibility of it coming to a sudden and terrible end seems as absurd as the scarifying apocalyptics of science fiction. We see a photograph of the Queen leaving Buckingham Palace; another of footballers leaping in a goal mouth. Above a book review there is a drawing of an Oxford college; and on another page we read of a parliamentary debate on the future of the House of Lords. But if a mistake were made by one of many Russians or Americans, if one of

From Philip Toynbee, A FEARFUL CHOICE (London, 1959), pp. 9–22. Reprinted by permission of Victor Gollancz, Ltd. and Wayne State University Press.

them lost his nerve and his head, the Queen and Buckingham Palace would be pulverised together; the footballers of England would be killed or maimed or condemned to a slow death by radiation; no more books would be read and the ancient colleges would be in ruins. The future of the House of Lords would be decided.

The monstrous inflation of our rhetoric contributes to this failure of the English mind to understand the condition of the times. "The Edge of the Abyss." "The Age of Terror." "The End of Civilisation as We Know It." Many of us have been guilty of using these glib phrases in the past when we have declaimed against some policy of our political opponents. Like the shepherd-boy we are paying now for having cried "Wolf!" many times too often. Yet somehow the Englishman's calm incredulity in the face of warning prophets *must* be shattered; he must be made, not to panic, but to pass through terror. The bland assurance of survival which proved a useful quality under the threat of German invasion is a fearful danger to us at a time when the rockets might fall at any moment and obliterate in an instant of time the incredulous together with the prophets.

There is a simple test for deciding whether or not we have truly contemplated the reality of nuclear warfare. Have we decided how we are to kill the other members of our household in the event of our being less injured than they are? This will sound morbid and melodramatic to most English ears, but in reality we ought already to be making sober plans for killing off our injured before disposing of ourselves. If nuclear war begins, a great many rockets are likely to fall on this country simultaneously. Those who are fortunate enough to live in the "safest" areas — London, East Anglia — can reasonably expect to be killed outright. But over most of the country there will probably be a chaos of people dying in isolation from each other, and in great agony. In most areas there will probably be no organised rescue work and no prospect of any organised rescue work. Much needless anguish can be avoided if we are at least prepared with our methods of euthanasia.

At the moment of writing we know that many bomb-bearing rockets are aimed at this country from Russian territory. We know that these rockets are effective and accurate. We can assume that the rocket-batteries are manned throughout the twenty-four hours.

We also know that American bombers are constantly in the air above England carrying Hydrogen bombs which can be made active within a few minutes. We know that the Americans wish to establish their own perpetually-manned rocket batteries in this country and in other countries of Western Europe. In fact, we know that we have now reached the in some ways familiar situation of two hostile but adjacent countries with tension running high between them. There are many points of resemblance between the present diplomatic and military relations of America and Russia and the relations between, for example, Israel and Jordan today or Bulgaria and Serbia before the 1914 war. We know that this older situation is one which leads to constant frontier incidents. Shots are suddenly exchanged; a few soldiers or civilians are killed on either side of the frontier. These incidents are not necessarily due to bad-will even on the part of the soldier or junior officer who is responsible for causing them. They are often due to panic, or to mistaking an order. And when they occurred in the cases we have known before they never led to war unless the government of one or both countries desired a war.

It is here that the parallel breaks down. If an "incident" should happen on the present frontier between America and Russia it must lead not only to war but to the total destruction of this country and perhaps of the human race. If one Russian rocket commander mistakes an order; if one American bomber pilot suddenly finds the strain too much for his mind, it is inevitable that rockets and bombers will be massively launched from both sides. That is the meaning of the word "deterrent" which both sides use so freely.

We should consider an individual Russian rocket in position, or an individual American bomber flying above this country with a Hydrogen bomb. In personnel these entities amount to small military units, each in the immediate charge of a junior military commander. Above these men are slightly less junior officers, who are in charge of rocket batteries and bomber squadrons; and the chain of military command extends upwards to the Kremlin on one side, the White House on the other. There are therefore a very large number of men on both sides who could bring about the certain destruction of this country, the possible destruction of the world, simply by giving a single order.

Nobody in his senses can believe that either the Russian or the American government wants to wage a nuclear war. The cynical but telling point must be made that we are for the first time in a situation in which the men who order a war are likely to be killed or maimed in it within a few hours of its outbreak. The White House and the Kremlin are both in the front line, since it is known that Moscow is within reach of American bombers and Washington within reach of Russian intercontinental missiles and rocket-carrying submarines. But the leaders of Russia and America, no less than all their subordinates in the chains of command which reach down to bomber pilots and rocket commanders, are capable of making a mistake or of losing their nerve. We know, for example, that there was a false invasion scare in this country during the last war. To this day nobody is sure of its origin, but we know that nation-wide action was taken as a result of it.

In fact, if we think purely in terms of probability it is surely at least as likely as not that mutual fear will lead to accidental war in the near future *if the present situation continues.* If it continues indefinitely it is nearly a statistical certainty that a mistake will be made and that the devastation will begin.

* * *

We should try to be as clear as we can about the meaning of the word "deterrent." It has become one of those magic talismans much favoured by politicians which often assume false meanings by constant and confident repetition. For example, the word is often used as if it were a synonym for "defence." We read in the press of American "Defence Plans" for Europe — as if the bombers and rockets which are being stationed here could, in a physical sense, *prevent* their Russian equivalents from falling on us. As if, in fact, these weapons were defensive in the sense that a shield is defensive, or the steel plating of a battle-ship. But there is no defence against a rocket once it has been launched. It may miss its object: it cannot be destroyed or deflected from its object by its intended recipients.

The most, and the worst, we can expect is that if a nuclear war breaks out we may be able to throw back at the Russians something of the horror and devastation which they have inflicted on us. Assume that Russian rockets have fallen on this country. Assume further that some means of retaliation have survived the initial attack. Why, at this point, should we make use of those means? The only motive for doing so would be a motive of childish and wicked revenge. For we would already have lost the war in the only sense which has any meaning. We would have lost our cities, our countryside, many if not most of our families and friends, our health probably forever, perhaps our limbs. Once the rockets have fallen on us there will be nothing left to lose for the survivors. Some of them *may* still be able to make millions of innocent Russians suffer the agony which millions of innocent Englishmen have already suffered. Why should they do so?

It would be wicked and pointless to launch a nuclear attack on Russia *before* we have ourselves been attacked. Wicked for obvious reasons; pointless because we would immediately get back a great deal more than we were able to give. It would be wicked and pointless to launch a nuclear attack on Russia *after* we had ourselves been attacked. Wicked for obvious reasons; pointless because we would no longer have anything to gain by it. We would only be contributing to the general destruction of the world, in the manner of Hitler trying to bring down all Germany and Europe in his fall.

There are therefore no circumstances in which we could use these weapons without behaving both wickedly and insanely. What sort of a "deterrent," then, are weapons which can never in any circumstances be used to our advantage — which can only be used as a futile act of revenge from the grave or as a means of putting us into the grave? They are of use to no one who possesses them, and they are a perpetual and appalling danger to us all.

A few years ago there was, indeed, a certain plausibility in the notion of "deterrents." It was believed at that time that a state of military and scientific equilibrium would be, or had been, reached between Russia and America. Each was thought capable of doing such destruction to the other that neither would dare to attack. It was assumed that tension, in this state of stalemate, would gradually decline, and that measures of disarmament would follow almost out of a mutual sense of the ridiculous.

To this it can be said that there must indeed have been at least an instant of parity between the two sides, since America was clearly the greater military power in the years after the war and Russia is clearly the greater power today. But that moment passed, of course, undiscerned and undiscernible. And if any such moment of theoretical parity were ever to exist again it too would pass undiscerned, since neither side, nor any third party, could possibly detect it. How is anyone to weigh, for example, a fleet of rocket-equipped submarines against a ring of land bases; or territorial advantages against technical advantages? Parity is a myth because neither side will ever be satisfied that a state of parity exists.

Nor is there any ultimate ceiling in the arms race against which both sides might be expected to arrive in the end. It is clear that a competition in technical advantages can continue indefinitely — or until that outbreak of unintended war which will end all questions of technical advantage. In this armaments race one side or the other will always be weaker.

*   *   *

At the moment, and in the foreseeable future, the West is the weaker of the two sides in the cold war. If the hourly danger of disaster is to be averted there is only one step which the West can take — which is to negotiate at once with the Russians and get the best terms which are available. It may be that the terms will be disadvantageous to us: there is very little reason to think that they will be crushing. The majority of Russian experts, including George Kennan and Edward Crankshaw, are agreed that the Russians hope to dominate the world not by military means but by commercial and political means. If they succeed in this aim then so much the worse for the West and the Western system. It was never intended by anyone to use nuclear weapons against *this* form of competition. Our proper weapons here are our brains, our industry and the virtues of our social and political faith. A competition with Russia in these terms would be a positively exhilarating experience.

Anyone who urges that we should accept even a slightly disadvantageous agreement for progressive disarmament is confronted at once with another of those dangerous and meaningless slogans which have been dinned into our ears over the years. "We must," we are always told, "negotiate from *strength*." The first reason why this is now a meaningless slogan is that we have not *got* the strength any longer. Nor is there any reason why Russia should ever lose her present advantage. It is naïve in the extreme to suppose that Russia will mark time in technical development while the West catches up; and the only reason why Russia did once overtake and pass the West was that the West was taking things easy in the confidence of her innate scientific and technical superiority. But it's clear that neither side will ever take it easy again, and there is no reason to think that Russia will lose her present advantage.

But if the West did make some miraculous discovery which suddenly gave her the advantage, the position would be not better but worse. For it would then be *Russia* which would refuse to negotiate from weakness, and on Russia we can have no influence whatever. As George Kennan has insisted, it is a great and fatal illusion of the

West to think that the Russians can be awed into making an agreement advantageous to the West. For years after the war they were patently weaker than America, and during those years they were at their most intransigent.

Parity, then, is a myth. Superiority is not only unlikely to be attained but if attained would make an agreement harder, not easier to reach. And on any day during the West's frantic attempt to catch up the tension of the race may lead to sudden disaster. There is therefore nothing for it but to negotiate from comparative weakness. It is childish to say that the Russians *ought* to behave differently. So far as we are concerned Russian attitudes are a fact of nature. If we know that they will not negotiate except from a strength which they are likely to keep for many years to come, then we must negotiate without superior strength; and we must do so at once. When it is a question of saving the world "Why should it be *me?*" is the cry of a dangerous child. We believe that we are wiser and larger-minded than the Russians, and it is in this way that we can show it.

It is very unlikely that these negotiations will lead the West into a position of serious disadvantage. And it is hard to believe that the Russians, armed with whatever slight advantage they may gain, will immediately embark on a path of military conquest. Their recent experience in Eastern Europe has been an unhappy one for them, and it is most unlikely that it has given them an appetite for occupying vast new territories. Why should they wish to attempt such an appalling military and political task when they have so much to do at home and when they are so confident of their ability to dominate the world by other means?

But it is at least conceivable that if the West accepted Russian terms now the result would be the total domination of the world by Russia within a few years. No one can honestly recommend this plea for a negotiated agreement without admitting that this is a possible result, however improbable. Would that result be worse than the nuclear war which is the almost inevitable result of an indefinitely continued arms race?

In answering this question much confusion has been caused by quoting examples of ignoble surrender in the past, and in particular the example of appeasement in the nineteen-thirties. In fact, of course, the present situation is unique in history and nothing from the past can instruct us on how we should now conduct ourselves. There was a choice in 1939 of fighting an arduous and bloody war or of submitting to a régime of total insanity and evil. It is generally felt that the choice of fighting the war was the morally right one — though many highly moral pacifists have disagreed with this. The present choice is of an entirely different kind. We can choose a course which will almost certainly lead to nuclear war. Nuclear war will mean the certain destruction of these islands at an unspeakable cost in human anguish. It will mean the certain destruction of cities in Russia and America at an equivalent cost. It will mean the certain deformation of future generations and the possible destruction of the whole human race. Even if some human beings survive the nuclear bombardment it is possible that many centuries will pass before any form of civilisation is re-established.

(Nobody, of course, and least of all a scientific layman, can accurately predict the results of the war, but this seems to be a fair guess at probabilities and possibilities. I believe that no scientist would say that these guesses are *ludicrous*.)

That is one choice.

The other choice involves, in the first place, the possibility of giving Russia a small immediate advantage over the West. It involves the further possibility that Russia will gradually dominate the world by political and economic means. It involves the extremely remote possibility that Russia will carry out a military occupation of the world. It is hard to see how anyone can believe that the worst of these possibilities is a more appalling prospect than the worst possible result of continuing the arms race. It is not a question of making a personal choice in favour of death rather than Russian domination; that choice is always available to the individual in any case. It is a question of allowing the human race to survive, possibly under the domination of a régime which most of us detest, or of allowing it to destroy itself in appalling and prolonged anguish.

We now believe that the thousand-year Reich is a myth; and the major lesson of the post-Stalin epoch is that even communist régimes are incapable of totally denaturalising human nature. An attempted communist domination of such fantastically indigestible morsels as Paris, London, Rome and New York would almost certainly result in a violent indigestion and a radical change in the nature of the dominating power. The Orwell nightmare of an everlasting tyranny seems to be truly a nightmare rather than a probable future for mankind.

It seems, then, that the worst, and least probable, result of adopting the choice of life rather than death would be a severe set-back to human freedom. In terms of history, as well as in terms of human misery, this would be a trivial reverse compared with the horrifying probabilities of nuclear war.

*   *   *

If it is right to choose the immediate acceptance of the best available terms, what methods are available to us for persuading the Americans to make this choice? The methods *of* persuasion, first of all. The attempt to demonstrate the case by argument. But if this fails we must employ the sanction of a unilateral withdrawal from the nuclear arms race. In the event of an American refusal we must renounce the use and possession of our own nuclear weapons and we must refuse to allow the continued presence of American arms on our soil. We must try — which should be no difficult task — to persuade the other countries of Western Europe to follow our example. We must try to build up a neutral bloc throughout the world dedicated to the repudiation of all nuclear weapons.

This is a drastic step which would have many unfortunate economic results for us. It would be bitterly resented in America as the betrayal of an alliance. But it is better to betray an alliance than to betray the human race, and it is better to save America from destruction against her will rather than to abet her in the destruction of us all. The result of this action would, of course, be far more advantageous to Russia than would the result of an agreement negotiated with her now by the united western alliance. Russian world domination would be made more probable; but this greater probability makes no difference at all to the earlier argument for choosing the lesser evil. A nuclear war would be equally excluded by this second-best method since America would be incapable of waging one and Russia would have no conceivable motive for waging one.

*   *   *

It is obvious, surely, that this is an issue which has nothing whatever to do with party politics and nothing whatever to do with our estimations of American and Russian society. In the terrible context of nuclear war even the vital differences between Communism and Western freedom become almost unimportant. We would infinitely prefer our Western system of freedom and privacy to prevail in the world; and if we are spared we shall have an opportunity of trying to ensure that it does so. But even if it didn't prevail *mankind* would still be given the opportunity of prevailing. Mr. Kennan has said that anything would be better than a policy which led inevitably to nuclear war. But surely anything is better than a policy which allows for the *possibility* of nuclear war.

The issue has nothing to do with politics. It has little to do with causes and highmindedness. Those who have had at least a partial vision of our destruction are like people who have leant out of the window of an express train and seen that a bridge is down a little further along the line. They are urging the driver and their fellow-passengers that the train should be stopped. But the others reply, many of them from behind their newspapers, that the train can't possibly be stopped because they have important engagements in the city. As for the bridge, it may not be down after all, and even if it is the train will probably manage to jump across it somehow. Besides, it does no good to the reputation of our railways if express trains are to be halted in this way. And finally, we ought surely to be aware that there is another express train coming in the opposite direction which will certainly fall down into the river just as soon as we do.

At the very least, then, let those who wish to continue with the arms-race be prepared with competent methods of killing off their mutilated families before killing their mutilated selves. Only when we see that they have made these preparations shall we be able to believe that they have faced the implications of their policy.

b   Richard Löwenthal (of the Observer), A Reply

PHILIP TOYNBEE'S memorandum starts from anxieties which in some degree must be shared by all, and it contains plausible arguments at some points. But the essence of the case he puts forward is that unconditional surrender to the Soviet rulers is the only safe alternative to race suicide. I believe this case to be based on false premises, faulty logic and a warped sense of values.

From Ibid., pp. 28–34. Reprinted by permission of Victor Gollancz, Ltd. and Wayne State University Press.

First, to remove a misunderstanding. Toynbee tries at times to hide the real meaning of his argument before himself and his readers by calling for "negotiation" with the Russians. But nowhere in his more than three thousand words does he give the slightest hint of what he wishes to negotiate about; apparently he has not given it a thought. As he wants to remove all risk of nuclear war, and remove it immediately, negotiation would presumably aim at the destruction of all nuclear weapons and their means of delivery, and a ban on their future production. Toynbee himself says that for the sake of this result, he would accept whatever accompanying conditions the Soviets would impose. But the Soviets have never been willing to accept effective total inspection on their territory, such as a total removal of the threat would require; and there is not the slightest reason why they should now accept it if faced with a partner offering Toynbee's terms. All he could effectively make sure of, then, is that the West would really abolish the weapon, and the Soviets might say they would do so. He might think that with the West atomically disarmed and wide open, the Soviets would have no more motive to keep the horror in readiness — especially as they are superior in conventional forces. But in any future political crisis they could always threaten to activate it again and thus impose additional terms. Hence Toynbee's plea really amounts to unconditional surrender — at a single stroke or in stages.

I think he would not really contest the logic of this; he says explicitly that if necessary he would be prepared to face that risk. But in the circumstances, it is a little disingenuous to talk of "negotiation."

Second, what would surrender to the Soviets imply? Toynbee refers to the opinion of most Soviet experts, including Kennan, that the Communists expect to win the world by political and economic means rather than by military conquest; he thinks this means by competition rather than by occupation. There is confusion here. Soviet policy aims to extend its domination without the risk of major war; but it has never hesitated to use force or the threat of force as a means of policy. If his proposal was adopted by the West, the Soviets would have unlimited possibilities of expanding their domination by political blackmail *without* war — ultimately, at their own pace, all over the world. For "without war" would not, in this case, mean "without force"; and there is ultimately no means of resisting a monopoly of force in the hands of a ruthlessly determined power.

Again, Toynbee recognises this as a possible consequence, and is prepared to accept it. But he describes it as an unlikely contingency, whereas it is, given the nature of the Soviet régime, a necessary consequence of his policy. He consoles himself by the thought that totalitarian world domination would not last for ever, and might rather result in a modification of the victorious régime. Such a modification is, of course, conceivable; but the initial victory, wiping out all dissidence, all right to organised disagreement, all tolerance on a world scale for the first time in human history, would be certain. I should hesitate to prophesy about further developments in these unparalleled conditions.

Now to the present situation. Here I disagree with Toynbee both about the relation of forces, about the function of the "deterrent," and about the risk of "accidents." I agree with him that the present is as good a time as any for negotiation with Russia — *real* negotiation, not surrender.

Toynbee assumes as self-evident that the Russians are at the moment militarily stronger than the West. This is not a vital point in the argument, as I do not hold that we should only negotiate while we have a position of marginal superiority — and the advantages now obtainable by either side are rather marginal. But as a matter of fact, the Western military leaders do not think that the Russians are actually stronger at present, and it is doubtful whether the Russians think so; at any rate they cannot be sure about it, any more than the West can. The best-informed Western view is that unless certain steps are taken by the West now, the Russians *will* be superior in two years time; that is the present key argument in the arms race. At any rate, the basic relation of strength is, and is likely to remain for a foreseeable time, one of *practical* parity — in the sense of a "balance of terror" assured by the knowledge that each side has the means to destroy the other, even if one or the other has these means in somewhat greater number or effectiveness.

In that sense, it is quite wrong to say that parity has disappeared overnight. And it is sheer sophistry to say that a deterrent is pointless because we should not use it before we were attacked, and could not benefit from it after we had been. The point of the deterrent is not that it is used, but that it deters; and it deters not only a nuclear all-out attack, but any serious war. If the Soviet experts are right in thinking that the Russians will primarily rely on political and economic means of expansion rather than war, the deterrent is one of the main reasons for that. And while it deters any serious aggression, both nuclear and conventional, it also greatly reduces the power of the Soviets to use the threat of such aggression as a weapon of political blackmail — and thus makes their political and economic methods conform more nearly to their own description of "peaceful competition."

All these gains from the possession of the deterrent still exist — and the risk of "accidents" has to be balanced against them. Toynbee assumes, because the number of people who might go mad is large, that the risk is very high — almost fifty-fifty. In fact, because the likelihood of this happening in any single case is extremely small, it is of course still very, very small even if this fraction is multiplied by the number of people concerned; and even then I should not regard automatic retaliation as certain. Still, the mere existence of *any* such risk, however small, is something new and very horrible, and it faces us wtih three questions: Whether we should rather choose surrender than accept any risk of this at all; whether the present policy involves us in an automatism where the risk is increasing all the time; or whether it is, on the contrary, possible to reduce this risk by policies short of surrender — policies of negotiation based on the retention of the deterrent.

The first of these questions is one of ultimate values, and cannot in its nature be resolved by argument. I shall just state baldly that no responsible policy has ever been possible which did not imply grave risks, and that I am consciously prepared to run the continued risk of "race suicide by accident" rather than accept the alternative certainty of race slavery by design. But I can only make this choice because I believe that the risk need not automatically increase, but may be deliberately reduced.

This brings me to Toynbee's parable of the express train and the bridge. It is evidently founded on the assumption that the risk is growing all the time — because, as we have all been told in innumerable meetings and pamphlets, "every arms race ends ultimately in war." I believe on the contrary that this is one of those unquestioned platitudes which have no basis whatever in historical fact. The example which its purveyors usually have in mind is the first world war; but while one particular arms race — the dreadnought competition — strongly contributed to Britain's alignment with the Franco-Russian alliance, the war did not start because of it, but because of a territorial conflict in an explosive area which was considered vital for the balance between the hostile alliances. In fact, a number of conflicts between the major powers before 1914 had been settled without war despite the arms race, while in the Balkans there had been local wars leading up to the big clash without a significant arms race! The arms race is a symptom, not a cause; it can be stopped if diplomacy succeeds in dealing with the danger areas.

In other words, it is true we all sit in that train; it is true that somewhere in front a bridge is down; but *the train ain't moving!* Of course, it *could* start moving if a madman got hold of the engine, and it is a devilish uncomfortable feeling to sit in a train in such a position, however small the risk may be statistically. But the need is not for a sudden desperate gesture, such as pulling the communication cord, nor would it really help to get out and try to walk to our destination, taking a solemn pledge never to use trains again. What we really want is a sensible driver with enough skill and initiative to shunt the train on to a different track, where the bridge is all right and the road forward is open.

By that I mean, of course, the alternative of real negotiation, in which the principal powers deliberately seek to reduce the risk of even an accidental clash. As we do not believe the Soviets aim at an atomic Pearl Harbour, we could stop such specially risky practices as the H-bomb air patrol or, on their side, the twenty-four-hour manning of rocket bases; even if they secretly broke that agreement, we should not be politically worse off — they could not use it for threats and we could restore the patrol if they did. We could negotiate steps to stop the spreading of nuclear weapons to further powers, including a British renunciation. We could above all try to end the most likely cause of accidental war — a revolutionary explosion in Europe involving the major powers — by negotiating a withdrawal of the latter from the borderline.

All this, however difficult, could be done — and that means that it should be done, and that we must press for it as rational means for reducing the risk. But it must be done not in a spirit of panic and surrender to avert imminent catastrophe, but in a spirit of cool, patient negotiation, based on sober calculations of the balance of power — and that means on the continued possession of the deterrent by both sides.